How to Live With and
Take Loving Care of Your Cat

THE GOOD CAT BOOK

Mordecai Siegal

SIMON AND SCHUSTER

NEW YORK

Copyright © 1981 by Mordecai Siegal
All rights reserved
including the right of reproduction
in whole or in part in any form
Published by Simon and Schuster
A Division of Gulf & Western Corporation
Simon & Schuster Building
Rockefeller Center
1230 Avenue of the Americas
New York, New York 10020

SIMON AND SCHUSTER and colophon are trademarks of Simon & Schuster.
Designed by Eve Kirch
Manufactured in the United States of America

1   3   5   7   9   10   8   6   4   2

Library of Congress Cataloging in Publication Data

Siegal, Mordecai.
The good cat book.
Includes index.
1. Cats.   I. Title.
SF442.S48   636.8   80-29638
ISBN 0-671-24640-2

to max, for clawing to pieces my good chair
and for the years and years of love,
laughter and learning,
your pal, m.

Contents

Part Two. A Who's Who of Uncommon Cats

Foreword

By Richard H. Gebhardt, former President
The Cat Fanciers' Association, Inc.

Mordecai Siegal is an extraordinary individual. I have spent many hours with him and have observed firsthand his great talent for understanding animals, the needs of animals, and the needs of pet owners. He has many fine books to his credit, and *The Good Cat Book* will surely take its place as one of the best cat publications for the American pet owner. Mr. Siegal is in touch with the real cat world, and his book reflects it. The book also expresses many of my own views as I look at the cat world and its owners.

The central message of *The Good Cat Book* is that the relationship between owner and cat should be a happy one. With this goal always in mind, Mr. Siegal provides insightful, interesting, and lucid information on how to achieve it. The cat seeker must seriously consider the right kind of cat to buy. He or she must also think about the time involved in caring for a cat or a pair of cats. Too often the choice of a particular breed is based on all the wrong reasons, and vanity is usually at the top of that list.

You may look for a cat that will enhance your home or yourself. This is fine, unless it happens to be a kitten from a breed that you are unable to cope with as it develops into a mature cat. Lots of coat on a cat is glamorous, but it also requires a great deal of work. Some cats are more devoted than others and want to be with you every minute.

You may find others too talkative for you. All these aspects must be given serious consideration. An honest breeder, one who cares where his or her precious kittens are placed, can be an excellent source of information and can help the prospective cat owner answer a great variety of questions regarding cat breeds, behavior, and care.

   The Good Cat Book will help you avoid many unpleasant experiences. It is a down-to-earth guide and reference book that will be of immeasurable value to even the most experienced cat fancier. *The Good Cat Book* will surely make you a better cat owner. Mordecai Siegal's approach to the subject of owning and caring for cats will contribute greatly to the pleasure of cat owners and to the happiness of their cats. It will ensure these wonderful animals a healthier and happier life . . . which is the most important consideration of all.

Silva-Wyte Cattery
Denville, New Jersey

Acknowledgments

Few books are ever the result of one person's effort. *The Good Cat Book* owes much to the talents, expertise, and generosity of many good friends and colleagues. To them I extend a heartfelt expression of gratitude and respect. Without their help and encouragement I could not have completed the task.

THE PHOTOGRAPHERS

The largest number of photographs for this work were taken by Jane Howard, who is rapidly becoming one of the better known photographers of felines in the United States. Her photographs have appeared in many books, newspapers and magazines both in the United States and abroad. She is primarily self-taught and ascribes her success to patience and love of the subject matter.

Alice Su has developed a fine reputation for animal photography, and her photographs of cats handsomely grace the pages of this book.

Susan Brooks has contributed many useful and interesting pictures seen throughout. Several were originally used by The Bide-A-Wee Home Association for their animal welfare efforts.

Larry Kalstone's grooming photographs are extremely valuable and will prove to be of lasting value to many cat owners now and in years to come.

Many thanks for the photographs of Jamison L. Wallace, Crezentia and Ted Allen, Deirdre Drohan, Scott Barry, Terence A. Gili, Vance Allen, Jeff Goldwater, Craig Moran, Jaye Apperson, Ron

13

Karafin, Jayne Langdon, Jim Cooper, and the Eastman Kodak Company.

A special acknowledgment to a leading gallery photographer, Mr. John Hacker, for his kind advice and enthusiasm.

THE EXPERTS

Much of the research for the nutritional chapter was furnished by Dr. Jim Corbin, Professor of Animal Science, University of Illinois at Urbana-Champaign; Dr. Mark Morris, Jr., Mark Morris Associates of Topeka, Kansas; Catherine G. Fabricant, Cornell University; Geoffrey Broderick, DVM; Patricia P. Scott, Ph.D., courtesy of Gaines Professional Services.

Important to the completeness of *The Good Cat Book* was the invaluable assistance and kindness of the Cat Fanciers' Association, Inc. Most helpful were Richard H. Gebhardt, president; Marna Fogarty, editor-in-chief of the CFA Yearbook; and Jean Baker Rose, executive director.

With much pleasure a very grateful author wishes to thank: Judith Star, American Humane Education Society (MSPCA); Ellen Yanow, Tree House Animal Foundation; Claude Ramsey, Morris Animal Foundation; Shirlee Kalstone, author and grooming expert; Walter Chimel, Gaines Dog Research Center; Carl Nowicki, American Animal Hospital Association; William L. Brisby, Moorpark College; Eda LeShan; Gunther Gebel-Williams, Ringling Brothers–Barnum & Bailey Circus; Kenneth J. Feld, executive vice-president, Ringling Brothers–Barnum & Bailey Combined Shows, Inc.; Nini Finkelstein, Solters & Roskin; Pat Stewart, I. D. Pet; David Agee, Garland STPM Press; James Craig, *Columbus Dispatch;* Brunson Caito (Mary Caito & Kathleen Brunson), *Columbus Dispatch;* Frank McSweeney; Marcia Higgins; Mel Berger; Patricia Warren and Reg Riedel, Foxtail Cattery; Tom Torio, Torio Cattery; J. E. Kachler and S. G. Sulloway, Sankachi's Bombays and Burmese; Carolyn and Gerald Osier, Wil-o-glen Cattery; Edward Lowe, manufacturer of Kitty Litter and Tidy Cat; Jerry Benisatto of Felines of Distinction; Susan Siegel, DVM; William Kay, DVM, director, Animal Medical Center, New York City; Sandy Stewart and friends; Joya Staack and Melissa; Frederic W. Hills, Senior Editor; Jim Ramsay, Associate Editor; and David Abramowitz.

Special thanks to the late Fred Honig.

PART ONE

Loving Care

1

The Perfect Purr

There's really two men inside of this skin.
It isn't a cat at all. —Groucho Marx

There is a cat named Max who once survived the rinse cycle of a Maytag. Max is the Inspector Clouseau of cats, who rarely makes it from the kitchen sink to his dish atop the fridge without frantically digging into the door like Hillary on Everest. Occasionally he will spring from the floor to the dining table, miss, cling by his claws and then fall back to the floor. After an impervious lick of the coat he will walk away with the aplomb of an indicted official.

Max is a cat who falls from grace at least twice a day. The kink in his partial Siamese tail hooks onto lamp cords and window shade pulls with the most disastrous effects. On any morning he is capable of stepping into one's Cream of Wheat, pulling down a leaning bicycle, clawing a leather chair, and drenching the sleeve of a cashmere sweater. Max is a wool sucker.

How, one must query, does this imperfect cat keep his exalted position as family pet? A question easily answered. We love and adore him and he knows it. Somewhere buried in that fact lies the essence of his dignity, or so his family chooses to believe. He is our own true cat and we benefit greatly from his tender mercies. Bewhiskered, bemused and beyond reproach, our good cat moved in and decided to stay for a lifetime. And why not? The service is good, the bed is soft and the wakeup calls aren't too early.

Like Max, your good cat is as valuable as a child's hug or a warm cake. The sustenance provided lasts far longer than color TV and a house on the beach. When curled up on your lap the good cat can blot out the six o'clock news with its strikes, power failures, and failures of power. It is all accomplished with the cat's overwhelming indifference to everything save you. Governments fall while television devours itself. Coins have no silver and bicycles rust. Change seems to be the only constant factor as the world sees itself through Saran Wrap darkly. But your cat is constant, unyielding in its preferences and totally committed to a place and the people living there.

The feline presence is an important one and must not be dismissed with a nonchalant shrug. Your cat does much more than chase mice and eat your food. He is the mortal enemy of empty rooms. Soft, warm, needful, all cats, but especially yours, gives far more than he takes. That is what makes him good.

WHAT'S IN A CAT?

Your cat is not just another pretty face. Ten pounds of cat gets you 245 bones, thirty teeth, hundreds of muscles, one mouth, a tongue, a complete digestive system including the stomach, one nose, two lungs, two kidneys, a bladder, one liver, a complete reproductive system, several glands, a heart, two eyes, two ears, miles of blood vessels and nerve fibers, one brain, a spine, lots of water, skin, fur and the most finely honed predatory instincts in the animal kingdom.

According to the *Guinness Book of World Records* the heaviest cat weighed forty-two pounds. The oldest cat on record was thirty-seven years old. The largest litter consisted of twelve kittens. The greatest mouser captured twenty-two thousand mice over a twenty-three-year period.

The taxonomy or scientific classification of the domestic cat looks like this:

CLASS
  Mammalia

SUBCLASS
  Theria

INFRACLASS
  Eutheria

ORDER
  Carnivora

SUBORDER
  Fissipedia

INFRAORDER
  Aeluroidea

FAMILY
  Felidae

GENUS
  Felis

SPECIES
  Domestica

Here is a creature equipped with sharp fangs and hooked claws, a predatory flame burning beyond the eyes, an unrelinquished sense of freedom, a devotion to its own needs and desires, a stubborn refusal to bend to the human will. What kind of pet can such an animal make? Perhaps the best kind. Why did such figures as Napoleon and Hitler hate or fear cats, while many writers, painters, poets and others have proven their deep affection and identification with them? As a rule, those involved with power over others seem to have the least interest in cats. Those involved with freedom and the creative spirit seem to have the most interest. Mark Twain, Emile Zola, Edgar Allen Poe and Victor Hugo are but a few of those notables who not only wrote about cats but loved them enough to share a lifetime with them.

Never hug a cat . . . unless you mean it. The soft feline fur covering the warm stretchy flesh will set off a network of emotions like miles of toppling dominoes. Do not squeeze those soft paws or interrupt while Puss is staring at a wall. (Cats stare at walls so that humans will make fools of themselves trying to figure it out.) All this is contrived by your good cat to ensnare you emotionally while he or she pretends not to be involved. However, it is impossible to embrace a cat casually and not make a fool of yourself. The very essence of cats is emotional manipulation. It is possible that they have been programmed genetically with an instinctive understanding of the saying "A little rejection goes a long, long way." We play into their paws both positively and negatively. No one, repeat, no one is indifferent to cats. But love them or hate them, it is difficult to simply walk away from them. Caveat emptor!

Cats are living, breathing creatures like us and as such are subject to the realities of life's roulette wheel. Cats get sick, experience emotional disturbance, make noise, cost money, and sometimes tear apart intricate constructions. One must not take up residence with a feline while working off a wafer-thin dream about white kittens with red bows around their adorable necks. The puffy purr that bursts out of a satin chocolate box is soon forgotten after cleaning a loaded litter box or witnessing the first bout of sexual excitability.

There is much more to cats than Christmas card images or such scenes as Winston Churchill painting in a garden with a furry imp in his picnic basket. Cats, like most dogs, are companion animals that do their job with consummate skill. They are a manageable, allowable snatch of nature coexisting in our homes like miniature creatures of the wild, expressing all of their ferocity at catnip mice and squatting rubber plants. They can also be loyal friends, keeping loneliness at bay and alienation from the door, not to mention mice and other rodents.

In all of animal history there has not been another such superstar as the domestic cat. Imagine a creature that was worshipped as a god because it prevented famine by protecting the granaries of ancient Egypt from rodents. And then consider the fiery martyrdom of cats in medieval Europe, where they were considered tools of the Devil. During this bleak period cats were brutally murdered by the superstitiously fearful and almost hounded into extinction. And then, when the Great Plague of the latter part of the Middle Ages occurred, there were no cats to destroy the rat population and their deadly, bubonic fleas. The common cat might have prevented the Black Death of the fourteenth century and spared Europe the loss of two-thirds of its population.

Today, as in ancient times, the cat enjoys high status. We are told that thirty million American families own one or more cats. Several million of these are purebred animals resulting from careful selective breeding. Those cats that are lucky enough to have homes are there through sheer demagoguery and reign as absolute autocrats. So the wheel has turned full circle, as we seem to have returned to something like cat worship once again. This is true unless you walk through the thousands of animal shelters where millions of abandoned cats innocently wait for new homes or euthanasia. It is a toss of loaded dice for these unlucky creatures. There are many reasons for this sad situation, not the least of which have to do with indiscriminate breeding, unacceptable human behavior, and the lack of reality on the part of many who never dreamed that cuddly kittens grow up to be large cats with physical and emotional needs.

The Good Cat Book has been written to help cats and humans enjoy twenty years of pleasant association through loving care. It is not enough to open a can of cat food and dump it on a plate. An informed cat person will enjoy a long, fulfilling relationship with a truly unique and valuable member of the animal kingdom.

The Good Cat Book will, it is hoped, do its part in preventing the increase of unwanted cats and the inevitable cruelty that ensues when they are abandoned. This can be accomplished by acquainting prospective cat owners, new cat owners and even experienced cat owners with the demands of ownership. Loving your cat is a good start, but it is not enough. Understanding cat behavior and learning how to cope with it are more to the point. These pages are for those who want to live with cats, but need facts and instruction. How to live with and take care of your cat is no mystery. It is simply a matter of information and the desire to base your life with your cat on a realistic foundation.

ON CHOOSING A CAT

If you are about to begin the task of selecting a cat, there are some guidelines that help. One must decide whether a purebred or random-bred cat is wanted. The differences lie in the predictability of physical characteristics and a few of the behavioral characteristics. Certain features of a purebred cat will fall within given parameters of conformity. These features have to do with body size, body shape, length of the haircoat, color, shape of the face, and other factors. One need only look at a photograph of a typical breed specimen to get a general idea of the kitten's look as a mature cat. A random-bred cat, however, might grow up to be more or less than expected in size, shape, color, and even in coat length.

Some behavioral characteristics are associated with pure breeds, but the purebred is subject to the same environmental influences as a random-bred animal. For example, Persian cats are considered docile and quite easygoing as a breed. However, whether a specific Persian adjusts to humans or not, learns to catch mice, learns to kill what it catches, learns to eat what it kills, and so on, depends on early influences, such as education from the mother cat and early socializing with human beings. In these matters of learning, a random-bred kitten is on an equal footing with a purebred kitten.

Once you have resolved whether you desire a purebred or a random-bred cat, the cat's early education and other environmental influ-

ences need to be considered. Ideally, a kitten is at its most adaptive if it stays with its mother and litter for ten weeks. During these ten weeks it should be handled and played with daily by one or more loving, caressing humans. A kitten thus reared will learn much of what it needs to know from its mother and littermates in addition to adapting to the human/pet lifestyle through human contact.

There is one other non-genetic factor that has a bearing on the temperament and adaptability of the youngster: the temperament and personality of its mother. According to Paul Leyhausen in his *Cat Behavior: The Predatory and Social Behavior of Domestic and Wild Cats,* "Kittens first learn to fear certain enemies through their mother's warning behavior. Kittens reared by very trusting and pampered domestic cats show no fear toward any living creatures." (See "Selected Readings" at the end of this book.) The implications of the behavioral influence of an even-tempered cat on her kittens are obvious. One can conclude that kittens reared by a sweet and loving cat are likely to be good companion animals. Leyhausen informs us that these factors are a matter of genuine learning and not of imprinting processes.

SELECTING A HEALTHY KITTEN

Although a kitten should stay with mother and litter for at least ten weeks, this is often not possible, especially when dealing with orphaned or abandoned animals. Kittens begin to be weaned away from their mother's milk at about four weeks of age and by eight weeks are ingesting whole food or at least a combination of the two, depending on when the flow of mother's milk begins to slow. A fully weaned kitten usually sustains the transition from litter to human social environment best. For that reason examine your prospective pet's mouth and look for a full set of bright, pointed teeth set in clear, pink gums. If the teeth have only partially emerged, weaning has not yet been accomplished and the infant should remain with Momma.

The best way to judge a kitten is to see her with her litter. Observe how she interacts with the others; do not take one that is apparently shy, cowering away from you and the rest of the world. A shy, nervous kitten is adorable and heart-rending but can be quite a problem as a full-grown cat (a point that will be dealt with in more detail in Chapter 3). It is also important to know that shy behavior is sometimes a manifestation of poor health.

The opposite end of the behavioral spectrum is overaggressiveness, which should also be avoided when making a selection. A litter of kittens, especially past six weeks of age, plays rough-and-tumble games like those of baby lions. However, now and again there is a tough guy who goes well beyond the limits of exuberant play and displays hostile and potentially dangerous behavior. It is not too difficult to distinguish play fighting from the real thing. Watch for a sullen facial expression, stiffened body, straight legs and arched back, contracted pupils of the eyes, and ears flattened against the side of the head. A kitten in this state can be dangerous to other members of the litter and possibly to humans as well. Observe how he deals with his littermates, and project that behavior onto a fully grown cat. It is best to avoid this little tough guy.

Once you've spotted the kitten you like, who seems to behave like a normal, even-tempered youngster, ask the breeder to bring him or her to you for inspection. If the kitten is not frightened, you're off to a good start. Hold the animal up and examine it for coat condition. The coat should be clean, have a slight sheen and be free of fleas. A dirty coat means something is wrong; constant scratching may indicate flea or mite infestation. Small bare patches or red spots indicate ringworm or one of the various forms of mange.

Be wary of liquid discharges from the eyes, the ears, the nose, the anus or the genitalia. This can indicate disease or poor health. The eyes should be clear, the nose clean and perhaps moist but not running. Unclean ear passages can be a sign of mites, parasites that are difficult to get rid of. Signs of diarrhea indicate that the kitten is not well. By comparing one kitten with the others in the litter you can judge if it is under- or overweight. This, of course, is also a health factor. A clean, lively, alert kitten that does not seem to be nervous is exactly the sort of healthy animal to select.

CHOOSING THE RIGHT SEX

In the wild, cats are not at all like dogs (who live in packs that are socially organized according to rank). Wild cats of both sexes are pretty much equal and behave similarly except during mating, pregnancy and cub rearing. Both males and females travel alone, maintain separate territories and hunting ranges, hunt and feed alone, and form no permanent social structures. The only species of cat that does form something like a pack is the lion. Of course all cats come together to mate, and females do stay with their cubs until they are capable of surviving on their own. Domestic cats behave similarly, and both males and females make ideal house pets provided they have been altered surgically so that they cannot create offspring.

It is strongly recommended to the reader to have a veterinarian perform the spaying of females or the castrating of males. If this is accomplished, there will be no difference between having a male or a female house cat. A whole male cat past puberty begins "spraying" around his territory (your home) with sexually scented urine that is unbearably pungent. In addition, a whole male cat is more apt to roam, claim outdoor territory, and enter into unbelievably violent encounters with other males. The cat pays with his hide, but you pay the vet bills.

An unspayed female characteristically goes into "heat" (estrus)

Male or female? Female (on left): A dot above and a slit below. Male (on right): A dot above and a dot below. The mature male cat develops protruding testicles between the two dots.

twice a year, but many domestic female cats experience the heat cycle on a continual basis or at least more than twice a year. This is probably the result of domestication and its contemporary influences. The radical behavior changes of a female in season can be quite disturbing to the novice cat owner. Her postures and vocalizing are designed to attract the attention of the males in the area. However, humans subjected to this behavior may become frightened or at least puzzled if they have never seen it before. A complete ovariohysterectomy after puberty will end this behavior and relieve the pet owner of the responsibilities connected with unwanted kittens.

HOW TO GET A CAT

There are a number of different ways to get a cat. It all depends on what kind of cat you want, how much you want to spend, and whether you want to show the cat or just have it share its remarkable life with you.

Adoption

Throughout this country there is a loosely formed network of people who rescue abandoned and lost cats and dogs. They often advertise in local newspapers offering pets free of charge to those who are willing to give them good homes. These well-intentioned volunteers are sometimes negatively referred to as "humaniacs," "cat ladies," or worse. Whether one agrees with their philosophy and sense of priorities or not, the fact remains that otherwise doomed animals by the thousands are rescued by these people, given medical attention, altered, fed, cleaned and placed in good homes. If you are fortunate enough to find such a network in your community, by all means acquire your new pet through it. The animal you receive will enjoy a clean bill of health from a veterinarian and the chore and expense of altering will have been taken care of. There is usually very little or no money involved, although of course a contribution is usually appreciated.

Another, more traditional method of adopting a cat is to visit your community animal shelters, pounds and SPCA-type organizations. This is still the best bargain in town when it comes to buying a cat. The cost varies from community to community, but the price is always

reasonable and the animals usually are in good health. If the cat is too young for neutering when you get it, the organization requires that you agree to have the operation done at the proper time.

Although there are always some kittens available at these shelters, there are more grown cats than anything else. Do not fail to consider rescuing a fully grown cat. Kittenhood is a wonderful experience, but it has its disadvantages. A fully grown cat has a great deal to offer the prospective pet owner. Many grown cats make easy adjustments to new homes and are every bit as affectionate as very young ones. As a rule, a grown cat is calmer and more sedate than a kitten, and this can be a distinct advantage. A grown feline more than likely will be the one to adopt you. The humane element of this choice is well worth consideration.

Most cats and kittens at adoption shelters are random-bred, but

now and again there does appear a purebred animal. So, be it kitten or adult, alley cat or aristocrat, check with all the agencies in your community before spending a lot of money. Check your Yellow Pages under Animal Shelters or ask your information operator for your local agencies.

Breeders

There are several kinds of cat breeders. The *backyard breeder* is an amateur and, as such, is best avoided. Such people do not have much knowledge or technical skill and do not breed their animals selectively. Consequently they set loose into the world even more kittens for which there are no homes. The barest health essentials are usually ignored and it's anyone's guess as to the soundness of the resulting kittens. It is a risk at best and a detriment to the cause of reducing the tragically large animal population.

Commercial breeders supply pet shops with kittens in large quantities. Profit is the only consideration, which brings into serious question the true quality and health of the animals made available. In the interest of accuracy, it should be said that some commercial breeders are quite responsible in their activities and function fairly and competently.

Non-commercial breeders are usually members of the Cat Fancy and appear to be more knowledgeable and have more integrity as a group than most other types of cat breeders. Although breaking even financially is often a consideration, more often pride in the quality of the animals produced and the pleasure derived from them motivates non-commercial breeders. Here, pedigreed cats of the most interesting and beautiful breeds are produced and brought into the world with the greatest selection and care possible. Each kitten is registered with one of the various cat registering organizations and is kept with her mother and litter for a proper length of time. She is finally allowed

to be taken to a new home, provided the humans involved appear to be kind, thoughtful and humane. These breeders also supply most of the brilliant cats seen in cat shows throughout the world. Non-commercial breeders are very fussy about who gets their cats. Although there are unfortunate exceptions, this is how the large majority of breeders function.

The very best of the non-commercial and commercial breeders can be found by contacting any of the various cat registering organizations or cat specialty magazines. (See lists at the back of this book.)

Pet Shops

Some pet shops sell random-bred and purebred kittens, although the proprietors realize the great availability through other sources. By charging a reasonable fee for the cat they hope to encourage the customer to return for more expensive supplies such as toys, books, collars, food, and so on. The hit-or-miss risk of getting a pet shop kitten is much the same as that involved in acquiring a pet from a backyard breeder. Let the buyer beware.

Cats Who Choose You

There is one source of cats that has no official name or sanction even though thousands are acquired this way. Like magic, some cats simply appear at your window sill or doorway and walk right into your life, knocking over a flower arrangement and taking up residence in your umbrella stand. Lost or abandoned strays are sometimes lucky enough, or perceptive enough, to claim and adopt the right household. It happens and is worth mentioning. It is, of course, your moral responsibility to attempt to find out if the cat has strayed from some other happy home. If no owner is found, consider yourself blessed. Cats who choose their owners can be particularly loyal and affectionate.

But no matter how you finally get a cat to move in with you it is important to know what you can expect for the next twenty years or so. For that reason it is suggested that you keep your copy of *The Good Cat Book* close by.

2

In the Beginning ... Kittens

Bringing home your very first kitten is one of the few threads of childhood allowed a grown man or woman. With the arrival of a kitten there is delicious excitement within, reminiscent of nursery rhymes and bubble gum expectations. Like a little fur glove, the precious bud curls up in the palm of your hand with mewing breaths and transports you back to thumb-sucking joy. But kittens are more than meows wrapped in fur. They are highly complicated mechanisms with genetically ordained destinies. They are what they are. They breathe the same air we do and their needs are much the same as ours. We are all of the same mammal class. Once the feline elf lies against your chest, the feelings of childhood dissolve and blend wih the tender emotions of parenthood. It is now time to stop thinking of the new kitten as a toy and relate to him as a living, breathing baby that needs love, sustenance and firm guidance. You are all that stands between this helpless, vulnerable babe and the forces of harsh reality. You are the protector and the provider, the teacher and the judge, the font of physical and emotional nourishment. Make no mistake, it is a large responsibility. But some day, when your kitten has grown to cathood, he will find a way, some unspoken way, to say thanks for this life.

THE FIRST DAY

Before the kitten arrives, certain preparations must be made. It would be a great mistake to attempt to solve the most fundamental problems of kitten care while trying to manage a lively bundle of mischievous curiosity. You need to consider such matters as food, equipment, toileting, grooming, behavior (yours and the cat's), and even learning how to hold the youngster. Preparation and essential knowledge will vastly improve the quality of the first day and the first night with your new member of the family.

Kittenproofing Your Home

It is imperative that your new kitten not be allowed to get out of the house. There is no one more curious than a kitten in a new home. Curiosity can kill. Check your living space for avenues of escape such as holes, broken doors, faulty screens or open windows. This is especially important for apartment dwellers living in high places. A two- to three-inch opening is all that's necessary for a kitten (or a grown cat) to squeeze through. The great outdoors is no place for a grown cat, much less a defenseless kitten.

Allow no opportunity for the kitten to fall into water. If you own a swimming pool, do not let the little cat out of the house for a minute. Keep the lid of the toilet down. Never leave the tub unless the stopper is out and the water is drained. The same applies for washing machines, sinks and pails. Speaking of washing machines, always close the door to the clothes dryer. A tumble-dried kitten is neither fluffy nor amusing. It is a common accident that results in death.

Take a walk around your premises and look for dangling cords, wires, ropes, shade pulls, venetian blind strings, fishing tackle, vacuum cleaner tubes, TV antenna cable, and even leather thongs on pot handles. They all appeal to a young cat as devices for exercise and play. But they all represent hidden death traps for a frisky mischief-maker. Put dangerous objects away. Fold up excess cords and tape them to a wall or under a table. Bits of yarn, string and ribbon are easily swallowed and can cause blockages, constipation and various stomach ailments. Keep this material off the floor and tables.

Electrical cords offer a double dose of trouble. A kitten is likely

to attack a dangling wire and pull down the appliance on top of himself. This can happen with toasters, blenders, electric frying pans (while in use), coffee pots and juicers. If the youngster is not scalded or brained, he could be electrocuted by plunging his tiny razorlike teeth into the wire. This is true of any electric device with a wire plugged into a wall receptacle.

Often without knowing it, owners of every household maintain a well-stocked supply of poisons. Many household cleaners are poisonous to humans as well as to animals. Small animals and children are especially vulnerable to common poisons because small doses can make them seriously ill. Poisons most available for kittens to get into include lead (as in paints, ceramics, paperweights), petroleum distillates (such as kerosene), detergents, lye, cleansers, mothballs, insecticides, and all medications, including aspirin, sleeping pills, tranquilizers and various cold remedies. It goes without saying that mind-altering drugs used by humans are lethal in most cases for small animals. Methadone, LSD, marijuana, heroin, amphetamines and all the various things that are sniffed, from cocaine to glue, can kill a kitten or grown cat. It is bad enough to have an animal get at them through carelessness, but it is a cruel and inhumane crime to feed drugs purposely to an animal.

Keep your kitten out of your garage or basement where it might get into antifreeze and all the other poisonous fluids used for your automobile. Antifreeze has an attractive color and sweet taste. Cats, dogs and even small children are attracted to it. They will lick it off the floor if given the opportunity. Antifreeze will cause death. Some plants are poisonous and must be considered when bringing a kitten into your house. (See Chapter 7.) If there are children in the house, they must be made aware of the dangers caused by some of their toys. Bicycles, tricycles, skateboards, and all other toys with wheels represent a potential hazard. Do not leave any plastic bags lying around for the kitten to get into. All plastic bags can cause immediate suffocation. Before you close your refrigerator door, make sure the kitten hasn't jumped in. Never allow the kitten to be around during the operation of any machinery, from the vacuum cleaner to the lawn mower to the radio-operated garage door.

The Cat Bed

When you provide a bed for your new kitten you will be appealing to his sense of territory, thus satisfying a basic cat need. Over the years he will try sleeping in every conceivable place in your home, from your personal bed to the sofa to the silver drawer. But he will always return to the one place that is personally scented and securely located. A small wicker or plastic basketlike bed with a soft pillow or blanket is all that is necessary. Most cats appreciate one that is covered so that it is somewhat like a small cave. Tall, carpet-covered poles with enclosed platforms at the top are brilliantly conceived for the cat who can have everything. But it really doesn't matter whether you spend hundreds of dollars or simply line a cardboard carton with something soft. The point is to give the new kitten a place of his own, some place to hang his tail and call home. Try to locate the cat bed in some snug corner on a higher level than the floor.

Litter Box and Rake

Without going into the matter of housebreaking here (see Chapter 5), it is sufficient to say that you will need what amounts to a toilet for your new kitten. Here, you have several options. The most common toileting device is a plastic cat pan ranging from eighteen inches to three feet in length. These come in many shapes and styles. Some have A-frame covers with a round hole for an entrance in the front.

These are probably more for the human's sense of the aesthetic, although they do afford the cat a feeling of privacy. It has been this author's experience that some cats feel uncomfortable or perhaps vulnerable being trapped inside while relieving themselves. A large plastic pan with no cover is always acceptable to the cat, provided it is cleaned every day.

You will need some rakelike tool to clean the litter pan every day, as often as necessary. A very popular tool, basically a cooking utensil, has proved itself equally useful in the toilet. It is an aluminum (or plastic) slotted spatula about ten inches long. It will remove fecal material without taking the gravel.

The litter material used in the pan is inexpensive and available everywhere from the supermarket to the pet store. A wide variety is offered, from plain granulated clay to chlorophyll-coated pellets. Many experienced cat people use plain sand. Richard Gebhardt, president of the Cat Fanciers Association, has mentioned using shredded newspapers exclusively. He feels that constant changing of the paper helps to prevent sickness and disease. It is probably best to allow your cat to make the decision. Try different materials and brand names and watch the cat use them. Many cats, for example, refuse to use scented litters, while others will not accept a change once you've started with one or the other.

Food, Bowls, and So On

Be prepared to feed your kitten. Have the food in the house before the kitten arrives. The best method is to obtain a one-week supply of the food that the kitten has been getting. If you are planning to change your new pet's diet (see Chapter 4), have the new food in the cupboard as well. Introduce the new food gradually, along with the regular diet. For two days, replace 25 percent of the regular diet with the new food and mix thoroughly. For two more days, replace 50 percent of the original diet with the new diet. For the next two days, substitute 75 percent of the regular diet with the new food and mix well. On the seventh day, feed the new diet exclusively. Feed the kitten in a very calm, relaxed atmosphere. Subdued lighting and one or no human beings present is not unreasonable. Stomach upset and poor nutritional utilization are often caused in kittens and grown cats by stress induced by their immediate surroundings and emotional state.

The food and water containers you select can be almost anything you choose. Plastic containers are not recommended because they can be chewed through and can be easily knocked about and tipped over. Some ceramic bowls are not fired hot enough in the kiln, thus allowing the lead content of the glaze to leach through and possibly cause lead poisoning. Most American-made ceramics do not have this problem. Stainless steel dishes inserted into a holder are excellent, as are any weighted bowls. Many seasoned pet owners use a simple flat plate so that the cat's whiskers (which are very sensitive) do not have to touch anything. A flat plate also allows the cat to do what she likes best with food—separate one morsel from the others. It is not a bad idea to place the flat plate on a medium-sized plastic tray like the ones used in fast-food restaurants. Whichever you select, your kitten will need a container for food and a bowl for water. Water must always be available, twenty-four hours a day, seven days a week.

Leash, Collar and ID Tag

A leash is completely unnecessary unless you plan to teach your kitten to walk with you outdoors. A lightweight nylon or leather lead is the only thing to consider. (See Chapter 5.) The newly developed Sogo Flexi 2 reel* is an intriguing lightweight leash device. It is an automatic, self-retracting nylon leash that extends fifteen feet from a high-density plastic case that weighs less than a pound. It has a brake and a locking mechanism that allow you to control the length of the leash while giving the cat more opportunity to roam. The proper equipment to accompany a leash is a cat harness. These are made of leather and are quite inexpensive.

A collar is necessary only when an ID tag or license display is important. It should not be used with a leash. If you plan to show your cat, it is best not to use a collar at all, as it may affect the coat around the neck area. Although a kitten should be introduced to the idea of a collar early, it is best to start out with something innocuous, such as a light piece of ribbon tied loosely around the neck. If the ribbon does not distract the animal you may replace it with something thicker in a day or two, such as a band of cloth. Introduce the collar one or two days later. Incidentally, a collar should be breakable by the cat or made of elastic so that it cannot strangle the animal when snagged on

* May be obtained from Sogo, 55 Sutter Street, Suite 512, San Francisco, CA 94104.

something. Some collars have a short length of elastic sewn onto the leather, while some newer ones are made with Velcro tape so that the collar will actually break away with pressure.*

Have an ID tag made up at your local pet supply store. A proper tag should be made of a sturdy metal so that the engraved information cannot be rubbed off. The tag must have your name, address and telephone number in addition to the cat's name. An excellent adjunct to the ID tag is a tattoo identification (see Chapter 7).

Scratch Post

This is a *must-have* accessory for cat ownership. (Cat claws and how to clip them will be discussed at length in Chapter 6.) Do not bring the kitten into the house without first having a scratch post ready. Scratching with their claws is a physiological necessity for all cats. Unless you set the proper pattern of behavior early (by that I mean *immediately*), your cat is going to scratch whatever is handy and appealing, and it will be extremely difficult to break the habit. Many a cat and her owner have been parted on this issue. An untrained cat with an urge to dig her claws into something is capable of destroying thousands of dollars worth of furniture, carpeting, curtains and bedding.

Tom Torio, who breeds the most glorious Turkish Angoras at the Torio Cattery in Flushing, New York, states that the first thing his kittens see is a disposable scratch post. While they are still in the nest they are encouraged to use it. This type is made with corrugated cardboard and is rubbed with a small amount of catnip. Once the kittens begin using this, says Torio, they almost never scratch anyplace else. The result is that no one who acquires a kitten from the Torio Cattery ever has a scratching problem, provided they always have a cardboard scratch post on hand.

Most scratch posts are vertical pieces of wood, sitting on a square pedestal with all surfaces covered with carpet, canvas or burlap. These are fine but are only effective if they are tall enough for the cat to stretch up to its full height when standing on its back legs and still have room to scratch with its front paws. Many of these posts are simply too short and will never be used by the cat. An effective scratch post can simply be a log lying horizontally or leaning vertically against the wall (provided it is secured to the floor). Tree bark feels good on

* Cat collars utilizing the unique Velcro "breakaway" material can be purchased from Petsavers, 8477 DeLongpre Avenue, Los Angeles, CA 90069.

the claws. Posts made of cork are excellent. However, the cardboard posts with their corrugated fillers rubbed with catnip seem to give the very best results. This author's cat can testify. The cat enjoys his post so much that he even naps on it. Such posts are available in pet supply shops, supermarkets and grocery stores.

Toys

Kittens that are held by humans and are given toys at an early age to awaken their sense of play grow into happy, intelligent creatures. Whatever the potential of the cat, it can be best achieved through early affection and stimulation. Toys are very important because they stimulate and provoke play. Kitten-play in the early life of a cat is the equivalent of grade school for a child.

Although play is an important means of exercise for domestic cats, it is primarily a learning and practicing process for activities connected with survival. Obviously the need for survival techniques no longer exists for pampered house cats, but genetic programming has not caught up with the realities of pet life. The tendency to learn the techniques for survival is strong and to some extent genetically organized. Whether the cat ever really learns the specifics is quite another matter. Some cats chase mice and others do not. Some will fight while others acquiesce. These specific behaviors are determined by early education from the mother and littermates, as are other behaviors

pertaining to dominance and subordinance, mating, gender and territory.

What a kitten is rehearsing during play is a drama of survival fighting, sexual behavior, territorial defense, and all those activities connected with hunting, which include tracking, trailing, stalking, capturing prey, and the killing and eating of prey. In kittens, however, what begins as a serious drama always turns into a howling good comedy.

When selecting toys for kittens and grown cats, try to get something that will provoke the various activities described above. For example, the single most attractive toy for a cat is a Ping-Pong ball. It is small like a mouse, it moves in quick, unpredictable motions, and it has a spectacular sound when bounced. In other words, many senses and instinctive responses are called into play. *Animal News* of Santa Rosa, California, suggests dropping a walnut into an empty Kleenex box and giving it to your cat as a toy. The cat will regard the walnut as a mouse and manipulate it with both paws. What joy.

The toys most frequently purchased for cats in stores are little felt mice that are advertised as catnip mice (or other similar toys). The truth of the matter is that most of these items are manufactured in the Orient and do not contain catnip at all. They are sprayed with some substance that is of fleeting interest to the cat and are filled with some chopped plant or tree bark that resembles catnip in appearance. If catnip is your reason for purchasing these toys, you are not getting what you paid for. Without true catnip it is merely an expensive colored piece of felt that just lies there while your cat pursues a Baggie tie or a brown paper bag, having much more fun with these "freebie" toys. However, some cats do enjoy felt mice. It's worth trying with yours.

A string or a rope is a good toy as long as you hold one end and work it like a snake. Put it safely away when you're not around to prevent your pet from swallowing it. Be careful of toys with metal whistles or bells, sharp objects, or small buttons. A cat toy should be safe and not have anything that can be swallowed on it.

Peacock feathers are wonderful; they offer movement, shape and texture. Waving the feather before the cat's eyes in a bouncing motion, tickling the nose and feet, all stimulate the hunter in your cat and will divert the animal for quite a while. Hard rubber balls, large sewing spools or almost anything that will roll makes an excellent toy. Containers such as cardboard boxes, large pots, paper bags, straw hats or even wastebaskets appeal to a cat's inherent need to practice hiding and escape.

Some scratch posts come equipped with a rubber ball attached to the top by an elastic string. These can be great fun and often keep the cat's interest focused on the scratch post instead of your furniture, and isn't that a good thing. The finest cat toy available, the one that offers the most play (if you will play too), is a crumpled sheet of paper.

Comb and Brush

Short-haired kittens require a natural-bristle or rubber-type brush only. As the kitten matures a comb will be a useful addition. Long-haired cats and kittens need a stainless steel comb with blunt, round-edge teeth, designed for cats, plus a natural-bristle brush. Although combing and brushing are not truly necessary for most kittens, it is advisable to start grooming as close to weaning as possible. There are several reasons for this.

Nothing helps the new owner establish an affectionate rapport with a kitten better than holding and touching the animal as he is brushed or combed. The very gesture of grooming, if done properly, is like a series of caresses, and at an early age is viewed by the pet as such. If you wait until the animal matures to begin grooming, you may have difficulty persuading him to be still. By combing or brushing a kitten for no more than a minute at a time, two or three times a week, in the early part of his life you will teach your cat to accept grooming as a normal part of his routine. (See Chapter 6.) This does not mean that the cat (young or old) will not rebel and try to avoid the process. You must be firm and not give in to intimidation or blackmail. Place the cat on a table covered with a towel (for traction). Keep him facing away from you and hold him by the back of his neck as you comb or brush with the lay of the fur. Be gentle and sensitive with your grooming tool and talk to the animal in a soothing tone of voice. Make the experience as pleasant as possible.

Cat Carrier

You will need a special container to transport the cat from one place to another. Although you may think an ordinary box will do, you are sure to change your mind after your first trip to the veterinarian's office, as your cat demonstrates a Houdini-like ability to escape confinement. Both you and the cat will appreciate a sturdily constructed

carrier that keeps the cat in and other animals out. The best part of the cat carrier is the luggage-type handle that makes it easy to carry. Carrying cases come in many styles and vary in price. A case that is built to take the weight of your cat without breaking at the handle and is *well* ventilated will serve the purpose.

Do not be fooled on the question of size. Naturally, large cats need larger carriers. But cats do not desire spaces that are too much larger than the size of their bodies when being transported. A snug area with just enough room to move around allows for maximum utilization of body heat and comforts the animal when being moved about. *This does not apply when shipping an animal.* Shipping is a different matter altogether that requires shipping crates and a different criterion.

During warm weather cat carriers can induce heat prostration if they are not properly ventilated. Always line the bottom of the carrier with a towel or newspaper for comfort, traction and hygiene. Keep the carrier clean at all times. It is my policy never to transport the cat in a carrier when the weather is extremely hot and humid. If you must, then a small plastic sack of ice cubes wrapped in a towel and placed in the corner of the carrier can be a help in preventing heat prostration.

THE ARRIVAL

A new arrival, kitten or grown cat, causes quite a stir in any household. Children in particular are the most excitable. The objective is to get the introductions over with as quickly and as quietly as possible. Avoid loud noises, bright lights, too much handling of the new arrival, and misplaced attention and affection. From the cat's point of view she is in danger, or at least in a state of anxiety caused by the uncertainty of her situation. She doesn't know where she is or who these creatures are and whether they are going to bring harm or not. It is your job to convince this animal that she is in good hands.

How to Hold Your Cat

Avoid holding a cat in any way that scares the animal. He may panic and try to squirm away, and in the process you may be severely scratched or the cat may have a bad fall. This is easily avoided when you know how to pick him up.

Slide your hand along the belly and up to the chest; stop when your fingers are just behind the front legs. Place the cat's rear end and back legs in the open palm of your other hand. Be firm but gentle and it will be almost impossible to lose the animal.

Exploring

With no one but yourself in the immediate area, allow the cat to take a look and a sniff at the new home. Instead of giving the cat the complete run of the house, take her into one room at a time, allowing her to see the entire territory and range. But do not let the newcomer roam too far away from you. It is especially useful to show her the litter pan (see Chapter 5) and then the food bowl. Have a bowl of water waiting in the place where it will always be. Follow the cat around and speak in a soft tone of voice.

It is now time for the first feeding. Get out the food and place it in the bowl. Do not bring the food to the cat; do it the other way around. This is the time to establish desirable habits. Show her where to eat and drink, where her toilet is, the scratch post, and where she is to sleep.

By the way, it is a good idea to select the cat's name right away and to begin using it immediately. Naming a cat is such a subjective matter that it hardly bears mentioning. No matter what elaborate or comical or literary name you choose, have a one-syllable call-name in addition, because that is the one you will probably use most of the time. Pets learn one-syllable names quickly and respond best to them.

On the first day, nothing more than an introduction to the family and to those areas pertaining to the cat should be emphasized. Feed, water and toilet the animal. Allow her to explore one room at a time. Keep her away from other household pets and children (if possible), and then give her some rest. Talk to her gently and use her name as often as you can. Do not play with the cat too energetically. Do not take the animal outdoors and do not bring any friends or neighbors in to see the newcomer. A sedate, restful environment is best for the first day. It is quite likely that your new kitten is going to go directly under a sofa and hide for a while. You will need to tolerate this; regard it as an expression of anxiety, not a personal rejection. It is natural for all cats to seek a dark, safe spot when they think they might be in danger. Do not move the furniture or force the situation in any way. You might make some very gentle, playful sounds and gestures. Let the animal hide if she insists until meal time. You might have to offer some food on your finger as an enticement to come out. If she accepts the food, get her to follow you to her food place (or carry her there). Be relaxed and soothing in your tone and manner. After she has eaten, take her to the litter pan, and from there to her bed for a nap. If the kitten insists on hiding under the sofa, be patient. She will venture out sooner or later.

THE FIRST NIGHT

There is stillness. The lamp has cooled and the silence of the evening has flowed into the sounds of night, which are all but hidden from those asleep in their beds. The hum of the refrigerator, the flip of a digital clock, a squeak from within the wall and drops of water from the sink are all that disturb the nocturnal silence. One dreams and incorporates the night life of the house as sleep continues.

There is a disturbing, unfamiliar sound of frantic scratching against paper and plastic. Sleep's crust is broken and your eyes part. It sounds like raccoons at a bag of chicken bones. Something tips over and a banging, bumping noise is heard as things roll around the floor. You get to the kitchen, turn on the light and are shocked to find the garbage pail knocked over. Cans and bottles and coffee grounds and oil-soaked lettuce leaves and bits of peas and Kleenex tissues are spewed everywhere. Sitting in the middle of an empty donut box, licking the crumbs off his nose, is your new family member. His eyes are two fish ponds. He lookes up in surprise and wonders what you're doing there. You make a move in his direction and he scampers away, back to the safe comfort underneath the sofa.

After you clean up the mess and make some disciplinary statements to the dark void under the couch, you turn out the light and go back to bed. No sooner do the sheets warm up than a kitteny mew is heard throughout the house. It gets louder, sharper and more anguished as each note ascends and one desperate octave is piled on top of another. You call out the cat's name and soothingly tell him everything is all right. Suddenly, and without warning, the little cat jumps onto the bed and scrambles across your face. Finally, the kitten discovers your blanket and curls up on top of your feet, bedding down for the night. It is gratifying that the noise has stopped. However, if you move your legs you will certainly disturb the cat and start the cycle all over again. With a certainty of muscle cramps in the morning, you accept your fate and stare up at the ceiling in hopes of getting back to your warm, toasty sleep. There is a long night ahead.

The first week with your new cat will probably be difficult at night. This is a time for adjustment to the new home coupled with activities related to the growth and development of kittens. It is, I believe, the most difficult time for the first-time cat owner. It is also a time, however, when kittens are the most charming, the most humorous and the most endearing. Telling stories about the first weeks with your kitten is equal to discussing army basic training, summer camp or that first week in college. They were all terrible at the time, but awfully funny in retrospect. As the cat tears the bindings off your new Britannica, tell yourself that you're going to "dine out" on this experience. It will help.

If you remove a kitten from his litter, his mother, and his familiar surroundings, he is going to be disoriented and anxious. Even a kitten from a pet shop is going to need time to make the transition from one environment to another.

In the natural setting, wild cats are raised by their mothers and, to some degree, by their littermates. They are taught how to survive by the mother and by exposure to the harsh realities of their environment. Up until the twelfth week, wild cubs are fed by the mother. After that she takes them out on hunting trips where they learn to fend for themselves. It is not until after the fifth month that the cubs go off to find their individual destinies. By that time the youngsters have been given a fine education and it is natural for them to leave the comfort and safety of the mother's bosom.

The same emotions are involved if you take a domestic kitten away from his mother and litter at an early age or if a wild cub becomes permanently lost before the proper time to leave the lair. There is a great fear of danger and vulnerability. In either case the youngster continually cries out for his mother. It is not a cry of sentimental longing for a lifestyle that is over. The cry is real and the fear is fully justified from the kitten's point of view. A kitten or a cub on his own is in grave danger and he knows it. Try to remember this during the period of adjustment when you first take up with a cat. It is your goal to convince the kitten that he *is* home, that he is safe.

The other irritating nighttime activity is play behavior. Although cats are not truly nocturnal creatures, they are very well equipped for conditions approaching darkness. They see better in dim light than most mammals do, and they can make superb hunting decisions based on a touch of one of their ultra-sensitive whiskers. It has also been suggested that cats, like owls, recognize ultraviolet rays given off in

darkness from the bodies of some animals. His response to the subtle vibrations caused by prey animals plus his remarkable hearing capacity make the cat a keen night hunter.

It is all too common for kittens and even grown cats to make a routine out of play rituals in the middle of the night. Play is practice for prey-catching techniques, hunting methods, fighting behavior, escape behavior, sexual activity, and simply for exercise and fun. The feline technique for hunting is to stalk and ambush, utilizing maximum energy in an instantaneous rush of bursting effort as he pounces on his prey. These behaviors are mostly practiced when cats play, especially at night when no one is observing them. Domestic kittens habitually use even more energy in play than they would when actually hunting. It is little wonder, then, that their nocturnal behavior tends to keep the family awake. Worse yet, the play can become destructive to possessions and property. Garbage pails, lamp cords, books, magazines, clothing, all should be placed out of harm's way before you retire for the evening.

One way to cope with the playful new kitten is to confine the animal to one room for the night. The best place is where the food, water, scratch post and litter pan are located. The only problem with this is the cat's anxiety. Some kittens will adjust to being confined in one room alone for the evening and some will not (for a while, anyway). You can choose to confine the kitten in your room (with the door closed) if you do not mind his sleeping with you in the bed. Take the new cat bed in with you and place it on the floor and see if the cat will use it. Every kitten is an individual and requires a separate solution for most problems. I have heard of some kittens' being confined to a large cage at night with a hot-water bottle wrapped in a towel and a ticking alarm clock as a substitute mother. Perhaps you can acquire a toy or object from his former nest so that the odor from that familiar place is ever-present. It could be a comfort. Trial and error is the only solution. Some kittens are comforted by a softly playing radio tuned to an all-night talk show. Soft music may work, too. It is a fact that young kittens will either cry all night or get into as much mischief as you allow. Of course they will sleep intermittently. A kitten that has been socialized properly at the earliest time will make the quickest adjustment to the new home. In any event, the worst will be over in one to two weeks in most cases and one night in others. Good luck and good night.

3

The Tiger Within
(Behavior)

Cats are like children. Just when you think you've learned everything, there is yet one more delightful surprise. Considering all the research accomplished on cat behavior and the vast army of experts who have developed great knowledgeability on the subject, there is still so very much to be learned (or discovered). In nine lifetimes you will never know as much about your cat as your cat knows about you. The truth of the matter is that there are very few absolutes regarding the will and the ways of the domestic feline. Research, observation and experience can supply information on some aspects of cat behavior. But there are no hard and fast truisms that can be applied to all cats. Every one of them, down to the last raspy-tongued ankle-grabber, is a unique individual with his or her own eccentricities. In a sense, cats make their own rules and thereby define themselves as they go along. The novice cat owner will discover, as the more experienced one has already learned, that it is easier and more profitable to understand one's self in relation to cats than to pursue absolutes of feline behavior.

Set a cat loose in the human environment and watch our needs and desires rise to the surface like an underwater vessel coming from beneath the icecap. We want to be loved and we want not to be alone. There are infinite variations of these needs and some of them are quite complicated. But they always add up to giving and receiving. In Life's Theater the cat is the eternal understudy, standing in for absent children, parents, lovers, companions and roommates. Sometimes, only sometimes, they are set into the human mosaic as a cat, understood and accepted along purely feline terms.

On occasion humans experience a second or two of suspicion that perhaps they are using their cats unfairly or unwisely. Is it cruel to regard a pet as something close to human? It is a question for each of us to answer him- or herself. It is hard to consider talking to your cat or preparing her a home-cooked meal as inhumane or a wanton violation of her needs. The carpeted cat trees and goo-gooing are purely a matter of taste and hardly a matter for the conscience. Your author wishes to state categorically that cats, like humans, also need the warmth of concern and the nourishment of affection. They too want to be loved and less alone in the world.

But the cat is, after all, a cat. The human who lives with one owes it to himself or herself, and to the cat for that matter, to understand something about the nature of the felid spirit. This scant information is not being offered so that the reader can attempt to change the family cat's nature (indeed, that's almost impossible), but rather as a guided tour through an intricate and fascinating experience. Your cat is a unique creature. It offers no apology for its uncompromising and sometimes contradictory behavior. Cats understand humans to be quite mad and accept this as a matter of reality. For humans to understand cats is to accept cat reality, such as it is.

There can be no doubt that much of the domestic cat's basic behavior is similar if not identical to the basic behavior of most species of wild cats. The primary difference, of course, is the domestic cat's total acceptance of the human/pet lifestyle. With few exceptions cats raised in the wild will not tolerate close proximity to humans, while almost all domestic cats relish the relationship with humans. It is part of the felid nature to live in self-imposed solitude, marking territory and hunting, socializing only during mating and cub rearing. Why, then, will our pet cats tolerate life in a household with a troupe of humans, dogs and even other cats? One can only guess.

Paul Leyhausen in his important work, *Cat Behavior*, offers the following explanation:

> Why animals, who in the wild shun or even fight their
> conspecifics [fellow cats] except during mating periods and thus
> apparently feel no need of other social contact, should have this

capacity for close relationships with man is difficult to say. One can only make the following surmise. The bond between siblings and the link between mother and young weaken during a specific developmental period and finally sever altogether. In cats, however, they can sometimes be preserved long beyond the normal time. In many other mammals too, juvenile habits do not disappear altogether even in normal cases and may occasionally reappear in the adult animal. They are merely suppressed by other adult activities which have not yet developed when it is young. Among adult cats the social sector is fully occupied with guarding territory, defense, rivalry, and mating, and one or another of the corresponding activities is always elicited by an adult conspecific at such strength that, although a residue of propensities for juvenile activities is still there, these get no chance to express themselves.*

According to Leyhausen, then, long, enduring relationships between humans and domestic cats develop along lines similar to those between parent and child, or among siblings. The instant a human assumes the responsibility of feeding and caring for a cat, he or she is eliciting a form of juvenile dependency from the animal. This juvenile behavior may always be there but in a dormant state waiting for the proper conditions. Leyhausen continues,

> With a little skill and the necessary sympathetic understanding, a person may be capable of triggering off the residue of a cat's propensities for juvenile activities and even of resuscitating them, because he does not elicit defense and/or attack as uncompromisingly as an adult cat almost always does. Thus genuine and lasting friendship, of a kind which may never occur between cats themselves, is possible between humans and members of various species of solitary cats.

Taking Leyhausen's hypothesis one step further, we can see in the domestic cat a paradox of behavior. The skill of the solitary hunter produces an adult capable of instant self-sufficiency. The acceptance of loving care produces an eternal kitten. Therefore, our beloved

---

* Reprinted from the English-language edition by permission of Garland STPM Press, New York City.

house cats are both independent and dependent at the same time. It may be the only difference between wild and domestic cats other than size. It may also be a bit of their mystery.

A general understanding of basic cat behavior can make life much more pleasant for those who have taken in cats as members of the family. Although some traits can be altered through environmental manipulation, the primary objective here is to understand what is *natural* or *unnatural* in the family cat's behavior. When they are understood, many characteristics of the cat cease to be objectionable and help the owner appreciate the inner qualities as well as the external aesthetics. The need to scratch, to dig around the litter box, to present a dead mouse at your feet are but a few examples.

There are several major areas of feline behavior that are most important for the cat owner to understand. Naturally, these topics must, by necessity, be dealt with in an abbreviated manner, and the details of some aspects left out entirely. Volumes have been written on the subject and there will surely be more to come. However, this chapter will at least open the door and give the feline devotee a brief but useful understanding of his or her friend, the cat. The most important aspects of cat behavior, domestic and wild, are territory; dealing with prey animals; mating; and social behavior.

TERRITORY

Much has been written about territory and animals. The term *territory* simply refers to an area an animal regularly inhabits. The animal behaves as though the area is an extension of itself; it may accept some interlopers or it may attempt to drive them away. Territory is sometimes inherited, won in combat, or discovered and claimed after its abandonment by a previous animal.

Territory is not always a fixed bit of real estate. Sometimes it is simply the area that an animal finds itself in at the moment. Territory can also be an area an animal claims during a given season or a particular time of the day. For cats, however, territories are loosely fixed areas influenced by time, space and other creatures.

We are told by Edward O. Wilson in *Sociobiology:* "Nearly all vertebrates and a large number of the behaviorally most advanced invertebrates, conduct their lives according to precise rules of land tenure, spacing, and dominance. These rules mediate the struggle for competitive superiority. They are enabling devices that raise personal

or inclusive genetic fitness." In other words, territory is claimed and defended (often aggressively) as an instinctive drive for the purpose of species or individual survival. Most mammals inherently struggle for territory in order to protect their food supply. These instincts for territory are especially imbued in the cat. Despite the many generations of domesticity in the typical house cat, the instinct to claim and defend territory is quite strong.

There are two important locations which define a cat's territory. The first is the *core area* or *immediate home*, which receives the heaviest use. The immediate home area is where most daily activities take place. It also contains the lair, the safest sleeping area in the entire territory. In domesticity, the core area may be an entire house, one room in an apartment, or perhaps a portion of a room. The second element is the *home* or *outer range*. This is a vague, loosely defined area composed of interconnecting pathways and trails leading to water, resting places, scent posts, emergency retreats and favorite sunning spots. It is also where most hunting takes place. The home range may be an entire valley or portion of a mountain range for some of the larger wild cats. For domestic cats it may be a basement, a kitchen, back alley or yard.

Male cats claim larger territories than females. Female cats are especially intolerant of territorial intrusions from other female cats. Quite frequently the outer ranges of neighboring cats overlap, a situation that is tolerated because the territoriality of cats also has to do with time-and-place rather than just place alone. Neighboring cats may hunt the same terrain but at different times. They will try to avoid each other at all costs. This scheduling of use of space prevents confrontations and inevitable fighting. It is quite a different situation from sharing of common territory by two or more cats who live with a human family. Here an informal order of rank and superiority coupled with the cats' juvenile tendencies help maintain order and a pleasant atmosphere.

Animal behaviors regarding territory vary from casual to intense. All cats, wild and domestic, have strong sets of responses concerning the acquisition and defense of territory. Domestic cats rarely have the opportunity to choose their territory. Even so, once they are brought to a place, they relate to it as their wild cousins do. Animals who graze in a herd (*e.g.*, wildebeests) and those who hunt in a pack (*e.g.*, wolves) travel vast distances in a sprawling, ill-defined territory, creating a great overlap of ranges. Consequently, their attitude toward territory is much more casual than that of cats.

With the exception of lions, cats in the wild live and hunt alone. Their hunting techniques involve stalking and ambushing, lunging and pouncing. Their territories are smaller and more exclusive than those of other mammals. Few cats in the wild can afford to tolerate an incursion into their territory by another cat. This fact is of vital importance to cat owners because it explains why their pets may become upset with a new cat, a human they do not trust, visiting cats, or a move to a new house. From the family cat's point of view, any change affecting territory is a threat to survival.

These tendencies are made apparent by the degree of emotion shown when the cat's territory is violated or moved. The most common expression of emotional distress is to urinate and defecate in various parts of the new premises (read territory) instead of in the litter box. Sometimes she behaves as though she is depressed (and she may well be). An unhappy cat may make low, throaty sounds you never heard before and might even start clawing the furniture, the walls, the curtains or you. Although relationships with humans and other animals become very important to domestic cats, loss of territory is of greater importance. It is taken as a catastrophe. While a domestic cat assumes she will survive without you, instinct indicates that the cat is in jeopardy with the loss of established territory. This grievous fear is usually not based in fact, because the human has simply exchanged one territory for another. But the cat doesn't know this; it takes great patience and much extra attention to convince the cat she is still safe when she is uprooted from her territory and moved somewhere else.

An extremely important aspect of territory for the cat owner to understand has to do with *marking*. This refers to the acts by which a cat in the wild or at home leaves his or her mark or individual sign of identity in various parts of the immediate home or the home range, or on another cat's territory. Researchers are not sure of the reasons for territory marking and can only offer educated guesses.

Some believe it is used as a boundary demarcation so that wandering or visiting cats will know they are trespassing. However, few cats have ever been reported to turn in the opposite direction on coming upon a territory mark. Leyhausen believes it may be a guide for cats to avoid each other, which prevents sudden clashes. Another aspect of territory marking is message-sending with a special function for mating, a perfumed billet-doux as it were.

Territory marking is accomplished in several ways. The most common and least understood by novice cat owners has to do with the cat's toileting habits. All cats, male and female, *spray* as a means of marking. When a cat marks territory or asserts itself, which are closely related, it may spray urine against some vertical object, defecate, scratch or claw something, paw-wipe, or vocalize. Quite often more than one of these methods are employed at the same time. This information can be of some help to the cat owner who doesn't understand why the family cat has suddenly "gone berserk" with unacceptable behavior.

It has been thought for a long time that the spraying of urine by male cats is eliminated once the animal has been castrated. It is one of the primary reasons pet owners have this surgical procedure done. Information from experienced cat owners indicates this is not necessarily the case. Altering a male usually but not always prevents spraying.

When this author's present cat first arrived, he quickly established a behavior pattern that included defecation (in the litter box, luckily) followed by mad dashes across the apartment at various odd hours while sounding the most disturbing *mmrowls* at the family dog. This was met with alarm and dismay by the rest of the household. To this day that cat continues to assert itself in this manner. However, it is now a source of warm amusement for the family, who have become quite blasé and only mildly interested.

Most male cats (some females, too), at various times, will back up against a wall, a window, a piece of furniture or some outdoor object and spray urine. In the case of unaltered male cats this urine usually is quite pungent and upsets everyone who comes in contact with it. Sometimes cats rub their faces in it and then rub against other objects. Every breed of cat, every species of cat, behaves in this manner. It is the most common form of marking, although defecation is also used for this purpose. Spraying may also be a form of sexual communication by either male or female.

Spraying urine and/or defecating can also be used by a cat as a sign of defiance to another cat after a nonviolent confrontation. This will occur at various spots already sprayed in the past as territory marks. In a litter box, the feces is usually buried beneath the sand. But on occasion the cat will bury the old feces and display the new feces on top of a mound of sand. This may be accompanied with a throaty sound and a mad dash from room to room. Sometimes the form of running is in a stiff, sideways gait that is not unlike the cat's arched display when preparing for a confrontation.

Marking territory or communicating the cat's presence is all too often accomplished by clawing visible scratches into a vertical object such as a tree, if you're lucky, or the arm of a sofa, if you're not. Although most scratching has to do with the need to remove the outer sheath of the claws, much of it has to do with assertion and the marking of territory.

Probably the most fascinating form of marking is vocal assertion. The large cats of the jungles and plains are the greatest of the vocalizers, but do not underestimate the domestic cat's powerful ability to manifest its roar. Vocalizing occurs between rival males when competing for a female in heat. There is much vocalization when two males are about to fight for territory. Sometimes vocalizing seems a lonely, haunting sound aimed at the sky, but it is in fact aimed at the near and far competition.

HOW CATS DEAL WITH PREY ANIMALS

It is not yet known if cats stalk, kill and eat prey animals simply because they are hungry or as an automatic reaction to stimuli. Researchers are not even certain if such a seemingly automatic reaction is learned or at least affected by experience. What is known is that all cats are intensely curious about scratching and high-pitched squealing noises. These stimuli do not necessarily have to be associated with any specific prey animal. According to Leyhausen, acoustic stimuli do not necessarily elicit prey-catching but simply the desire for prey-catching. The cat quickly moves to the source of the sound and investigates visually. All the hunting mechanisms, such as stalking, shift into gear at the first sighting of movement or sooner, if the cat is an experienced hunter.

A young, inexperienced cat tends to regard all creatures as "fellow cats." Leyhausen tells us that a cat and a mouse placed together do not necessarily automatically play out hunter/hunted roles. If the mouse moves slowly it will be sniffed but tolerated. However, if the mouse runs away from the cat swiftly, in a straight line, the cat will chase it and pounce upon it. This is true of any smaller animal running away from or at right angles to the cat. Conversely, when a smaller animal runs *to* the cat, the cat will hesitate and perhaps retreat. Leyhausen concludes that the cat's catching action is innately released by specific forms and directions of movement. He adds that only prey with fur or a furlike covering will elicit a killing bite. The prey's scent seems to have little or no bearing on stalking or killing. Scent is used by the cat primarily for the purposes of mating and ingesting food, although experienced cats are drawn to the dried urine spots left behind by mice as they run and cats will sniff along this type of trail.

The following table indicates the components of behavior toward prey.

COMPONENTS OF PREY BEHAVIOR

SENSORY SPHERE	SIGN STIMULI	ACTIVITY ELICITED
Hearing	Rustling and scratching sounds, squeaking call-notes	* Appetence for prey-catching
Sight	Not too large object moving beside or away from cat	Approach to prey (stalking-run, creeping in, watching, springing, grasping)
Touch	Furlike surface of object seized	Killing bite
Sight	Recognizable head-and-body shape of prey object	** Taxes of grasping, killing, picking up to carry around
Probably smell	Not known	Cutting open
Probably taste and/or touch	Not known	Chewing and swallowing
Touch	Stimulation of whiskers by direction of hairs on prey	Taxes of cutting and eating

* In behavioral psychology: actions carried out to directly or indirectly satisfy a need.

** Plural of taxis: the responsive movement of an organism toward or away from an external stimulus.

From *Cat Behavior: The Predatory and Social Behavior of Domestic and Wild Cats* by Paul Leyhausen. Translated by Barbara A. Tonkin. Published by Garland STPM Press. Copyright © 1979.

Cats have a remarkable memory for the places they have traversed. A cat that experiences a hunting triumph at a particular location will remember that exact place and return again and again seeking another triumph, even after a long time lapse. This is an extremely important part of the cat's superb hunting ability and has obvious survival value.

Domestic cats can interact with captured prey in a manner that is sometimes construed as "cruel" or "heartless." It is behavior that is difficult to reconcile with the image of the pet cat who is cuddly and lovable. Cats appear to "play" with their captured prey until it mercifully dies. This instinctive behavior is programmed genetically and

The predator cat at work. Stoop-shouldered, it waits for the prey animal to move or show itself.

meant to be performed in front of kittens. Its purpose is to elicit the correct responses in kittens so that their hunting instincts might develop properly. Nature does not take into account the pet food industry or whether a male or female cat actually has kittens to teach. Both novice and experienced cat owners must understand that cats are *natural* creatures who behave with a strong survival instinct. Most living organisms have built into their behavior the drive to ensure the survival of their species. This is why most animals protect and teach their young what they know. Try to bear this in mind if you happen to witness your cat's behavior with captured prey. Consider what the captured animal probably does with *its* prey.

What constitutes the prey of domestic cats can be reduced to one simple rule: *A cat will be attracted to any living animal no bigger than itself.* Depending on the cat's aggressive inclinations, she is mostly interested in mice and rats. (It is important to note that few domestic cats will take on the full-grown Norway rat, which is the most common rat in the world.) Domestic cats are interested in most insects including houseflies, beetles, crickets and grasshoppers. They are also interested in frogs, toads, lizards, snakes, rabbits, shrews, moles, squirrels, and birds. With regard to birds, a reassuring note to bird and cat lovers is the fact that cats are capable of catching only old, sick or very young avians. Only on rare occasions do cats capture mature, healthy birds. What is often not appreciated is that at least three-fourths of all birds die as a result of nature's own control of the population/territory ratio. The primary factors that keep a bird population of any area relatively constant are cold, insufficient food and disease. Cats could not survive if they relied on a diet of birds exclusively.

In fact, cats perform a selective function when they prey on unprotected, old, sick or injured birds. By selecting out these birds from the population, they enhance the survival of the general population of birds. And, as stated above, the most common prey of the domestic cat is the mouse.

The method of catching her prey is what makes the cat, both domestic and wild, the consummate hunter of the entire animal kingdom. A cat usually hears her prey as the first signal. In a crouched posture she runs toward the sound. She then stops and observes in a special close-to-the-ground position. In the natural setting she would crouch behind grass, earth mounds or other forms of cover. The principal technique is to ambush the prey animal before it has the opportunity to escape. In a stooped-shoulder manner she waits for the prey to move or show itself. Domestic cats are quite patient and are capable of waiting long periods. Once the prey is sighted, the cat employs a stalking run, which again is very low to the ground. This enables her to get closer to the prey without having to give chase. More observation takes place as the claws unsheath; the tail lies flat and twitches from side to side at the tip, and the leg muscles contract in readiness to spring. Every sense the cat possesses goes into full operation, from extended whiskers to forward-pointing ears. With a wobbling motion of the hind legs the cat prepares to attack. She springs forward, low to the ground, and bounds to the victim in a shallow leap. The cat almost always catches the mouse with her paws at this stage.

If the pounce is unsuccessful, a chase ensues with all the advantage going to the cat. Once the mouse is caught, the cat strikes it from behind on the back and shoulder with one paw and holds it while she delivers a killing bite in front of the holding paw, directly on the nape of the prey's neck. This usually severs the spinal cord, effecting instant death. In the natural setting (and sometimes the domestic one as well), the cat commences to eat the animal.

Experienced cat owners know that not every cat will chase, catch, kill or eat mice. A domestic cat may perform none or one or any combination of these predatory elements. Although there is no way to be sure why this is true, there are some possible explanations for this behavior (or the lack of it). It is important to recognize that every cat has the inherent tendency to hunt for food. Whether or not these instincts are developed fully depends on several factors. They must be elicited at an early age by the mother, by the littermates and by prey itself. However, even if there is no early elicitation of the prey-catching behaviors, they will appear later with the onset of hunger or with the appearance of prey animals acting in a manner that provokes this behavior.

Leyhausen tells us that the first prey-catching movement is made by a kitten at about three weeks of age. This is a tentative forward grope with one paw, which is also how an adult cat investigates any new, fairly small object. Lying in wait, chasing, stalking, the stalking run, and the pounce onto the prey appear in rapid succession. These are completely developed by the time the mother cat brings the first live prey animals to the kittens in about their sixth week. In the fourth week the mother cat begins to carry dead prey into the nest, where the kittens watch her eat it. In the following weeks the kittens' reactions to the prey animal mature. Thus when the mother brings the first live prey animal into the nest, the kittens have at their disposal all of the instinctive movements for prey-catching. The killing bite is the last element to develop. This late development has survival value, for the kittens would surely injure each other while playing at prey-

What mouse sees from its hiding place.

catching if the response developed earlier. As they play with the first live prey animals brought into the nest by the mother, the ordered sequence leading to the killing bite—lying in wait, stalking, pouncing and seizing—establishes itself gradually, though occasionally it can happen quite suddenly.

Mother cats with kittens older than three weeks usually catch considerably more prey than at other times. These, we may presume, are for the benefit of the kittens who are now being weaned from breast milk to partially solid food. It is the behavior of the kittens themselves that stimulates the mother's hunting activity. From the fourth to the sixth weeks the mother brings dead prey animals to the nest and growls to attract the attention of the kittens. The growling may change into a coaxing purr and she will paw the dead animal several times before eating it, once she is certain that the kittens are watching. This very same behavior can be seen in domestic cats who do not have kittens. They may catch a mouse, kill it and then bring it to the feet of the human companion, who in this instance is serving as a substitute kitten. Males as well as females behave in this manner. It is less important for the human to "congratulate" the cat than it is simply to approach the cat and look at what it caught.

Interestingly, the killing bite is not taught by the mother, but rather elicited by the mother's behavior or that of a littermate. A live prey animal is brought into the nest and released by the mother. She swiftly catches the released animal as the kittens observe her. They do not learn from her example, as one would imagine; their inherent instincts to give chase and to capture the prey are triggered by the mother's behavior. She appeals to their sense of competition as they eventually try to beat her to the released prey during the several times it is released. The released prey elicits the kittens' prey-catching activity by running away, and its swift recapture by the older cat compels the kittens to be even quicker if they want to catch the prey before the mother seizes it again. This is what provides the needed excitation that leads to the killing bite. It is important to note that the keenest domestic cats never seize their prey with as much wild eagerness and determination as young male wild cats. (This is what makes them suitable as pets.) Yet the instinct to kill prey is often observed by the ninth week in domestic kittens.

If the mother cat does not bring live prey to the kittens during the critical period between their sixth and about their twentieth weeks the kittens either do not kill prey later in life or else learn to do so slowly and laboriously.

The development of the killing bite is connected with the growth of the canine teeth, which are the ones employed for this purpose. The deciduous or milk teeth are all in place by the fifth week and ready to function. During the transition from deciduous to permanent teeth there may be one or two weeks when the temporary canines are too weak to function and the permanent ones are not yet long enough. This happens sometime between the fourth and sixth months. In a natural setting, the litter of kittens breaks up as a family by the sixth month. This happily coincides with the development of all the permanent teeth.

One further statement on prey capture is essential for the owner of a domestic cat. All cats, both young and old, engage in play activity. Much of this play behavior is connected in one way or another with prey-catching activity. For reasons too complex for this work, cats tend to play with their captured prey, both before and after they have killed it. In the true play that cats indulge in (*without* prey animals), one can observe the various aspects of prey capture with or without toys or other animals. Here we often see a form of "overflow" energy involving all aspects of hunting and prey capture. Some cat owners refer to these energized spurts as the "nightly crazies," when the normally quiet animal suddenly dashes across the room in a crouched position. All elements of prey capture can be seen, including stalking, watching posture, creeping, pouncing, seizing with the teeth, carrying around, and tossing objects away. During the "crazies," more energy may be expended than if the cat or kitten were actually hunting. To the novice cat owner this is a startling and perplexing set of behaviors. It is probably safe to assume that all cat play mimics the dynamics of cat existence from prey capture to declarations of dominance to fighting over females and territory. It is harmless, fascinating and, more often than not, quite funny if not outright lovable.

MATING

When considering cat behavior it is impossible to ignore sexual urges and the drive to mate. Although the biological imperative of most living organisms is to procreate, it is the furthest thing from the mind of a sexually aroused cat. It would seem that the principal drive in all unaltered cats is to experience sex as frequently as possible. Females in heat and males aware of such females can think of nothing save the consummation of their potent urges. Because so much of the

Courtship . . . feline style. Two Russian Blues about to mate.

feline personality is overshadowed at these times by sexual appetite, it is of vital concern to the cat owner to become aware of the details of this behavior. This may help in deciding to have the whole male or female cat surgically sterilized.

Whole males (tomcats) exhibit great frustration if they are not permitted to mate as often as their bodies dictate. Purebred cats that are employed as studs should be mated frequently. Sexually frustrated males are hostile, restless, sometimes dangerous. They yowl and pace and spray their areas with an altogether unpleasant smelling urine. A frustrated tomcat makes the worst possible pet or home companion.

Unspayed females (queens) who are sexually aroused and not permitted to satisfy themselves are equally unpleasant to be around. Their vocalizing is continual, as are their physical entreaties to be allowed outdoors. In some instances unmated females remain in a constant state of heat. This can mean a nonstop display of vocalizations, rubbing, purring, and rolling behavior in addition to odorous glandular secretions deposited anywhere from the litter box to the carpet.

Sex between male and female cats is less violent when arranged by experienced, knowledgeable breeders. Here, a desired genetic selection is being sought in order to further the best qualities of two lines of a pure breed. The union is less violent because the female is presented to only one male and the encounter is on the male's own territory. Random matings of feral cats or cats that are permitted to roam outdoors are always violent, noisy, and somewhat bizarre to the human sensibility.

When the female goes into heat, most of the male cats in the area smell and hear her condition and become attracted and aroused. A collection of males begins to assemble around the lusty female. They travel through other cats' territories to get to the female, which sometimes causes violent confrontations. Although there may be a loosely formed order of dominance among the cats of the immediate vicinity, it is not honored by those of other areas. This creates a situation much like a time bomb. It will definitely explode. The question is when.

The female will ward off any male advances until she is quite ready for copulation. Until then, the competition for her attention will intensify. Once or more males will begin to circle and then the fights begin. One, two, three or even more tomcats may engage in savage fighting with unsheathed claws and slashing teeth, causing the most awful damage to each other.

The males confront each other with spiky coats and arched backs and hiss, spit and growl. After a choreography of slow approaches accompanied by threat vocalizations ranging from growls, to shrieks, one will finally spring at the other and aim its teeth at the nape of the neck as though it were after a prey animal. They slash and claw at one another, rolling furiously about, screaming and spitting. Suddenly they will break apart and move away for a needed rest. After a brief pause they will return for another confrontation, and repeat this blistering ritual several times until finally one of the participants does not return to the fight, thus accepting defeat. The fascinating element is that the victor does not always win the female. As the most dominant males are fighting, there may be one lower-ranking male who begins the courtship and quickly enjoys the female's favors while the others are still sorting themselves out.

The courtship between the male and the female cat is highly ritualized. There is the traditional pursuit and avoidance. He follows her but she moves away. If he fails to follow she stops and entices him with alluring gestures, rubbing, rolling and softly purring. If the male approaches too quickly or not at the correct moment, the female rebuffs him with hissing and spitting and a swipe with her paw. A nervous or impatient female is capable of rendering painful damage to a pursuing tom.

Once the female is ready she will crouch, rub her body against the ground and cozy up to the male. She may even tread or knead with her feet as she lowers the front of her body and raises the rear in a presenting posture. Her tail is shifted to one side, giving the male complete access to her vulva. At this point the male pounces as if she were prey, seizes her by the nape with a slight holding bite, and mounts her. He grasps her abdomen with his two front paws as his penis emerges from its protective sheath. His hind legs hold her in place as he attempts to make entry. Both male and female keep shifting positions to facilitate this. Several attempts are made until it is accomplished. Upon entry, ejaculation *and ovulation* take place within five to fifteen seconds. The male instantly pulls away, causing the barbs on the tip of his penis to tear slightly some inner tissue. It is believed that this sensation, be it intense pain or pleasure, creates a violent reaction in the female. She emits a screaming sound, frees herself from the male grip, and attempts to strike him with a slashing claw. Most often the experienced male springs away just in time to avoid injury. Both male and female will then relax and start over again within a short time. They may copulate as many as five or ten times in thirty minutes. The mating process can continue for twenty-four hours or even longer. During this time, the male may tire of her and allow the other waiting males to continue satisfying her needs. The female is almost certain to become pregnant because copulation stimulates ovulation in the female. Because ovulation occurs with each mating, and because more then one male may mate with a female in heat, it is possible for the kittens of a single litter to have different genetic fathers. Wondrous are the ways of cat reproduction!

Whole male cats will mate at almost any time, especially if they are on their own territory. A free-roaming tom will travel relatively great distances to "visit" a female in heat. Mature male cats must gratify their sexual appetites or suffer severe frustration. Mature females (eight months or older) usually experience estrus four times a year. Some cats go into season every thirty days while others may show a cycle that occurs only twice a year. Few generalities can be applied to all cats.

To those unprepared for it, feline sexuality is a disturbing surprise, to say the least. The human family agonizes over what they think is traumatic and painful for the cat. Often novice cat owners do not even know what they are looking at and contact the veterinarian, thinking they have a medical emergency.

The most logical response for humans to this behavior is the surgical sterilization of their pets. The terminology used is *neutering.* Male cats are *castrated* or *altered,* while female cats are *spayed* or given *ovariohysterectomies.* Depending on when the cat is neutered, many or most of the sexual behaviorisms will never develop. It is best to have males altered at or before six months of age. Females should be spayed shortly after their first estrus cycle, which is often between five and six months.

Because there is so much to enjoy and appreciate in the complexity of the feline personality, it is sad to see it all overpowered by the intense sexual behavior of unneutered cats. Fixed or altered cats are much pleasanter to live with and capable of showing all aspects of themselves. Even so, there is still some residual sexual behavior in neutered animals, including the male's occasional spraying (although the urine is not nearly so pungent or terrible-smelling, and not all do this). On the positive side is the cat (male or female) who rubs against your leg with affection and offers a mellow purr and a doe-eyed caress with the eyes. Love's labor is never lost.

SOCIAL BEHAVIOR

Living with a cat is a paradox. What is it that enables a creature of solitude and incredible independence to share its existence with humans and other animals? As we noted, Leyhausen suggests it may be human elicitation of juvenile tendencies and an encouragement of childlike dependency. Despite the loss of savage wildness and the exchange of total independence for domestic comforts and rewards, the typical house cat cannot escape the matrix of its felid behavior. A cat is always a cat, whether it's living in a split-level ranch, a twenty-floor high-rise, or in a mountain crevice taking the afternoon sun along the timberline. Relations with other cats in or out of its own territory remain unchanged in format if not in intensity.

When two strange cats meet, which almost never happens in the wild (except for mating), they cautiously sniff each other. They investigate the immediate area, using sight, sound and smell. They then turn back to each other. At first they appear to sniff each other's noses,

The human elicitation of juvenile tendencies in cats makes them perfect house pets.

although they do not actually touch. The whiskers act as feelers as they size up each other's nape and flanks and ultimately smell each other's anus. Although there is a slight resistance to this aspect of the investigation, one finally allows the other to continue smelling, provided the encounter remains friendly. Very often the friendliness ends when one moves a bit too quickly while examining the nape of the neck. Defensive postures quickly develop and one or both begin to hiss. From there the more assertive of the two will deliver a blow on the nose with its paw and send its opponent running. This automatically establishes a kind of social structure, with one cat dominant over the other. The encounter may repeat itself several times before the confrontation ends. Depending on the territoriality of the dominant cat, things may go very sour and result in a direct physical attack. This is highly likely if both cats are whole tomcats. The cat who is on its own territory is usually the dominant animal, at least in the beginning. In variations of this behavior, both animals will crouch, staring at each other for long periods. Extremely timid cats will run and hide as long as there is a strange cat in their territory.

In domesticity, two or more cats can share a territory with little or no difficulty.

The factors that permit cats to get along with each other are not fully known. Many experienced cat owners have perfectly delightful stories of cats who spend entire lifetimes together in peace and harmony. However, the dominance of one cat over another is usually subtle in manner and sometimes imperceptible to the enthusiastic cat lover, who translates animal actions into human terms. The use of the food bowls and litter box by a dominant cat can act as a guide to the degree of harmony in a multi-cat territory. In some hierarchical structures, a top cat emerges along with one or more low cats on the totem pole who behave in a cowering manner to all the others. Leyhausen says, "With cats there is nothing automatic about the buildup of such a social structure. It largely depends on the individual character of the animals concerned and there are also communities in which neither a definite top animal nor a pariah appears."

When two or more cats share a territory or a common home, only the gentlest form of dominance and subordination may manifest itself. Here are cats completely accustomed to one another without much need for the type of violent fights that cats are capable of engaging in. However, a strange cat entering the scene will certainly be examined and quite likely attacked.

Because domestic cats do not select their primary territory, but rather have it selected for them by humans, they seem to accept each other with much greater ease than their wild cousins. This is an extremely important aspect of domesticity. The denial of the primary decision in a cat's life probably has a subordinating effect. This may be what allows them to share a territory in domesticity with one or more cats.

Cat owners can greatly enhance their own and their cats' lifestyles by understanding and accepting the basics of cat behavior. The importance of territory applies to such everyday elements as feeding dishes, litter boxes, resting areas, toys, and hiding places. Allowing for predatory behavior, if only in the manner of play, is extremely important for the mental health of a house cat. Do not discourage prey capture in any form unless it is destructive to the home or anyone living in it. Sexual behavior cannot be avoided unless the animal is surgically sterilized, and even then not all of it can be eliminated. Matters of dominance, social harmony and aggressiveness must be dealt with sympathetically. By studying a cat's behavior one cannot help but comprehend its true nature and love it all the more. It is here that you will begin to perceive the dignity of your cat. In every dear kitten and sweet-faced tabby is a prehistoric fire reflected in tooth, claw and leap. Look for tigers burning brightly.

4

Food, Glorious Food

If you really want to feed your cat what he likes best, try a mouse sandwich with a fondue tray of grasshoppers, crickets, flies, beetles, moths and butterflies. Coarse grass or houseplant leaves make an excellent dessert to be washed down with seasoned water such as that found in flower vases and outdoor puddles. These are the things that cats enjoy most. Of course, domesticity has altered the menu a bit for the sake of the human sensibility. The prehistoric saber-toothed tiger liked nothing better than sinking its foot-long canines into fresh mastodon hide as, indeed, today's wild cats still hunt the cloven-hoofed grass eaters. The point is that it is impossible to feed a house cat what he would eat in the wild unless you devote your entire life to that pursuit.

Much is being discussed about "natural diets" and "health food diets" for cats and dogs, but unless you are determined to set the cat loose or to stalk the wild flora and fauna yourself, formulating such a diet is a task best left to the manufacturers of cat food. Although cats easily revert to the natural state, they would have a most difficult time finding a natural setting to accommodate their primitive instincts. Most cats live in urban areas where it is becoming difficult to find anything growing or moving about freely.

It is true that the cat is a carnivore, more than any other animal. But it cannot exist on an exclusively meat diet, which would cause serious nutritional deficiencies leading to disease and death. A fine balance of protein, carbohydrates, fat, water, vitamins and minerals is obtained when the cat kills and eats its prey. The entire carcass is consumed, including the bones and the viscera. The viscera of rodents, birds, and insects contain plant foods such as leaves, stems, roots and grains. It is, in effect, a vegetable tray accompanying the steak tartare. Duplicating this important variety and nutritional balance in your kitchen is not impossible, but it is extremely complicated and difficult.

COMMERCIAL CAT FOOD

Commercial cat foods are being produced in greater variety every year, and it is apparent that they are being named to appeal to the owner/shopper. It is best to pay more attention to the contents listed on the label.

Dry, Cereal Type

Dry cat food is a cereal-based source of nutrition consisting of grains or cereals mixed with combinations of meat, fish and/or dairy products. The premium brands have added vitamins and minerals, balanced to meet the nutritional requirements of cats.

Dry cat food is a highly controversial subject among cat owners, breeders, veterinarians and even researchers. It is believed by some and not by others to be an element in Feline Urologic Syndrome (FUS), which is one of the more common and, unfortunately, lethal illnesses in cats. (See Chapter 7.) Although no one can be sure if dry cat food actually causes FUS, most experts agree that dry-type food should not be fed to any cat with a predisposition toward that disease. Some veterinarians believe that the intake of water in large quantities is necessary in preventing and treating FUS. They hold that cereals do not promote a sufficient intake of moisture. Others suggest that the ash content of cat food is either a cause or an aggravating factor in FUS.

One researcher believes FUS is caused by a herpes virus, while other researchers are convinced it has to do with high magnesium intake. High ash content (minerals) is also a possible factor. Some veterinarians believe there is no relationship whatsoever between FUS and a cat's diet; others disagree. Richard Gebhardt, president of the Cat Fanciers Association, believes that some cats can tolerate dry food while others cannot. He heartily concurs with the view that any cat with a tendency to show symptoms of FUS should not be fed dry cat food.

Aside from any medical considerations, dry cat food is the most economical form of commercial food for cats. Because of the high density of the food, the pet owner is not purchasing large quantities of water. The moisture content of dry food is 10 percent. Canned foods contain between 70 and 76 percent water, making it necessary to feed the cat larger portions in order to maintain adequate nutrition. Cost, therefore, becomes a great consideration.

Cats do seem to find canned cat food more palatable, possibly because of the resemblance to fresh game. Certainly the high moisture content of canned food is a factor. However, cats are generally reluctant to eat solid chunks from a fluid mixture. Many cats love to crunch their food and one of the easiest ways of feeding is to select a top-quality dry-food product, put it in a bowl in a quiet, convenient place and let the cat eat whenever the mood prevails.

Soft-Moist Cat Food

This most recent and extremely popular form of commercial cat food comes in various colors and is soft to the touch, yet it does not require refrigeration. It is often made to resemble hamburger, stew meat or meat granules. Cats tend to be attracted to the look, smell and taste of it. Unlike the sugar preservation process used in similar food for dogs, phosphoric acid is utilized by most manufacturers to control bacterial growth in soft-moist cat food. (However, some brands use sucrose [sugar] as a preservative because it is felt that phosphoric acid plays a role in Feline Urologic Syndrome.) It is made with many protein sources; it may feature only one as the overall flavoring, such as beef or tuna, or may offer flavor mixtures. This form of pet food is more expensive than dry food, but not as expensive as canned "gourmet" types. It is designed to provide complete nutrition.

Canned Ration

Canned cat food is by far the most popular form of food used to feed house cats. The ingredients always consist of some form of protein (most often fish), along with various grains and vitamin and mineral supplements. These are cooked in the can and preserved through the traditional canning process. Canned food is much more expensive than other forms because of the extremely high water content. You actually buy close to 75 percent water when purchasing canned cat food. Many canned ration cat foods, especially those composed primarily of fish, contain levels of minerals (ash) well in excess of feline requirements. It is a good idea to compare the mineral content on the label of any canned cat food you might select with the nutritional requirements for cats given in the charts at the end of this chapter.

Canned Gourmet Cat Food

Of the canned foods, these are the most expensive and, interestingly, the most popular. They come in such flavors as kidney, liver, chicken, shrimp, tuna, beef and in hundreds of varieties of these ingredients. Most canned gourmet cat foods are not balanced diets despite the fact that some have added vitamins and minerals. It is a mistake to feed a cat any one food exclusively, but it is a serious mistake to feed it a gourmet canned cat food and nothing else. This form of commercial food should be used only as one part of an overall feeding program.

Canned Prescribed Diets

There is a variety of canned pet foods that is available only through a veterinarian and is formulated for the dietary management of cats with special medical or physical conditions. Although several leading pet-food manufacturers have created foods for various stages of life for dogs (such as Gaines Cycle 1, 2, 3, and 4), only Prescription Diet and Cadillac brands have canned formulations for various medical conditions for cats. Consult your veterinarian for more information.

HOW TO FEED YOUR CAT

Cats, like humans, need different kinds of food at different times in their lives. The following section will provide you with a valuable set of guidelines for providing your cat with optimal nutrition throughout its life.

Kittens

From birth to weaning, which usually means from day one to day twenty-eight (or thereabouts), mother's milk is the only source of nourishment. This is adequate if the mother cat (queen) has an ample supply for the entire litter. Important antibodies are present in the mother cat's milk for the first twenty-four to thirty-six hours. This first milk is called *colostrum.* In addition to providing immunities, it also supplies protein, vitamins and various nutrients to the newborn kittens. It is essential that the kittens receive colostrum as soon as possible. If the kittens are orphaned or rejected for any reason, it is imperative to supply milk as quickly as possible if the animals are to live. There are several high-quality milk-substitute products available for orphaned newborn kittens. It is important to understand that cat milk has a greater quantity of protein and fat than cow milk. For that reason the latter cannot meet the nutritional requirements of kittens.

When nursing an orphaned kitten, bear in mind that the animal needs direct stimulation to help him digest food for the first two weeks of his life. You will have to burp the little cat by gently patting his back and then help him to urinate and defecate by rubbing him on the belly. Normally, the mother cat would do this with her tongue. Follow the directions on the milk-substitute product that apply to the kitten's age. Quantities and time schedules will be supplied. Most nursing kittens require four or five feedings a day and receive just under two teaspoons per feeding. These commercial products often come with nipples and bottles to implement feeding. One of the finest nursing kitten products is KMR from Borden. Their Small Animal Nurser set has everything you will need.*

By four weeks of age the kitten is ready to begin being weaned away from a milk-only diet through the gradual introduction of whole food. For two or three weeks a commercially prepared cereal product for weaning kittens should be introduced. Mix it with tepid whole or evaporated milk and feed a small quantity four times a day between nursing sessions with the mother or scheduled milk-substitute feedings. By the sixth week you may begin introducing small quantities of scraped meat or boiled white fish or chicken.

* Ask for their very informative booklet, "The Borden Guide for the Care and Feeding of Orphan and Rejected Kittens." KMR Borden Chemical, Pet Products, Box 419, Norfolk, VA 23501

The growth rate of kittens is accelerated during the first twenty-one weeks. In the first three weeks a kitten's birth weight usually triples. Many cats, however, do not reach full maturity for fifteen to eighteen months. An eight-week-old kitten, fully weaned, requires four meals a day—the more mixed the diet, the better. A minimum of four to five ounces of food per day should be provided for each kitten. Vary the diet from meal to meal with dry food designed for kittens, cooked egg yolk, small quantities of whole milk (provided it does not cause indigestion), strained meats (baby food), cooked white fish, cooked chicken (white meat), and a very small quantity of cooked liver. By five months a kitten should be provided with no less than six ounces of food daily.

At five months of age, switch from four to three meals a day. Three feedings a day are desirable for kittens up to eight months of age. The feeding habits of cats can make grown men and women weep. Many cats, when allowed, will become addicted to or will insist on one or two foods or brands of food. This can be dangerous if the food is not a balanced diet or if, for some medical reason, the diet must be changed. This is why a varied diet should be fed to the average house cat for its entire life. Try to avoid any addictions or fixations to any one type of food. Never try to humanize the cat diet in order to make it more palatable. Human preferences and cat preferences are different, although cats will sometimes eat human foods because of the attention that goes along with it. Please bear in mind that every cat is different and only the most general rules apply to all. To some extent allow the insane dictates of your own cat to determine food quantities, feeding schedules, and types of food offered.

CLEAN, FRESH WATER MUST BE AVAILABLE TO THE CAT AT ALL TIMES. THIS IS IMPORTANT FOR THE ENTIRE LIFE OF THE CAT.

One of the most subjective and controversial matters pertaining to cat nutrition is that of vitamin and mineral supplementation. Pet-food manufacturers claim that such supplements are not necessary because vitamins and minerals are already added to their products. Vitamin and mineral supplement manufacturers claim that supplements are necessary because there is no way of knowing if the individual cat's needs are being satisfied by the food or if the cat is eating enough of the food to satisfy its vitamin and mineral requirements.

For several reasons this author, quite subjectively, recommends a vitamin and mineral supplement for cats from birth to death. Cats

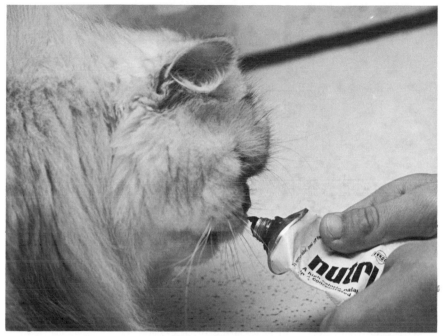

Some vitamin supplements come in a tube. Because of their gelatinous base, they are very appealing to most cats.

require, on the average, more than twice the amount of B-complex vitamins as dogs. Cats cannot convert some of the amino acids of protein into needed vitamins (specifically, tryptophan into niacin). However, it is important never to oversupplement. The theory that if one amount is healthy for the animal then ten times that amount must be better is not true. As a matter of fact, oversupplementation can be damaging.

The best vitamin products are usually those prescribed by a veterinarian and obtained in his or her office. Although over-the-counter products are better than nothing, they never have the quantities of vitamins and minerals obtained in prescription products. For kittens with no teeth there is a liquid supplement called Lixotinic, which is given once a day in .25 cc doses. Once the kitten's teeth have come in and it is capable of chewing, Pet-Tabs Feline is recommended. This product is a palatable, chewable tablet and is perfectly balanced. Both Lixotinic and Pet-Tabs Feline are manufactured by Beecham Laboratories. Another fine supplement manufacturer is Norden Laboratories, which makes Felobits. This product must also be obtained from a veterinarian.

Adults

When feeding adult cats, the average pet owner has two choices that are apparent and one that is not so obvious. Most owners resort to commercially prepared cat food. This is certainly a convenient and economically sound option. Premium-quality cat food will sustain life and promote growth. The second option is preparing food at home in one's own kitchen. This too can be a viable choice, provided a careful study is made of the individual cat's nutritional requirements. Homemade food should, of course, consist of the proper proportions of protein, carbohydrates, fats, vitamins and minerals. It can and is being produced in home kitchens all over America. The third and not so obvious option is to combine commercial cat food with food prepared in the kitchen. This combination, coupled with a vitamin and mineral supplement, not only gives the cat the necessary variety, but also assures a maximum of nutritional requirements that will promote growth, maintenance, and resistance to disease.

If you are going to feed your adult cat commercial cat food exclusively, select one or more brands that state on the label that they provide a complete and balanced diet. Give your pet a vitamin and

mineral supplement. Feed the cat twice or three times a day—a total of five to eight ounces of canned food; up to three or four ounces total of dry food (or simply leave it up to the cat); or from two to four ounces total of soft-moist food. Even here you can vary the diet by constantly switching brands and types.

Homemade cat food will require studying the charts at the end of this chapter, plus learning about the nutritional values of the foods you give your cat. Once you know the nutritional value of human foods (not supplied in this book), match them up against the nutritional requirements for cats (see charts) and work out a sensible diet. Here too, the keynote is variety. It is especially important to add vitamin and mineral supplements with homemade diets for cats.

When feeding a combination of commercial cat food and home-prepared food, one should feed the cat twice a day—once in the morning and once in the early evening. Vitamin and mineral supplements are helpful; so is one teaspoonful of corn oil, bacon fat or butter. The morning meal should consist of either one or two ounces of dry, cereal-type cat food * or an occasional cooked egg or raw egg yolk. (Never feed the cat raw egg white because it contains an enzyme that destroys the nutrient biotin.) The evening meal may consist of a canned ration or canned "gourmet" food at least four times a week. For the remaining evening meals, try raw organ meat such as liver or kidney, or hamburger. A ten-pound adult male cat (unneutered) requires no less than 8.5 ounces of premium canned ration daily. Neutered cats require 7.5 ounces. Adult cats require about thirty-six calories of food for every pound of body weight. This may vary from cat to cat. Remember to provide fresh water at all times.

When feeding canned food, serve it at room temperature to keep the food appealing and digestible. Do not overfeed your pet or allow it to become obese. Overweight cats have shorter life spans and greater health problems. Within the bounds of reason, feed your cat on a regular schedule. Consistent routines, including regular feedings, help keep your pet secure and anxiety-free.

Probably the single most common mistake made by cat owners and even some veterinarians is to provide cats with a food that is balanced for, intended for, and manufactured for dogs. This is a great mistake because the nutritional requirements for dogs are much dif-

---

* For cats with a predisposition to FUS (see Chapter 7), substitute canned ration or canned "gourmet"-type food for dry cereal-type food.

ferent than those for cats. Cats require more than twice the amount of B-complex vitamins that dogs need. Conversely, cats readily absorb iron from meat, while it is usually more difficult for dogs to assimilate iron from the diet. Also, as noted earlier, cats cannot convert some of the amino acids of protein into needed vitamins.

A proper cat food contains over 50 percent more protein than dog food. Cat food should also contain approximately 25 to 30 percent fat, on a dry-weight basis. The minimal fat requirement for dogs, according to a National Academy of Science study, is 5 percent.

Here are some tips concerning human foods: All fish must be cooked before feeding to house pets. Most cats like fish, but it can be addictive to the exclusion of all other forms of protein. Be judicious in the quantity given and the frequency with which it is fed. Excessive amounts of canned fish can bring about an ailment known as steatitis, which can be fatal. Milk is not essential in the cat's diet. However, pregnant or lactating queens do need an added source of calcium. Some cats will drink milk, but most cannot digest it properly because of a lack of necessary enzymes. Diarrhea is usually the result. Other good calcium sources are cheese, yogurt, canned sockeye salmon, cottage cheese, collard greens, kale, turnip greens. Tomato juice is beneficial for acidifying the urine in cats with a predisposition to cystitis. (See Chapter 7.) Cooked vegetables offer some vitamins and minerals and are desirable if the cat likes them. Most dry cat foods do not contain a sufficient amount of fat—dry foods with this much fat would tend to become rancid if stored for too long a time. Consequently, a teaspoon of vegetable oil, animal fat or butter once a day is of great benefit to the cat. Too much liver (raw or cooked) is difficult for cats to digest, and provides an excess of vitamin A, which adversely affects bone structure.

UNDERSTANDING YOUR CAT'S NUTRITION

It is possible to provide an optimum level of balanced nutrients for cats without becoming a nutrition specialist. Regulating your cat's intake of excellent commercial pet foods will achieve optimum nutrient consumption economically and conveniently. A general knowledge of cats' nutritional requirements will help the cat owner to better understand his or her cat and the problems that are likely to be encountered.

More has been learned about nutrition of cats during the past fifteen years than was learned previously throughout history. At the rate research is progressing, it is safe to estimate that the facts learned about cats during the next fifteen years will be equally dramatic.

All cats, regardless of their size, shape, age and activity, require the same forty-three–plus nutrients, but in varying amounts. These nutrients, except for vitamin C, are the same nutrients that are needed by humans. Humans normally obtain proper nutrients through a wide variety in the dietary selection. Feline nutritional requirements demand the same variety of foods. Unfortunately many cats may consume only one product during their entire life, so this product should at least be nutritionally balanced.

Optimum nutrition is the provision of that quality and quantity of food that will permit the cat to obtain and retain the most desirable body condition for the circumstances in which it lives.

Cats should carry enough weight so that they do not have an emaciated look; however, they should not be obese if they are to live long, healthy lives as pets or, in the case of females, to be healthy, productive queens in a cattery. (The cattery owner knows that cats, like other breeding animals, should be moderately muscular for optimum and prolonged breeding production. Obesity precludes this.) Today the average cat lives better and longer than ever before because of:

1. Improved pediatric care.
2. More effective biologics to control infectious diseases.
3. Effective anthelmintics (internal parasite remedies), insecticides, mitocides, fungicides.
4. Improved diagnostic procedures.
5. Increased veterinary skill and knowledge.
6. Better education of cat owners.
7. Confinement.
8. Genetic selectivity.
9. Superior nutrition.

Energy

Cats expend energy in every form of body activity, and this energy is obtained either from oxidation of food or from the mobilization of their own stored body sources of energy. The utilization of energy obtained from food is influenced by the type of food consumed, how recent the last feeding was, the quantity of food stored in the body and the amount of exercise.

The energy (calories) remaining after fecal and urinary loss and the heat gain associated with digestion are available for maintenance, voluntary activity and storage within the body. Since energy comes from proteins, carbohydrates and fats, measuring the energy content of a ration is not easy. More than 95 percent of most types of fats are digested by the cat, and fats contribute more than 2.25 times as much energy as an equal weight of carbohydrates and/or proteins. Not all absorbed nutrients capable of supplying energy are used by the cat to the same extent.

The energy requirements of cats vary. Size, age, activity, state of health, and the environmental temperature all influence these requirements. The energy requirement of a cat per unit of body weight decreases as the cat's weight increases. This means a small kitten requires more energy per pound of body weight than does a large cat. Part of this is related to the higher ratio of skin surface to body volume in the smaller animal, surface through which the energy can be lost. This is the same principle that enables crushed ice to cool liquids more rapidly than an uncrushed ice cube.

The cat that is restricted to a small apartment or house will use much less energy than a cat that is accustomed to roaming the neighborhood and fields. The lactating queen may use up to three times as much energy during heavy milk production while nursing a large litter as she will use during a non-lactating period. A young kitten uses up to three times as much energy per unit of body weight as does an adult cat that is not very active.

Most cats on a self-feeding (*ad libitum*) diet will consume the quantity of food and thus the calories needed to maintain their body weight; this amount varies from individual to individual. Some cats appear to require less than half as much energy per unit of body weight for maintenance as do others. Normally, it is recommended that 0.5 ounce of dry food be provided for each pound of body weight of each cat daily. The quantity of soft-moist food consumed will be slightly more than dry food. If canned foods are fed, the quantity will be approximately 1 to 1.5 ounces for each pound of body weight each day.

Protein

Protein supplies amino acids that are essential to a cat's growth and health. The most common protein sources are fish, meat, vegetables, and eggs. The amino acid composition of the proteins can be influenced by source of the protein and the food-processing methods.

Egg protein is probably the best-known source of balanced amino acids for cats. Other proteins from fish, meats, and vegetable sources, available in commercial rations, approximate the amino acids found in egg protein. Such better-quality proteins are well digested and absorbed. While moderate heat treatment in processing does not significantly reduce the value of the proteins, excessive heat may destroy some protein values.

Protein forms tissues such as hair and muscle ligaments and is combined with carbohydrates, fats and minerals in the cat's body to form enzymes, hormones, various body fluids and antibodies. A specific level of protein is needed by the normal cat to continue normal body processes. A ration containing, on an air-dry basis, 30 to 35 percent protein, about 8 percent fat, and 40 percent carbohydrates can meet the protein requirements for a normal cat. Although the minimum level found in good commercial diets is approximately 30 percent, the extra 5 percent is recommended since the added protein seems to help increase disease-fighting antibody production. A large excess of protein can be tolerated fairly well by the majority of normal cats. Excess nitrogen is broken away from the protein or amino acid molecules and is eliminated through the urine. Most of the remaining excess protein is metabolized as energy in the body or may be converted and stored as fat. While this excess protein may not be harmful to young, normal cats, it may be extremely harmful to cats with liver damage and may be harmful to older cats with impaired circulation. Cats with liver and kidney damage tend to accumulate excess nitrogen in the body, and it is dangerous to feed them an extremely high protein diet (too much meat).

The cat owner, if he or she decides to feed extra meat, fish and other protein sources to the cat, should cook these foods before adding them to the bowl. Uncooked egg white, for example, contains an anti-biotin enzyme that is harmful to the cat. Most fresh fish contain an anti-thiamin enzyme. This can cause a thiamin deficiency in the cat, resulting in anorexia (loss of appetite), paralysis, abnormal reflexes, convulsions and a general breakdown of the nervous system. Cook all fish! Cook all eggs (especially the white)!

Carbohydrates

Most cat foods include carbohydrates, which are usually the most inexpensive sources of energy. When properly prepared, carbohydrates are well utilized by normal cats. Some starches, like those from oats, corn and other grains, are poorly digested unless first subjected to heat treatment. Carbohydrates also supply much of the fibrous portions of the ration. Fiber has specific functions in the digestive tract: some is digested and used as energy; other fibers absorb significant quantities of water and produce softer droppings than do nonfibrous rations. Fiber is helpful in stimulating and maintaining intestinal action, especially in the senile or inactive cat. Although not absolutely essential nutritionally to cats, fiber helps control the condition of the cat's digestive tract. Without the fiber present, the intestinal tone of inactive older cats often becomes sluggish, with the result that the ingested food may accumulate in bunches, causing constipation and other problems. Fiber helps keep the intestinal contents more uniformly distributed throughout the intestinal tract, since it acts like thousands of tiny sponges that pick up and hold water, thus helping to prevent both diarrhea and constipation.

Some sugars are effectively used and tolerated by normal cats, but others, such as milk sugar (lactose), may be poorly utilized by some cats. Some cats, particularly older cats, cannot synthesize adequate quantities of the enzyme lactase that is required for the digestion of milk sugar. This is why some cats tend to scour (have diarrhea) when given too much cow's milk, which is high in lactose. Young kittens and cats like cow's milk, but sometimes cannot digest it properly. Cats with diabetes may not tolerate foods containing sucrose at levels sometimes used as a preservative in some brands of soft-moist foods.

Fats

Fats are included in the cat's diet to provide a concentrated source of energy and the fatty acids that are needed by the body, as a taste factor, and as a carrier for fat-soluble vitamins A, D, E and K.

Fats are made up of smaller components called fatty acids. Most fats contain many different kinds of fatty acids. Some of these have a high melting point; these fatty acids are usually found in the fat from cattle, sheep and horses. Other fats contain a large quantity of low-melting-point fatty acids which are mostly semi-solid or liquid at household temperatures. These fatty acids are found in the fats of pork and chicken, and in highly unsaturated vegetable fats, such as corn oil. The source of dietary fats determines to some extent the type of fat deposited in the cat's body and the resulting body-fat firmness.

Most fatty acids in cereals are highly unsaturated. Thus some cereal grains are good sources of fatty acids. Fish contain an extremely high proportion of unsaturated fatty acids of a type that oxidizes rapidly and, unless processed with care, can produce a vitamin E deficiency and lead to steatitis, or "yellow fat disease," in cats. This condition may be precipitated by feeding stale wheat-germ oil, or cod-liver oil or other fish oils that are in the process of going rancid. It can be prevented by supplying adequate vitamin E in the diet, adding antioxidants during processing, carefully controlling the processing of the fish, and avoiding feeding stale or rancid oils.

Vitamins

Vitamins play a dynamic role in body processes of cats. They take part in the release of energy from foods, promote normal growth of different kinds of tissue, and are essential to the proper functioning of nerves and muscles. Vitamins are required in extremely small quantities, but are essential for life. More than a dozen major vitamins essential to the cat diet have been identified and analyzed. They are broadly categorized into two groups, depending on their solubility. One group includes the "fat-soluble" vitamins A, D, E, and K, and the other includes the "water-soluble" B-complex and C vitamins. Knowing this can help the cat owner understand the nutritional needs of his or her cat. Some vitamins can be synthesized within the body from other food nutrients, while other vitamins must be present in the diet. Fat-soluble vitamins tend to oxidize easily. This means that fats that are becoming rancid or that have been oxidized excessively may be devoid of these vitamins. This is why old or rancid fats or oils should not be fed to cats. Cats seem to have a much greater tendency to exhibit muscular disintegration than other animals as a result of eating rancid fats.

Following is a summary of the essential vitamins, including some of their functions and foods that are dependable sources.

Vitamin A. Vitamin A is necessary for normal growth, reproduction, physical maintenance of tissues, hearing and vision, particularly in dim light. It also helps keep the skin and inner linings of the body healthy and resistant to infection. It occurs only in foods of animal origin. Many vegetables and fruits, particularly the green and yellow ones, contain a substance called carotene that most animals can change into vitamin A. However, the cat seems to have an extremely poor ability to use carotene as a source of vitamin A. Cats can utilize vitamin A from chemical or animal sources efficiently.

A deficiency of vitamin A leads to emaciation and tissue malfunction. Large coarse skin lesions may indicate that the cat is not receiving adequate vitamin A. This may be the result of a deficiency of vitamin A in the ration, or it may be due to a particular cat's inability to absorb the vitamin A and/or the fat that is available in the diet. Extra vitamin A can be supplied in the cat's ration and even applied topically to the skin lesions. Since cats lick their skin so much, they may remove the vitamin A from the skin and absorb it internally. Vitamin A can also be absorbed through the skin in some circumstances, although this is an inefficient route. Signs of vitamin A deficiency include loss of appetite; poor growth; skin lesions, dryness, scaling, and scratching; and weak and affected eyes. A severe, prolonged deficiency may aggravate respiratory infections and can be fatal to the cat.

Liver is an outstanding source of vitamin A. Significant amounts are also found in eggs, butter, whole milk, and cheese made with whole milk.

Vitamin D. Vitamin D is important in building strong bones and teeth because it enables the body to use calcium and phosphorus. It is primarily associated with calcium absorption, transportation and deposition within the body. Kittens on a diet with an imbalanced calcium-to-phosphorus ratio and inadequate vitamin D are susceptible to rickets. Vitamin D requirements are reportedly much lower for adult cats, and there appears to be more danger of overdosing with vitamin D than of deficiencies.

Calcium absorption from the digestive tract is influenced by the amount of vitamin D in the cat's diet, the dietary fat level, and body stores of vitamin D. Vitamin D is necessary for the effective passage of calcium across or through the intestinal wall and into the bloodstream. This nutrient may be produced in the skin by radiation from the sun acting on the fat (cholesterol) on the skin. This process occurs in most animals, including humans, and it is thought that the cat can produce vitamin D efficiently by this route, although it has not been fully confirmed. Vitamin D_3 from animal sources and vitamin D_2 from irradiated plant sterols are both effectively utilized by the cat.

A severe vitamin D deficiency will prevent normal calcification of the bones of cats even when ample calcium is present, resulting in rickets, improperly calcified bones, irregular teeth, and other skeletal defects. An excess of vitamin D may cause calcium to be deposited in large quantities in the heart, lungs, muscles and blood vessels. An extreme excess of vitamin D can kill animals, and cats have died because of excessive quantities of vitamin D added to their diets.

Few foods contain much vitamin D naturally. Milk with vitamin D added is a practical source if your cat is one who can tolerate it. Small amounts of vitamin D are present in egg yolk, butter, and liver. Larger amounts occur in sardines, salmon, herring, and tuna. Direct sunlight is another source.

Vitamin K. Vitamin K is considered the anti-hemorrhagic (anti-bleeding) vitamin. It is synthesized in the intestinal tract of cats and other animals under normal conditions. When certain drugs are given or when specific stress occurs, vitamin K may not be produced in quantities sufficient for normal requirements. This is why vitamin K_1 (menadione bisulfite) is added to commercial cat foods. When bacteriostats are administered orally or included in the diet, added vitamin K is warranted. Like other fat-soluble vitamins (A, D, and E), K requires fat intake and bile salts in order to be absorbed and utilized. Vitamin K is found in green vegetables and is also synthesized by bacteria in the intestine. Consult a veterinarian before giving *added* K to your cat.

Vitamin E. In human nutrition vitamin E is one of the more controversial issues. Many have claimed that vitamin E can promote physical endurance, enhance sexual potency, prevent heart attacks, protect against air pollution, and slow the aging process. Discovered about fifty years ago, the vitamin has also been described as a cure, preventive, or treatment of cancer, muscular dystrophy, ulcers, burns, and skin disorders. The dangers of promoting vitamin supplementation lie in its use as a substitute for *medical* therapies in already existing illnesses. Vitamin E, in this author's opinion, should be taken as a preventive against vitamin E deficiency. If it is to be used as a medical therapy it is recommended that a veterinarian be consulted first. Approximately 50 IU of vitamin E per kilogram of food is usually recommended as a minimum for cats.

Vitamin E is called the "anti-sterility" vitamin. It is a biological anti-oxidant and is considered necessary for several body functions. In cases of vitamin E deficiency, the ovum becomes fertilized but fails to become implanted in the uterus. The developing embryo may either die of "starvation" or just pass out of the tract. Too often, vitamin E is destroyed in the body by feeding wheat-germ oil, or cod-liver or other fish oil that is going or has gone rancid.

Muscular and nerve degeneration resulting from steatitis (yellow fat disease), which in turn is associated with a vitamin E deficiency, has been described in cats and mink. In the acute phase, steatitis is characterized by a general soreness, anorexia (loss of appetite), depression, signs of pain, and constant elevated temperatures of 104° to 105°F. *Neutrophilia* (an increase in the white cell count of the blood) is common. Body fat on biopsy is generally found to be firm and light yellow to dark brown in color. Fats in the process of becoming rancid apparently destroy vitamin E in the ration and in the animal's body. If wheat-germ oil, cod-liver oil, or other unsaturated fats or oils must be fed by the cat owner, these oils should be kept in the refrigerator after the container has been opened in order to retard oxidative rancidity. Any such oil that you even remotely suspect to be stale should be thrown out.

One reason little is known about vitamin E is that E deficiency is almost impossible to produce in human subjects. To withdraw all sources of vitamin E is almost to withdraw food itself, since the vitamin is present to some extent in most foods and in large amounts in vegetable fats and oils. The major sources of vitamin E are unrefined soybean, cottonseed and corn oils; wheat germ; whole grains; and nuts. It is also found in smaller quantities in green vegetables, beans and eggs.

Biotin. Biotin is generally thought to be produced by intestinal synthesis in normal cats. In cats with *miliary eczema* (small skin lesions), English researchers have indicated that dietary biotin has produced eczema remission and improved haircoats.

Biotin is inactivated by an enzyme, avidin, in raw egg white. This is the main reason that raw eggs should not be fed to cats, since they might produce a biotin deficiency. Simply cook all eggs before feeding. Biotin is found in many foods including egg yolk, milk, liver and yeast.

Thiamin (B_1). The cat has an unusually high requirement for thiamin. Some of the thiamin in canned cat foods is destroyed by processing. In addition, some raw fish contain an enzyme, thiaminase, which inactivates thiamin. When a thiamin deficiency is suspected, the daily dosage should be 1.6 mg per 100 gm dry diet consumed. Although cooking destroys thiaminase in fish, this enzyme may already have destroyed the thiamin that once was present. Therefore, fish is an unreliable source of thiamin.

Thiamin helps convert glucose into energy or fat. When thiamin is reduced in the cat's body, the animal's energy level is seriously reduced. Thiamin deficiencies in cats produce anorexia (appetite loss), vomiting, weight loss, dehydration, paralysis, prostration, abnormal reflexes, convulsions and cardiac disorders.

Extra carbohydrates, such as bread and potatoes, and extra exercise increase the cat's requirements for thiamin. The need for thiamin is decreased slightly when higher levels of fat are added; thus, composition of the diet influences the vitamin requirement.

Sources of thiamin include whole grains (especially wheat germ and rice polish), brewer's yeast, pork, milk, nuts, liver, peas, soybeans and dried beans.

Riboflavin (B₂). Riboflavin is one of three B vitamins (thiamin, riboflavin and niacin) that play a central role in the release of energy from food. They also help promote proper functioning of nerves, normal appetite, good digestion and healthy skin. Riboflavin is used in many body processes, especially those involving healthy skin, eyes, and the linings of the mouth and digestive tract.

If a deficiency of riboflavin occurs, cats will develop anorexia (appetite loss) with a resulting emaciation that, unless riboflavin is again supplied, will lead to death. Loss of hair around and on the head sometimes occurs in riboflavin deficiencies, and cataracts have been observed in some deficiency experiments. In the domestic setting, however, deficiency does not occur on ordinary diets and is only encountered in abnormal situations where the cat has been severely deprived, coupled with a heavy demand for riboflavin, as in lactation, or infection during the growth period.

The daily requirement of riboflavin lies between 0.15 and 2 mg according to the diet and metabolic demands. The principal sources of riboflavin are liver, brewer's yeast, and milk. Whole grains and green vegetables are also good sources of this nutrient. If the greens are cooked, the water-soluble vitamins will leach into the cooking water, which should therefore be fed along with the vegetables.

Niacin (B₃). Signs indicating a deficiency of niacin include dermatitis, loss of appetite, ulcers, and other abnormalities, including diarrhea, emaciation, and redness of the buccal (cheek) cavity. Severe deficiency can be fatal. Unlike most other animals, the cat does not have the ability to convert the amino acid tryptophan to niacin. Since niacin is available in commercial cat foods and stable in the diet, there is almost no opportunity to see a true niacin deficiency when modern commercial rations are provided.

Niacin sources include brewer's yeast, wheat germ, liver, and kidney. Whole grains, fish, eggs, meat and nuts are also good sources.

Pyridoxine (B₆). Pyridoxine is one of several co-enzymes that help metabolize amino acids. This vitamin also helps make possible the utilization of carbohydrates in the body. In animals with a pyridoxine deficiency, slow growth, convulsions and hyperexcitability are produced. Kidney lesions and the formation of oxalate calculi (stones in the bladder, urethra or kidneys) have been associated with a vitamin B_6 deficiency. The best sources of pyridoxine are meat, egg yolks, liver, whole grains, brewer's yeast, heart, and blackstrap molasses. Canning, exposure to light, and excessive storage time tend to destroy its potency.

Pantothenic Acid. A deficiency of pantothenic acid is accompanied by weight loss, fatty deposits in the liver, and disturbances of metabolism. The modern pet owner will probably never observe a deficiency of pantothenic acid, since it is available in commercial cat foods, is stable, and is also synthesized to some extent in the digestive tract.

Excellent pantothenic acid sources are brewer's yeast, liver, kidney, heart, wheat germ and whole grains.

Choline. This nutrient, which is part of the B complex, is important in the metabolizing of fats and in many biochemical reactions. Choline deficiency in cats has been characterized by weight loss, fatty deposits in the liver, and hypoalbuminemia (an abnormally low concentration of certain proteins in the blood). Choline is obtained from liver, kidney, wheat germ, brewer's yeast and egg yolk.

Vitamin B_{12} (Cyanocobalamin). Vitamin B_{12} is essential for the function of all cells in the body, but especially for bone marrow, the central nervous system, and the intestinal tract. It is retained in the liver and kidneys and is important in metabolizing nucleic acids and folic acid. Vitamin B_{12} is of primary importance in red blood cell formation. It is essential to the prevention and cure of some types of anemia and is necessary for the development of young healthy kittens. The precise level of vitamin B_{12} required by cats is not known. However, the synthesis of vitamin B_{12} by intestinal bacteria combined with the B_{12} found in the ingredients used to make cat foods helps ensure that a deficiency will not occur. Vitamin B_{12} is found in whole grains, meat, fish, yeast and liver.

Vitamin C. Vitamin C is another of the controversial elements of nutrition. For several decades experts have been telling us that vitamin C supplementation in cats is unnecessary except in very unusual conditions. This very essential nutrient was traditionally thought to be manufactured or synthesized within the tissues of cats. However some experts now feel that there are individual differences among cats and that it is impossible to know which cats create their vitamin C and which do not, or if it is being synthesized in adequate quantities.*

Patricia P. Scott, Ph.D., in her chapter, "The Nutritional Requirements of Cats," (from "Gaines Basic Guide to Canine Nutrition") makes the following observations:

> Cats, unlike humans, are able to manufacture ascorbic acid (vitamin C) from glucose, and can thus normally exist satisfactorily on a diet free from this vitamin. However, ascorbate production may be severely depressed during infectious illness, thus leading to a conditioned deficiency. Ascorbic acid also acts as an important antioxidant outside the body and is useful in protecting processed foods from oxidation. Some breeders emphasize the importance of including a source of vitamin C in the diet.

Dr. R. G. Broderick recommends that 250 mg of vitamin C be given four times a day. Dr. Louis L. Vine in his book, *Common Sense Book of Complete Cat Care,* states, "The overfeeding of some vitamins has not been proven harmful but it is still in question. I would not feed a cat an excessive amount of any vitamin unless instructed to do so by your veterinarian."

Vitamin C helps create *collagen,* a gelatinous material that helps hold the body's cells in place. It also assists in normal tooth and bone formation and aids in healing wounds. Probably the most controversial questions about vitamin C concern its role in aiding the body's own immunological mechanisms. The argument between Dr. Linus Pauling, Nobel Laureate in molecular biology, and much of the American medical community centers on the efficacy of vitamin C in treating the common cold and other ailments, with Pauling as the major proponent of megadoses of vitamin C.

---

* Dr. R. Geoffrey Broderick of Veterinary Nutritional Associates, Huntington, N.Y., has been conducting his own research with vitamin C and cats. He states, "Vitamin C should be supplemented in all animals to insure that they have adequate vitamin C. It will boost their own immunological mechanism. We don't know how much vitamin C your cat makes. Some produce more than others. They all have biochemical individuality so they all produce it at different rates. I give them all vitamin C. It can't hurt. It can only help." Dr. Broderick is the creator and manufacturer of Cornucopia Natural Pet Foods.

Natural sources of vitamin C are citrus fruits (oranges, grapefruit, lemons, limes, and so on, and their juices). Fresh strawberries are very high in vitamin C. Other important sources include tomatoes (and tomato juice); broccoli; Brussels sprouts; cabbage; cantaloupe; cauliflower; green peppers; some dark-green leafy vegetables, such as collards, kale, mustard greens, spinach, and turnip greens; potatoes and sweet potatoes, especially when baked in the jacket; and watermelon. Cats are unpredictable animals and may be interested in eating any one or all of these, or none at all.

Water

Life cannot be sustained without the intake of water. It is as important as air to the mammalian body. The body's need for water exceeds its need for food. In the wild, cats do not usually drink more than once every twenty-four hours because they obtain most of their fluid intake from the carcasses of their prey, which are 70 percent water.

About one-half to two-thirds of the body is made up of water. It is the main component of body fluids, secretions, and excretions. It carries food materials from one part of the body to the other. Water is the solvent for most products of digestion. It holds them in solution and permits them to pass through the intestinal wall into the bloodstream for use throughout the body. Water helps regulate body temperature, aids digestion, and helps sustain health with its effect on all body cells. Only with a generous intake of water can these bodily tasks be performed with any degree of competency. A light sprinkling of salt on your cat's food encourages this.

Minerals

Minerals are necessary in the cat's diet and enter practically every phase of body activity. Cats would not live very long on a diet devoid of minerals. Minerals maintain the acid-base balance and tissue condition within the body and help regulate most body activities.

According to Dr. Mark Morris, Jr., in *Feline Dietetics,* "The requirement and ratio of many minerals in a diet can be affected by a change in only one. Because of this interrelationship, minerals always should be considered as a group, not as separate entities, in clinical application. The total mineral requirement in the diet (as well as for most of the minerals on an individual basis) is lower for cats than most other carnivores."

Calcium and Phosphorus. Calcium is the most abundant mineral element in the body. Most of the body's calcium is found in bones and teeth. Combined with phosphorus in an exact ratio it is largely responsible for the hardness of these structures. When a deficiency or imbalance occurs, poor bone growth or maintenance results.

The small amount of calcium in other body tissues and fluids aids in the proper functioning of the heart, muscles, and nerves, and helps the blood coagulate during bleeding. Bone formation seems to be optimum when the levels of calcium and phosphorus are adequate and when such associated nutrients as magnesium, vitamin D, choline, fluorine, and manganese are present in adequate and balanced quantities. A large excess of calcium can produce a phosphorus deficiency and, conversely, a large excess of phosphorus can produce a calcium deficiency. Some foods have a very poor calcium-phosphorus balance. Lean meat contains approximately 0.1 percent calcium and 0.18 percent phosphorus. The proper ratio of minerals (with a ratio of 1.2 parts of calcium to 1 part of phosphorus generally being desirable) is extremely important. If a cat owner wants to add lean meat to the cat's diet, the meat should be supplemented with a good commercial diet that can contribute the needed calcium. Calcium or calcium-and-phosphorus supplements should be added to a cat's ration only in carefully controlled quantities. Any such supplementation should not include vitamin D, since this combination can, under some conditions, cause hypercalcemia (too much calcium in the blood, possibly leading to calcium deposits in body tissues)—unless, of course, your veterinarian recommends otherwise.

Magnesium. Magnesium in the diet helps maintain good skeletal growth, deposition of minerals in the right places, and maintenance of body secretions. Magnesium deficiency can produce many abnormalities. For example, deficiency can influence the deposit of too much calcium and calcium salts in soft muscle tissues, such as the heart and blood vessels. The calcium level in many organs of the cat may be increased if there is an insufficient quantity of magnesium in the diet. Many supplements fed to cats are deficient in magnesium, and it is easy to see how supplements that contain calcium and phosphorus but are deficient in magnesium could produce abnormalities in kittens and cats. The formation of urinary calculi (crystals) has been associated with both deficient and excess levels of magnesium. According to Scott, dietary magnesium levels should be kept as low as possible (see table at end of this chapter); the concentration of magnesium tends to be raised in fish-based dry cat foods when a high proportion of fish bone is included in the formulation.

Manganese. Manganese deficiencies in test animals have caused abnormal bone development, stunted growth, hyperactivity, sterility in females, and impotence in males. Manganese has long been known to be involved with bone growth, enzyme production, and temperament in animals. More needs to be studied about the effects of manganese in the diets of cats, although at present this nutrient is assumed to be essential.

Zinc. Zinc deficiencies in laboratory animals have induced skin abnormalities, poor fertility, immune mechanism failure and difficulty in healing. Zinc is a component of enzymes and hormones (such as insulin), and is necessary for normal bone, muscle and skin growth. Zinc is required at low levels and sufficient amounts are present in any good commercial diet or vitamin and mineral supplement.

Iron. Iron is needed by the cat's body in relatively small but vital amounts. It combines with protein to make hemoglobin, the red substance of blood that carries oxygen from the lungs to body cells and removes carbon dioxide from the cells. Iron also helps the cells obtain energy from food. An iron deficiency results in anemia. This is particularly true in cats that have certain parasite infections or other sustained blood losses. A deficiency of iron may be associated with coat-color changes. Some relatively insoluble forms of iron are not freely available to cats, while excess supplementation of other forms can be toxic. Iron deficiency can also result in hypothyroidism (an insufficiency of thyroid hormones). Clinical signs include stunted growth, edema, lethargy and thickened skin.

Only a few foods contain much iron. Liver is a particularly good source. Lean meats, heart, kidney, shellfish, dried beans and peas, dark-green vegetables, dried fruit, egg yolk and molasses also serve as good sources. Supplemental iron is seldom necessary for normal, healthy cats, and must never be given without veterinary supervision. In large doses it becomes far more dangerous to a cat's health than a deficiency.

Copper and Cobalt. Copper and cobalt deficiencies are uncommon in cats, who have the ability to utilize these elements from meat. Growing kittens reared more or less exclusively on cow's milk, which is poor in iron and copper, may suffer from anemia. Copper and cobalt are, with iron, necessary for the prevention of anemia. Copper helps in the incorporation of iron into hemoglobin, and cobalt (in the form of vitamin B_{12}) also stimulates hemoglobin production. These minerals are supplied in most commercial diets and supplements as trace mineral salts.

Sodium Chloride (Salt). Salt in the cat's diet is one of the most variable and in some ways the most troublesome of nutrients. Fresh meat contains very little salt, while water from some home soft-water conditioners may supply all of the sodium needed by normal cats. Salt helps to maintain proper fluid balance within the body, but an excess can put a strain on the kidneys in some cats. Salt is necessary for the production of gastric hydrochloric acid. Higher-than-normal levels of salt will increase water intake, with a subsequent increase in urine output and in milk production in the lactating female. For these reasons, supplementary salt is sometimes used to help combat urinary calculi and to increase milk production.

Potassium. Potassium is usually adequate in normal diets, but deficiencies result in poor growth, restlessness, poor nerve development and poor conduction of neural impulses.

Iodine and Other Trace Nutrients. Iodine is a nonmetallic element important to the formation of hormones secreted by the thyroid gland. When the thyroid does not function properly the result is fatigue, slowed pulse and a tendency to gain weight even though an average ration is ingested by the cat. In areas far from the seacoast where the soil is low in iodine, the inhabitants sometimes fail to get an adequate supply of this mineral. In many cases, enlarged (hyper-) thyroids are the result of an iodine deficiency. The use of iodized salt adequately supplies the cat's iodine needs.

Many additional trace nutrients, such as fluorine, nickel, chromium, molybdenum, silicon and others are apparently needed by cats. These trace nutrients seem to occur in sufficient concentrations in normal diets. Inducing specific deficiencies in test animals is not always easy, so the minimal requirements are not yet known. Some of the trace minerals are needed in remarkably small quantities and the toxic levels of some required nutrients can be reached very quickly.

Nutritional deficiencies are complex and may involve interactions between amino acids, minerals, and vitamins, or the presence of certain diseases. Different levels of the same nutrient will produce different responses and degrees of response in animals. This makes the recognition and treatment of some problems difficult, especially when they are the result of oversupplementation by the cat's owner.

HOW TO FEED A FAT CAT

When a fat cat lies on its cushion digesting a meal, it resembles the Hollywood Hills during an earthquake. If your cat reminds you of a two-humped camel or a four-legged turkey or a vicuña lap rug, perhaps it's time to rethink its diet. Some cats were born to be lean and svelte while others were destined to be square-shaped and muscular. But nature never intended any cat to resemble a miniature wart hog.

Everyone knows that cats are demanding creatures who know how to insist. The image of a finicky blackmailer who will not offer his affections unless you come across is not without foundation. Many cat owners simply cannot handle rejection and are at the mercy of their little tender-footed darlings. All too often the cat is fed a large quantity of food that is unbalanced and too fattening. Few owners see the harm of this, but it can be very damaging to the feline body.

We love our cats and tend to express our love with food. And why not? Isn't that how we operate with the people in our lives? But it is absolutely necessary to understand that food is not love. Food has only to do with nutrition. Too much food makes one fat whether one is a human, a cat or a praying mantis. The awful truth is that overweight mammals experience more osteoarthritis, heart disease, skin disorders, respiratory ailments, liver and pancreas stress and skeletal deficiencies, and have less resistance to viral or bacterial infections, than mammals of normal weight. Obesity also decreases the cat's tolerance of extreme summer heat and makes it more susceptible to diabetes. Fat cats are poor risks for surgery. First, fat itself interferes with access to various parts of the body that may require surgery. Second, overweight cats may experience a poor or even fatal reaction to anesthesia. Fat also makes it difficult for a veterinarian to examine the animal patient.

Obesity has three causes. Endocrine disorders may cause an animal to gain more weight than its frame was meant to hold. These and other medical dysfunctions creating obesity must be treated by a qualified veterinarian. The second cause has to do with the aging process. As a cat becomes older, its ability to metabolize food decreases along with its energy output. Despite this metabolic reduction, the quantity of food given (and eaten) is often the same as it was when the animal was younger. The result is obesity. The third cause is really so simple that few believe it. Overfeeding. When the caloric intake exceeds the energy requirements, fat is created and stored in the body. This is the most common explanation for obesity in cats. The only way for a cat to lose this excess fat is to eat fewer calories daily. If the cat is given fewer calories than it needs, it will draw from its own fat deposits around the body to create the needed energy. We're talking diet here.

If you haven't recoiled in horror at the word "diet," then the next step is to determine if your cat is overweight. The most obvious sign of obesity, of course, is the evidence of subcutaneous fat (just under the skin). One of the most common places for a cat to show this is around its jowls and neck. As a cat gains weight, its face appears to puff out and its neck develops a furl or two. The stomach becomes somewhat distended and sags like a pouch. (This is also the look of a queen that has recently delivered kittens.) Place your hands under your cat's belly and feel the rib cage. If you cannot feel each rib without pressing, the cat is overweight. (If you can *see* each rib, the cat is probably undernourished.) Of course, the best tool for determining obesity is the scale. With the exception of some large types, such as the Maine Coon Cat and other special breeds, the average mature cat should weigh between seven and ten pounds. Obviously, this does not apply to pregnant or lactating queens. Hold your cat and step on your bathroom scale. Next, weigh yourself without holding the cat. Deduct the second scale reading from the first to get the weight of the cat.

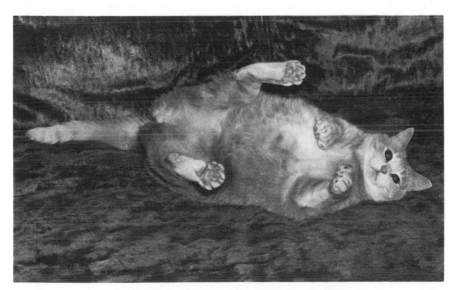

Perhaps it's time to rethink your cat's diet.

A Diet for Fat Cats

Once you have determined that your cat is overweight, it is best to have it examined by your veterinarian to be certain that there is no medical problem. Having ruled out any of the various medical possibilities, you may now select an "ideal weight" as a goal to reach through a reduction diet.

At this point you have several options. You may simply reduce the quantity of food given by 40 percent and try to live with your cat's complaints. Once the cat has achieved the "ideal weight," normalize the diet, but do not feed the same amount you did when the animal became obese. The average adult cat requires 8.5 ounces of canned ration per day or thirty-six calories per pound of body weight. A neutered cat requires no more than 7.5 ounces of canned ration per day or thirty-six calories per pound of body weight. (See table, "Daily Food Requirements of Cats According to Age," at the end of this chapter.) Whenever you place your cat on a reducing diet, supplement the diet with a high-quality vitamin and mineral product.

Another option, and a much superior one, is to offer your cat a homemade reducing diet. The major problem of placing a cat on a diet is the pangs of hunger and the demanding behavior they produce in the cat. This can be avoided if the animal is given approximately the same quantity of food it always gets, but with fewer calories. The following is a high-protein, low-fat diet that can be made in your own kitchen with very little trouble. It was created by Mark Morris, Jr., DVM, Ph.D., of Mark Morris Associates, Topeka, Kansas. Dr. Morris is one of America's foremost animal nutritionists.

Weight-Reduction Diet for Cats

1¼ lbs. pork liver, cooked and ground
1 cup cooked rice
1 tsp. corn oil
1 tsp. calcium carbonate * (to maintain a healthy calcium/ phosphorus ratio)
Vitamin–trace mineral supplement that supplies the minimum daily requirement of the cat

Combine all ingredients. They will yield 1¾ pounds of food. One pound of this recipe provides 534 calories. For variety you may substitute cooked white meat of chicken, ground beef (cooked or raw), or cooked fish for the pork liver.

* Calcium carbonate may be obtained from a pharmacy or a feed and grain store. Or, as a substitute, use the antacid product Tums. Crush two Tums tablets into powder and mix into the recipe.

Feed your cat the amount of food indicated in the "Feeding Guide." Maintain feeding this quantity of food until the cat achieves the optimum body weight you have selected. Dividing the food portion into two feedings a day is the best way to avoid hunger pangs and to achieve maximum food utilization by the cat's body. Do not be discouraged if no weight loss is observed for the first week or two. In the early stages of a diet, the fat content of the body's cell structure is slowly replaced by water. This creates the impression that nothing is changing. But in a short while your patience will be rewarded as the excess water begins to be passed from the body and reveals the loss of body fat.

ANALYSIS OF-WEIGHT REDUCTION DIET

Moisture	71.8%
Protein	15.3%
Fat	3.3%
Ash	1.4%
Calcium	0.2%
Phosphorus	0.2%

FEEDING GUIDE

Optimum Body Weight	Daily Feeding
5 lbs.	¼ lb. (134 calories)
7–8 lbs.	⅓ lb. (178 calories)
10 lbs.	½ lb. (267 calories)

Chinese Food for Fat Cats

Because weight watching can be tedious and somewhat unpleasant for both cats and cat owners, it is desirable to break the monotony and vary the diet of the reducing feline. In the cause of healthy nutritional diversion and in the spirit of good fun, the following recipes can be prepared at home and offered as a random, occasional change that may be enjoyed by any dieting member of the houschold from cats to humans. Because so many of our most popular breeds of cat are from Asia, the idea of Chinese food for dieting cats is not *entirely* absurd, especially if it is low in calories, low in fat, and high in protein. The following recipes have been formulated to please the palate of any cat in the process of losing weight by dieting. However, the

Author and his friend, Max, contemplating a "Shanghai Steamer."

food just may appeal to many cat owners as well, provided they enjoy Chinese cooking.

In preparing these recipes for your cat, the use of the traditional Chinese stir-fry pan known as the *wok* is helpful but not necessary. A large, wide frying pan will suffice. Either will permit you to push one ingredient to the side while stir-frying another until you are ready to mix everything together. These recipes can be prepared in any average American kitchen.

Kitten Shrimp and Green Treasure

4 oz. raw, peeled shrimp
Pinch *each* salt and sugar
½ tsp. peanut oil
½ cup cooked broccoli
2 water chestnuts
⅔ cup water with dissolved chicken bouillon cube
1 tsp. cornstarch

Shell the shrimp, wash them thoroughly and slice them in half lengthwise. Lightly salt and sugar them and stir-fry for 2 minutes in peanut oil. Set them aside in a dish. Cut cooked broccoli into small pieces (1 inch or less) and place them in pan with water chestnuts. Fry them, stirring constantly for three minutes. Return shrimp to pan and add water with chicken bouillon cube. Bring the mixture to a boil and add the cornstarch mixed with a small amount of cool water. Blend thoroughly and bring to a simmer for 3 minutes. Remove from pan and allow to cool. Feed to cat in two separate meals. Contains 173 calories.

Shanghai Steamer

3 oz. boned haddock
1 thin slice fresh ginger
1 dried Chinese mushroom, soaked overnight
⅓ cup raw bean sprouts
Pinch *each* salt and sugar
½ tsp. peanut or sesame oil
1 tbs. soy sauce
½ tsp. cornstarch
1 or 2 tsps. water

Place fish in wok or large pan. Cut ginger and Chinese mushroom into thin strips and lay on top of fish. Place bean sprouts on top of fish. Sprinkle pinch of salt and sugar over fish. In a small bowl blend oil, soy sauce, cornstarch and water. Pour into wok around the fish and cover tightly with an appropriate lid. On a medium flame allow fish to steam and simmer for 10 minutes. Remove from pan and allow to cool. Serve fish and vegetables with sauce in two separage meals. Contains approximately 150 calories.

Meow Shu Pork

2 oz. lean pork from shoulder
1 tbs. soy sauce
⅔ tsp. cornstarch
  Pinch *each* salt, sugar, and catnip
  (optional for human diners)
1 oz. bean sprouts

Mince pork fine. Place it in a bowl and add the soy sauce, cornstarch, salt, sugar and pinch of catnip. Knead the mixture thoroughly so that all ingredients blend evenly. On a board shape the doughy mixture into a small loaf. Place it in a steam basket; put the basket into a tightly covered pot with 1½ cups boiling water. Steam the loaf over medium heat for fifteen minutes. Remove it. Add bean sprouts to steamer and cook for two minutes. Allow the loaf to cool. Slice and serve over bed of bean sprouts. Serve in two separate meals. Contains 160 calories.

Chicken and Mandarin Whiskers

¼ cup celery
¼ cup bamboo shoots
1 dried Chinese mushroom, soaked overnight
2 to 3 oz. raw chicken meat (light or dark)
1 tsp. peanut or sesame oil
  Pinch *each* salt, pepper, and sugar
  Dash of dry sherry
¼ cup water with dissolved chicken bouillon cube
½ tsp. cornstarch mixed with 1 tsp. water

Slice celery, bamboo shoots, mushroom and chicken into small, thin sticks. Keep these ingredients separate from one another. Heat oil in wok and stir in celery. Add the bamboo shoots and the mushroom and stir-fry for 3 minutes. Add a pinch each of salt, pepper, and sugar plus a quick dash of dry sherry. Mix in the pan. Add water with bouillon and then cornstarch pre-mixed with water and stir as it comes to a boil. Boil for 2 minutes and pour into a dish. Wipe out wok with a cloth and sprinkle two drops of oil into it as it reheats. Toss the chicken into the wok plus a dash of dry sherry and a pinch each of salt, pepper, and sugar. Cook for 2 minutes; then return vegetable mixture to pan. Mix with chicken. Remove from wok and allow food to cool. Serve in two separate meals. Contains approximately 177 calories.

Paw Paw Egg

1 egg
¼ cup cooked rice
1 cup quickly steamed bean sprouts
   Garlic powder (optional)
   Pinch *each* salt, pepper, and
   sugar
   Catnip

Beat egg and fry gently on nonstick surface. (You may use a nonstick spray product inside the wok or frying pan.) Remove egg from pan and fold each end in. With a knife, cut into thin shreds. In a bowl combine egg with rice, bean sprouts, garlic, spices and a dusting of catnip. Feed in two separate meals. Contains 141 calories.

It is important to bear in mind that these recipes do not represent an *absolutely* balanced diet in every case. Always use a high-quality vitamin and mineral supplement designed for cats and use these recipes as an occasional break from the everyday routine. And please do not substitute Chinese food from restaurants. These are specially formulated to meet your cat's high protein needs.

DAILY FOOD REQUIREMENTS OF CATS ACCORDING TO AGE

Age	Expected Wt. lb.	Daily calorie/body wt. cal./lb.	Daily ration oz.
Newborn	0.26	172	1.1
5 weeks	1.1	113	2.9
10 weeks	2.2	91	4.7
20 weeks	4.4	59	6.1
30 weeks	6.6	45	7.1
Adult ♂	9.9	36	8.5
Adult ♀ (pregnant)	7.7	45	8.2
Adult ♀ (lactating)	5.5	113	14.7
Neuter ♂	8.8	36	7.5
Neuter ♀	5.5	36	4.7

♂ = Male
♀ = Female
   Adapted from "Gaines Basic Guide to Canine Nutrition with a chapter on the Nutritional Requirements of Cats." Courtesy of the Gaines Dog Research Center.

"IDEAL" RATIONS FOR CATS *

	Water %	Protein %	Fat %	Carb. %	Ash %	Calcium %	Cal./ 100g.
1. Newborn **	72	9.5	6.8	10	0.75	0.035	142
2. Kittens and Cats	70	14	10	5	1	0.6	150

* "Ideal" Rations for Cats refers to natural diets, which encompass mother's milk (for newborns) or food obtained from nature (for kittens and cats).
** The term "newborn" applies to the first five weeks of life.
Adapted from "Gaines Basic Guide to Canine Nutrition with a chapter on the Nutritional Requirements of Cats." Courtesy of the Gaines Dog Research Center.

RECOMMENDED NUTRIENT ALLOWANCES FOR CATS
(Percentage or Amount per Kilogram of Diet, Dry Basis [a])

Nutrient	Unit	Amount
Protein [b]	%	28
Fat [c]	%	9
Linoleic acid	%	1
Minerals		
Calcium	%	1
Phosphorus	%	0.8
Potassium	%	0.3
Sodium chloride [d]	%	0.5
Magnesium	%	0.05
Iron	mg	100
Copper	mg	5
Manganese	mg	10
Zinc [e]	mg	30
Iodine	mg	1
Selenium	mg	0.1

[a] "Dry Basis" refers to the value of all foods when measured without moisture.
Nutrient levels selected have satisfactorily maintained adult cats and have supported growth of kittens. It is probable that they would be adequate for gestation and lactation, but few such studies have been conducted. Since diet processing (such as extruding or retorting) may destroy or impair the availability of some nutrients, sufficient amounts of such nutrients should be included to ensure the presence of recommended allowances at the time the diet is eaten.
[b] Quality equivalent to that derived from unprocessed mammalian, avian, or fish muscle. Processing may lower protein quality and necessitate higher concentrations.

Nutrient	Unit	Amount
Vitamins		
VitaminA	IU	10,000
Vitamin D	IU	1,000
Vitamin E ^{f}	IU	80
Thiamin	mg	5
Riboflavin	mg	5
Pantothenic acid	mg	10
Niacin	mg	45
Pyridoxine	mg	4
Folic acid	mg	1.0
Biotin	mg	0.05
Vitamin B$_{12}$	mg	0.02
Choline	mg	2,000

^{c} No requirement for fat, apart from the need for essential fatty acids and as a carrier of fat-soluble vitamins, has been demonstrated. The figure of 9 percent fat is listed only because approximately this amount is necessary to develop a diet with the necessary caloric density of dry matter. Fat does favorably influence diet palatability.

^{d} Since reliable individual estimates of the need for sodium and chlorine are not available, the need for both elements has been expressed as a recommended allowance for sodium chloride.

^{e} When cats are fed vegetable-protein-based diets, zinc requirements may be in excess of 40 ppm (Aiken *et al.*, 1977).

^{f} Higher levels may be necessary when large concentrations of unsaturated fats, such as in tuna oil, are included in the diet.

From "Nutrient Requirements of Cats," Number 13, Revised 1978. National Research Council.

5

Gaining the Upper Paw (Training)

The potential for being well-behaved lies within the brain of every cat, like a rich vein of gold running through a layer of granite. Cats only *appear* to be stubborn. It is true, however, that their behavior patterns and traits are mostly predetermined and render them adaptive only to a point. Dogs are social animals, and are more than a little willing to please in exchange for human approval. Cats are not at all like that. They can become attached to a few humans when treated with care and affection and will reciprocate affection for affection after a fashion. The independent air of most cats is quite understandable and justified because of their natural ability to resort to predatory skills if forced to return to the wild state. However, house cats need humans to feed them, clean their litter boxes, let them in and out, supply the catnip, shield them from galloping dogs and clutchy children. It is within this domestic context that cat training becomes necessary.

Contrary to popular belief, most cats can be trained to some degree and, indeed, must be trained if they are going to share the same home with humans. Cats must be taught to use their litter pans or the outdoors for their toileting. They must be taught not to destroy furniture and human flesh with their claws. And it would certainly be

113

helpful for a house cat to learn not to climb the curtains as a substitute for trees. Cat tricks are not necessary, although some owners think they are amusing.

The problem is with the word *training* itself. Cats are never really trained as one understands the word, unless you are talking about the big cats performing in a circus. Training is more or less a form of behavior modification where the animal is conditioned to respond to a stimulus, especially when the desired response is outside the animal's usual range of behavior. For example, housebreaking a dog is training because it is natural for the dog to relieve himself anywhere except where he sleeps and eats. A trained dog will only relieve himself outdoors or indoors on newspaper and usually at one prescribed place. In the case of cats, however, it is probably more accurate to use the term *cat management* when describing cat training.

Managing your cat at home does not require the rigors of a complete obedience course as does the management of a pet dog. The following are the only demands you need make on your cat to enjoy a pleasant home life:

1. Litter box orientation.
2. Come when called.
3. Leash training.
4. "Sit."
5. "No."

It wouldn't matter if you were Tarzan or the stage manager of the Circus Maximus, no cat can be made to obey because he wants to please you or is terrified of you. It is only on the simplest level that cats accept the dominant/subordinate idea at all. With the exception of lions, cats in the wild are solitary figures stalking their prey in the lonely shadows of a variety of remote regions of the world. The hunt is not always successful and dinner isn't on the table at five every day. Like their undomesticated brethren, house cats are always in search of food because they cannot get it into their dear heads that the electric can opener whirls on a regular basis. And that's where man sticks his foot in the door.

Your little cat is, in a sense, constantly on the hunt. She'll go to almost any lengths to obtain food. She could even be persuaded to obey a command or two as long as there was a reward with a munch factor. Think of her as a politician looking for campaign funds. She'll do almost anything for a contribution. Bribery is the name of the game; to be sure, it is for a higher purpose.

One of the great trainers of large wild cats (and teacher of trainers) is William L. Brisby, director of the Institute for Wild and Exotic Animal Studies and department head, Exotic Animal Training and Management Program, Moorpark College, Moorpark, California. Mr. Brisby is a writer, lecturer, educator, naturalist, environmentalist and advisor to several museums and institutions of learning. He tells us that the same basic procedures are followed when training big cats and little cats. Of primary importance is to know the animal. This means that you must spend considerable time with your cat before starting a training (or management) program. It's important to learn individual peculiarities in order to determine how to motivate, reprimand, and get the cat to react. The most important thing is to learn the animal's native abilities. Each cat has its own gimmicks for getting what it wants and these can be useful in manipulating behavior.

Brisby works on what he calls the *hunger drive*. He feeds the normal diet necessary to maintain the animal in a healthy condition. However, for training purposes he reduces the ration a bit so that the cat's appetite is sharpened, just slightly. Although this author agrees with the effectiveness of the method, it is probably best simply to conduct training sessions for domestic cats before the daily feeding rather than to reduce the ration. Give the cat a basic diet that he gets whether he trains or not, says Brisby. Then find a food substance that he likes and use it as a supplement to the basic diet. Cats love yeast pills or little bits of cooked liver, for instance. Contrary to what most people think, cats work better when they are hungry. When working a lion or tiger in a show or demonstration, the trainer works it hungry because that's when the trainer is safe. When the big cats are full, they want to curl up and sleep and not be disturbed. The trainer gives them food rewards while they're working (very small amounts) and feeds them when it's over.

Brisby advises that one should start slowly when training a cat. Get the animal's confidence and take time to give him an opportunity to understand what you want. When teaching commands, you should develop a hand signal as well as a verbal signal (plus a clicker, bell or whistle to serve as a "bridge" between signal and reward). The cat must be told when he's doing something correctly in order to reinforce what he's learned. You start getting him used to the signal or bridge by feeding him the reward and following it immediately with a whistle or a click. It's best always to hand-feed the animal; never put the food in a pan as a training reward. Giving food rewards by hand helps the cat fix on you as the source of his food and makes him come to you for his meals and rewards. In this manner you work with him and get the behaviors you are looking for. In many instances the cat will walk toward you and do some stunts and tricks just to get your attention because he wants to be fed. This is perfectly normal behavior, particularly if he's just on the edge of hunger. Don't make the cat too hungry. In that case he won't think of anything but food.

By using the bridge consistently at the beginning of training, the cat will always associate the sound with the food reward, and this is the first breakthrough in training such animals. From there you start working the cat with the behaviors he offers or the ones you want him to do. By developing a cat's proper response to a bridge sound you can teach almost anything and expect good results.

The ideal training situation, according to Brisby, is to have the cat imprint on you from the very beginning of her life. Brisby claims that the best results occur when you start talking to the kitten (or the cub) around the fourth day of her life, even before her eyes have opened. You talk to her and caress her frequently so that imprinting on you takes place. (Imprinting is a learning process limited to a specific developmental period that leads to an extremely rapid conditioning. If the animal focuses on the imprinting object—in this case, you— during the very early or sensitive period, the animal will always prefer the imprinted object.)

William L. Brisby, Director of the Institute for Wild and Exotic Animal Studies at Moorpark College, Moorpark, California, as he becomes acquainted with a subject for training.

Some researchers maintain that the most important factor in a cat's ability to be educated is its opportunity to be socialized. In the earliest weeks of its life, a kitten should be handled and cuddled by a human several times a day. She should also be surrounded by objects such as toys, spools, balls and other objects of play to stimulate mental and physical activity. If these elements are introduced early in a kitten's life, she will be much more adaptive to living with and responding to human beings and possibly to other cats. Although kittens should stay with their mothers until weaned, loving human contact is essential as soon as possible. A socialized cat will respond to training more enthusiastically. It is almost never too late to socialize cats, even an older cat, to some degree.

When you are training an animal it is important to focus all of your concentration on the animal. The training environment must be quiet and offer no distractions for the trainer or the animal. Cats can get frightened quite easily by people coming up behind them, especially strangers. It is important that there be only pleasant associations with the training sessions. It is also worth mentioning that cats work best in their own territories. Do not train outdoors and do not train at locations other than in the cat's home. You must be the focus of attention and the only relief from boredom. Be patient and do not play with the cat during training sessions.

The cat should be worked every day. The length of each session depends on the attention span of the animal. Because no two animals are alike, you will have to determine this for yourself based on trial and error. Some cats will train no more than three minutes, but can tolerate three or four sessions a day, spaced well apart. There are other cats who will tolerate five-, ten- and even fifteen-minute sessions, but in this case you should limit the sessions to one a day. In each session, continue to work the animal as long as she will work readily. Always stop the minute the cat has performed a command sharply, no matter how short the session was. Do not push her to perform the command again. Always stop the first time she performs correctly and leave her with a good experience. The next day work her again and if she performs properly the first time, you can get her to repeat the action once. It is important not to bore the animal by having her constantly repeat something she has learned to do well.

It should be noted that whole tomcats and unspayed females are not very good candidates for training. It is almost impossible to train a male cat with a strong sexual urge. The same is true for a female during estrus. The management of cat behavior is best achieved when the pet has been surgically sterilized. A physically sick cat is also impossible to work with. Cancel all training sessions until the animal is well. Do not train the cat if *you* are not well, either. Otherwise your techniques may become sloppy, which will certainly carry over to the animal.

It is extremely important to understand what to do if the cat becomes panic-stricken for any reason. Never pick up a frightened or panicked cat. Leave him alone, get the area quiet, resolve the source of the animal's fright. Give the cat as much time to settle down as he needs. Even a small kitten can be nothing but a mass of claws and teeth if he is very upset. He has the tools and the ability to rip anyone wide open, exposing people and other pets to infection and the necessity for painful medical treatment.

LITTER BOX ORIENTATION

The most obvious function of the cat's eliminative processes of course has to do with digestion, nutrition and elimination of the body's waste materials. However, there is more to it than that. Cats use their body waste as scent posts for the purpose of marking off territory and also as a means of communicating with other cats. Females in heat and males looking for females mark off areas with their urine to attract each other. In this situation the urine contains glandular secretions that give it a special odor with sexual connotations. Body waste is also connected with health functions. Frequency of elimination and the quality of feces and urine are often indicative of the animal's state of health. All of these factors may be involved in your cat's litter box orientation. Therefore, when your cat suddenly stops using the litter box, it may not be a simple matter of training or spite or anything concerning discipline. A sick or emotionally upset cat will have housebreaking failures. Solving the underlying problem is the only way to get the animal back to using the proper toilet.

For the first two weeks of life the kitten has no physical ability to eliminate on his own. Elimination is accomplished with the help of the mother, who simply licks the underbelly, thus stimulating urination and defecation. She ingests the body waste from the kittens so that no detectable odor comes from the nest. This natural response promotes survival because it prevents enemies and predators from locating the litter by scent. Similarly, her own body waste is eliminated away from the nest and buried. It is for this reason and this reason exclusively that cats instinctively bury their body waste. For the pet owner it is a blessing since a cat's natural proclivity to keep odors to a minimum (with the exception of territorial and sexual marking) makes him the best of pets.

The first three weeks of kittenhood may be compared to the first eight months of a human baby's life. The kitten's eyes open, hearing begins and just about all physical functions begin to work without outside stimulation. The kitten begins to crawl and eventually gets himself outside of the nest for a look at the greater world. It is extraordinary that the youngster has already learned not to eliminate in his own nest. The mother is very strict about this and does not permit it. At this early age many kittens have already begun to travel a relatively far distance from the nest in order to relieve themselves and make infantile digging and burying gestures. All of this works to the advantage of humans who wish to live with cats as companion animals. Assuming a kitten has been with his mother and littermates for at least eight weeks, litter box orientation is an easy and quick process.

The Technique

Following each meal, after every nap and after strenuous play, place the kitten (or grown cat) in the litter box and take hold of the front paws. Push them forward and backward so that they have to make a scratching motion. On most occasions the instinct to eliminate will take over, although the cat will not always eliminate each time this is done. Do not force the issue. Allow the cat to hop out of the box for a few minutes' pause. Do not permit the animal to leave the room. It is advisable to close the door from the outset. Repeat the procedure. Depending on your cat's intelligence, mood and patience with you, she will eventually give the desired result.

The bathroom is the ideal location for your cat's litter box.

Supervision is important. Therefore, never give the cat the run of the house unless you are right there, watching for a mistake. If she sniffs one spot constantly, begins to circle or scratch the floor or carpet, it's time to transport her to the litter box quickly, close the door behind you and repeat the front paw scratching. Chances are it won't be necessary.

Confinement is a very important aspect of this technique. Keep the cat in the room with the litter box and nowhere else unless she is constantly supervised. Place a dish of water in with her, and perhaps a toy or two. Young kittens need a little time to learn to find the room with the box in it. Even a grown cat may decide to place a scent signal on the far wall of a new dining room simply because she hasn't been patterned to use the litter box yet. Also, kittens may not be able to control their small bladders while on the way to the room with the litter box. Very few cats will deliberately soil their living space if they can help it. They are too fastidious.

Confining the cat to one room helps her to pattern her behavior in the correct way by making the litter box more immediately available than any other place in the home. Once a cat soils an area outside the box, she will constantly be drawn back to the spot because of the odor. *Do not let this develop into a pattern because it will be extremely difficult to break.* When the cat makes a mistake, it is important to clean it up and destroy the urine scent as fast as you can. There are several products for sale in pet supply stores designed to eradicate urine stains and odors. Remember, the odor (imperceptible to humans) is the most important signal that you need to eradicate. The absolutely best product for this purpose is Nilodor, a highly concentrated odor neutralizer.

Normally, it is essential to keep the litter box clean by cleaning it out every day and changing the clay or sand very often (some owners change it every day). However, during the orientation period it is a good idea to leave the litter slightly soiled so that the scent will attract the cat.

Do not neglect or reject the idea of confinement. Even a cat who has always used a litter box should be confined when not supervised at least for the first twenty-four hours after moving into a new home. Continue to confine kittens until you are certain they know what to do and where to do it. It shouldn't take more than two or three days, if that long.

COME WHEN CALLED

It is now time to decide whether or not to use the *bridge* technique as suggested by William Brisby. As stated earlier, get the cat used to the signal or bridge by feeding a reward and then creating the sound either from a whistle (not too loud) or from a clicker, the small metal type used by children at Halloween (usually shaped like an animal or insect). Feed the cat a small reward and then click the clicker. Always hand-feed—offer the reward from the flat of your palm. Do this five or ten times and then quit for thirty minutes. Do it again for five or ten times and quit for the day. Repeat this procedure for three or four days. By now your cat should be accustomed to working with a bridge.

The next step is to reinforce the cat's responding to his name. A cat learns his own name by hearing it repeatedly and associating the name with something pleasant. One must never use the cat's name in vain, for punishment or for scolding. The cat's name is useful when you want him to come to you. If the association is negative, no cat will come running upon hearing you call. When teaching his name, stand back just a short distance from the cat while he is on the floor. Say the cat's name, pause for one second, drop the small food reward, pause for one second, click the clicker. When the cat finally eats the morsel, tell him what a good cat he is. Repeat these actions five or ten times, but on each occasion take two steps backward so that the cat is following you each time you call him. Give the cat two sessions for the day, half an hour apart, then quit. Repeat this step for three days.

At the next session place the cat in one end of the room and walk to the other. Call the cat by name and add the word "come." At the same time use a hand signal. Starting with your right arm hanging at your side, swing it upward and around as though beckoning so that it touches your left shoulder, then gently return to its original position at your side. After the execution of the hand signal, click the clicker. As the cat begins to move toward you, hold out your hand with the food reward sitting on the flat of your palm. Bend forward slightly so that the cat can lick the reward off your hand. As he does, congratulate him. This praise reinforces the food reward. Walk to the opposite end of the room and repeat the procedure. Do this five times if the cat performs well and ten times if he does not. Remember the procedure. Call the cat by name, adding the word "come": "Albert, come." At the same time use the hand signal. Immediately after the hand signal, click the clicker. Offer the reward on the flat of your hand and then give the praise. Once again, work the cat in two sessions, spaced apart, each day and do this for three days in a row. Miraculous as it may seem, you have now taught your cat to come when called.

WALKING ON A LEASH

How often does a cat get to enjoy canine prerogatives at a campfire, munching on barbecued hot dogs after vigorous backpacking? A trip to Yellowstone or even an outing in the building elevator is a pleasure never shared by the family cat. For those who enjoy the company of their cats, there is a way to take them almost anywhere. The key to cat travel is the leash and harness. Bear in mind that it is just as unnatural for a dog to be attached to a leash as it is for a cat. The dog makes the adjustment, and so can the cat.

Ideally, leash training is best initiated during kittenhood. However, there is no reason why grown cats cannot be trained to walk in tow if they are brought to it with patience, sensitivity and intelligence. The correct equipment, while simple, is absolutely essential. Unlike dogs, cats and kittens must not use collars with leashes. To prevent a collar from slipping off over the head, it would have to be buckled too tightly for comfort and safety, and the cat's negative reaction would be a natural one. This is the primary mistake that is often made when teaching a cat to walk with a leash. Instead of a collar, use a cat harness. A well-fitted *figure-eight harness* is best, accompanied by a long, lightweight leash. It is suggested the leash be made of nylon or webbed cloth. A leather leash is fine provided it is six feet long, light yet strong.

The initial problem is getting the cat to adapt to wearing this equipment. Some cats will not mind from the very beginning, while others will resist with obstinate vigor and take a long time to make the adjustment. Start with the harness. Give it to the cat as if it were a toy. Lay it at the cat's feet and allow her to sniff it, move it about and even use it in play. Once she is convinced the harness is not dangerous, put it on. Allow the cat to wear it for the better part of the day; repeat this for two days. It might even be a good idea to place it in the cat's bed so that she can claim it as her own "territory."

Next, tie a twelve-inch strip of cloth, rope or string to the harness and leave it on for five to ten hours. Do this for two days. Do not encourage the cat to play with the cloth if you can help it. Then hook the actual leash to the harness instead of the cloth strip. This will be different. The greater length and weight will annoy the animal. For the first day do not hook the leash to the harness for more than thirty minutes at a time. If the cat seems receptive, leave it hooked for as long as eight hours. Repeat this for two days.

You are now ready to pick up the leash in your hand and attempt to walk with the cat. It may go well in the beginning when you are both walking in the same direction. The problem begins when you exert just the slightest pressure and turn to walk in another direction. The cat will definitely balk and maybe dig in her paws (or claws), coming to a screeching halt. If she begins to fight the leash, lies down, or seems otherwise disturbed, be gentle and kind, using soft words, and coax her slowly to follow you. Perhaps an offer of her favorite type of food reward will help. Never, never drag her around on a leash; this will simply not produce the desired result. Never assume that your cat will walk like an obedience-trained dog. Walking with a cat is more like a negotiated settlement than a direct command. You both share in the decision as to which direction you will walk.

The moment of truth comes when the cat is to be taken outside for the first time wearing a harness and leash. It is important for you to know that, for the cat, being exposed on the sidewalk is more frightening than the unnatural sensation of being tethered. Hold the cat for as long as you must, even for the entire first experience. Next, kneel and entice her to come to you, using reassuring entreaties and food rewards. Be patient and very sensitive to her emotions. Eventually, the average, healthy cat will make the adjustment and walk as you walk.

You must be certain that your cat has a suitable temperament for this type of exercise. The very shy, cowering cat, who would rather be home under the bed than anywhere else in the world, is a very poor candidate for leash training. But if your cat is extremely curious, gregarious and somewhat adventurous, then by all means afford her the pleasure of your company by teaching her to walk with you on a leash. Be prepared to pick her up if a stray dog or other potential threat appears, or you may find yourself serving as an impromptu tree climbed by a terrified cat equipped with eighteen razor-sharp claws.

"SIT" (JUMP, SIT UP, DOWN)

The objective here is to get the cat to sit where you want him to, even if that means getting him to jump onto a chair or stool. Once the cat is seated, it is easy to get him to rise on his hind legs for you and then, on command, to leap back to the floor. This is not as difficult or as complicated as it might seem. You will simply employ the same principles of training as before. The sound bridge made with the clicker is important here because it is the link between your command and the cat's desire to be rewarded. For this reason it is important that the cat be somewhat hungry before and during the training sessions. As stated before, conduct the sessions before meals.

At the start of the session, work the cat in the manner described in the "Come When Called" section above. Once he comes to you, give him a food reward, immediately followed by a click (the bridge). Kneel down slowly, keeping his attention on you by staring in his eyes. Say "Sit," gently push his hind section down into a sitting position, give him a food reward, click the clicker, and offer him lavish praise. Repeat this five times and then quit. Conduct another session one or two hours later, doing the whole thing over again. Repeat this each day until the cat will sit on signal, without your having to push his rear end down.

The next step is to get him to jump onto a chair or stool and sit for you. While the cat is at one end of a room, set up a stool at the other end. In a friendly but firm voice say the cat's name, followed by "come." Don't forget to use your hand gesture. When the cat gets to you, kneel down and give him a food reward. Click the clicker immediately and praise him. Then say, "Sit." If he sits for you, give him a food reward; immediately click the clicker and praise him. Rise to your full height and hold out a food reward with your hand halfway up the length of the stool. The cat will probably try to reach for it while still in a sitting position. Say his name and "jump." If he starts to get poised as if he is going to jump, place the hand holding the food reward slightly above the height of the stool so that he must aim for the stool as a landing ledge in order to get at the reward. Allow your arm to slide up and down (like a trombone) so that the reward is an enticement for him to jump onto the stool. When he finally makes the jump, give him the reward instantly and click the clicker just as quickly. Praise the cat. It is important that the food reward be given immediately after he performs properly so that he associates the command with the reward. It is equally important that the bridge (the clicking sound) and the praise come instantly after the food reward is given, for the same reason. Repeat this sequence of stimulus-response-reward five times and then quit. Conduct another session one or two hours later and repeat the procedure. Do this for several days until the cat is performing the command sharply.

The next and final stage is to get the cat to *Come when called; Sit; Jump onto the stool, Sit and Jump Down.* Repeat the three steps, as above. When the cat gets up onto the stool and is given his reward for doing so, give him the command "Sit." He should respond readily. When he does, give him a food reward immediately, click the clicker, and praise him. Let him remain seated on the stool for fifteen seconds. Hold out a food reward in your hand, down near the floor (using the same trombone movement as before). Say his name and "down." When he jumps down, kneel and instantly give him the reward, click the clicker, and praise him. Repeat this five times, then quit. Repeat the procedure one or two hours later. Repeat this lesson every day until the cat is performing it with precision. It will not take too long.

"NO"

By the strictest definition, "No" is not really a command. "No" is more of a demand and quite often a discipline tool. When you use the term "No," the cat must stop what she is doing.

This term is essentially a negative one and is associated exclusively with discipline. Cats can be disciplined, and the sooner this is accomplished the better life is going to be for everyone. The object is to stop unwanted behavior before it becomes patterned. But all cats crave patterned routines, which means the family is going to have to exercise patience, consistency and loving authority. According to the Tree House Animal Foundation in Chicago, the cat must be caught in the act if she is going to be reprimanded in a way that teaches. A loud noise or a sharp "No" will get her attention and signal your displeasure. Most cats hate loud, sudden noises and will do almost anything to avoid them.

When your cat misbehaves (scratches the curtains or furniture) and you catch her in the act, you may do one of two things. You can "assault" her senses. For example, you can keep a water pistol handy and squirt it at the cat (not in the face) and say loudly, "No"; or slap your hand loudly with a magazine or stamp on the floor. Do not make any gestures that could be interpreted by the cat as a threat of violence. Terror will get you nothing. The second—and better—technique is to take the cat by the nape of the neck, pick her up, hold her out in midair with the bottom feet supported and shake her head. At the same time, use the word "No" with firm authority so that there can be no mistake about your meaning. Do not shake the cat's head too hard. This is the manner in which the mother chastises the kittens. It is perfectly acceptable as well as effective. The demand "No" can be administered in this fashion for all unacceptable behavior and can be used for healthy cats of all ages. However, there is more to do after the reprimand.

Your objective is to impress on the cat that you do not like what she just did. However, it is now time to teach her what she should be doing. In the case of scratching furniture, carry the furry offender to her scratch post. Gently squeeze the front paws until the claws show and rub them into the material, allowing her to get the feel of pulling on this area. (Of course, the scratch post must be sturdy enough and

Patience, kindness and communication are what's required when training cats . . . all cats.

tall enough for the animal to be able to reach up and stretch out on without tipping it over.) When a cat scratches, it is sharpening its claws and removing dead tissue. This is an important exercise for her. She may also be marking territory. You must redirect the activity to an acceptable location. Once you've redirected the cat's activity, she must be given praise for doing the correct thing. You may even give her a food reward. If you do, click your clicker to help motivate her into redirecting her activity where you want it. Rub the scratch post with catnip for a little added reinforcement to the demand.

Another aspect of unwanted behavior is attacking and destroying house plants. Because many plants are poisonous to cats, the damage can be to both cat and plant (see Chapter 7). It is natural for cats to eat greenery. When they are allowed outdoors, they can chomp on grass and they have no difficulty. But you must give the demand "No" when you catch the cat in the act of chewing on your favorite plant. Repeat the same techniques outlined above. The best way to redirect the cat's desire to eat plants is to supply her with something of her own. Commercial plant products that grow in their own containers and are ideal for cats to eat are sold in pet stores. Of course, you can sprinkle red pepper on your plants (leaves, stems and soil) and allow the reprimand to be a natural one. If your cat uses the soil in your planters as a litter box, pepper the soil heavily. An alternate solution is to place a grid of chicken wire over the dirt. You may use your water pistol to stop the cat as you say "No," or pick her up as described before and say "No" as you shake her. Redirection is absolutely essential and a reward, bridge and praise should immediately follow.

Other techniques for solving behavior problems are use of bad-tasting substances for chewing problems; balloons for scratching problems and to keep the cat off chairs and sofas; double-sided tape for covering up toilet "accidents."

If your cat has a tendency to chew clothing, lamp cords or anything else, simply coat the object with a product called Bitter Apple (obtainable in a pet store) or with Tabasco sauce. The unpleasant taste experience will stop the problem.

When a cat has chosen to claw the arm of a sofa, tape four or five tightly inflated balloons to the offended spot. The movement of the balloons is enough to stop the average cat. And if not, when the first balloon pops from being mauled, the sound should be frightening enough to break the habit. This technique is also good for areas where you don't want the cat sitting.

Once a cat urinates or defecates in a spot outside the litter box, she will be attracted to the same location by the scent. This will inspire the cat to repeat the same offending action. Cover the entire spot with double-sided tape. A tacky surface is just too unpleasant for a cat to cope with, due to its fastidious nature.

TRICKS

The question of cat tricks is a matter of the owner's personal taste and preference. Tricks are not very difficult to teach; it's a matter of observing what the animal likes to do on his own and then encouraging him to perform when asked. For example, many cats enjoy rolling over. If you can catch him in the act, give him a food reward, click your clicker and praise the animal. If you say "Roll over" every time the cat is about to do it and then reward him for doing so afterward, he will eventually roll over on command. The same applies to shaking hands, jumping on your shoulder, and retrieving, as well as the dubious feat of begging. Training your cat to practice the social amenities is much more important and of lasting value.

Cat tricks are merely the formalization by humans of various behaviors and individual quirks that some cats do automatically. In Elizabeth, New Jersey, Frank McSweeney, an animal lover all his life, has formalized the behavior of cats and dogs for quite some time. At one time his Siamese cat, Shanghai, and his fox terrier, Singapore, were a great performing team in and around the New Jersey–New York area. Although Singapore is gone, McSweeney and Shanghai can still be enticed to take their engaging "act" to any school, church, hospital, fair or other charitable institution.

Shanghai is a Seal Point Siamese who in 1974 was the All-American Glamour Kitty. First she was Ms. New Jersey; then she went on to Miami Beach, where she won the national contest, being judged superior to over thirty-five thousand entries. She was written up in over six hundred newspapers across the country. The event was covered by ABC, CBS, the Associated Press and United Press International. She is currently sixteen years old and still in show biz.

Shanghai's principal talent is not bolting away when facing a large crowd of people. You have to admit it is a rare quality in a cat. She will sit in a wagon and allow herself to be pulled around. As a matter of fact, sitting in various conveyances is a great part of Shanghai and McSweeney's act. She dresses up in her Glamour Kitty gown, robe and crown and poses for her big finale. McSweeney is an ex-Marine who drives a school bus for a living. Training performing animals is a heart-warming hobby as far as he is concerned. He has brought a smile to the faces of thousands of sick and disadvantaged children and a lump to the throats of many adults.

If you want to discuss the training of cats, there is no one better to talk to than Gunther Gebel-Williams, superstar of the Ringling Brothers and Barnum & Bailey Circus, who is a familiar face in American Express card commercials on TV. Anyone who gets into a circus ring with seventeen tigers at one time knows something about cat training.

"It takes years to train animals to perform tricks," says Gebel-Williams. He says he scours the planet looking for the most intelligent animals, and even breeds his own stock when he finds quality stud stock. He claims:

Trainer Frank McSweeney, and (left) Shanghai and (right) Singapore.

You have to have a relationship with each one, and know who gets along with whom. It is rather easy when you know your animals. You have to be always strong. You command animals with your presence. They must respect you. Without respect, it is all over. The most dangerous thing is the claws. Our skin is like paper. And when you're between two cats to break up a fight, it is not hard to get cut.

First you must find an animal and it must learn its name. Then you have to wait until it is old enough to begin training. It must be strong enough to protect itself from other cats or elephants. When you begin training you must be patient. You need to take time and in animal training, one year is nothing. It is all a matter of communication. It is all in your voice, your touch and in your personality. You must maintain the authority of your personality.

Gunther Gebel-Williams, superstar of the Ringling Brothers and Barnum &
Bailey Circus. Only a great trainer would parade around the center ring with
a leopard around his shoulders.

In every spare moment not taken up by rehearsing, performing, cleaning and feeding, Gunther can be found walking down the cages, talking to the animals, patting the ones that allow him to do it, checking on their mood and well-being. "When I say I feel very close to my animals, it's not only words. If I miss a morning with them, I feel bad. I do everything I can for them. If they are cold I cannot rest. They are like my family," says the trainer. Perhaps that is why Gunther Gebel-Williams is the greatest animal man in the Greatest Show on Earth.

Cats will not stop loving their owners when the owners decide to take control of the pets' behavior. In fact, it strengthens your rapport with your pet. Asserting yourself with a pet is not an act of cruelty. It isn't even a violation of your animal's true nature. Do not get caught up in the "Born Free" syndrome, where everything you do to and for your pet is taken as a violation of the animal's true inclinations. That attitude has hurt many animals and helped few. Having a well-trained pet is a happy circumstance for both four-legged and two-legged inhabitants of any given living space.

6

Looking Good
(Grooming)

When a cat looks good, it's because it's healthy. Good health is directly connected with the elements of nutrition, exercise, mental stability and, of course, grooming. A well-groomed, happy pet is a shining example of loving care, which increases the cat's opportunity for longevity.

EXERCISE

Young cats, old cats, thin cats and especially fat cats should exercise so that they may enjoy the benefits of weight control while strengthening and toning weak and sagging muscles. Without movement of some kind, cats will become listless and fatigued. Once a sedentary cat is placed on an exercise program, listlessness and fatigue are replaced by alertness and energy. Sleep is better and more restful. What's more, exercise can provide a stronger bond between one's self and one's pet. It is a release for pent-up energy and is also a form of recreation for any cat.

It is important that exercise involve most parts of the cat's body. A cat's physical activities should tax the power of the muscles and be extended long enough and strenuously enough to produce a sense of healthful fatigue. The exercise must be suited to the age and physical condition of the cat. It would be wise to consult a veterinarian before launching a program of increased physical activity. Some cats have conditions that could be aggravated by the wrong kind of exercise.

There is probably no greater physical activity for you or your cat than walking. Once you have taught your cat to walk on a leash (see Chapter 5), it is a relatively simple matter to take thirty minutes a day for a brisk walk indoors or outdoors. Brisk walking or even a form of cat jogging (start and stop intermittently) is good for the heart and lungs and develops endurance (for cat *and* owner).

Other forms of exercise for cats help improve the animal's strength, agility, flexibility, balance and muscle tone. These objectives can be achieved through play. You may use Ping-Pong balls, objects for retrieval, peacock feathers, strings, paper bags, and so on. (See "Toys" in Chapter 2.) Pipe cleaners, plastic bag ties, rope, loving children and other animals may all provide suitable exercise for any cat. Never leave your cat alone with such objects of play as string, yarn, plastic toys. Far too many cats swallow such seemingly innocent items and choke.

COAT CARE

Because owners of companion cats have no need for show grooming techniques as a rule and because the subject can fill a book of its own, only those grooming needs that keep a furry friend healthy and reasonably aesthetic are offered here.

Combing and Brushing

Although long-haired cats require more attention than short-haired ones, daily grooming is necessary for all. The most important aspect of grooming, as it applies to hygiene, is daily combing and brushing. This must be done every day to give the cat a good appearance as well as to avoid the ill effects of the animal's constant self-grooming. If you cannot comb or brush out your cat every day, try to do it at least three times a week.

Cats continually lick their coats clean with their tongues. They engage in this activity for a variety of reasons. Licking is often a healing process. It is also an important "displacement" gesture. In other words, preening takes the place of some other, usually instinctual, behavior that the animal is suppressing. A cat that enjoys clawing the furniture but also knows you will scold him for that behavior will lick himself until either you or the urge leaves. Feline self-grooming also helps prevent scents that might alert prey animals to the cat's presence. A sleek coat makes it easier to stalk through underbrush on a hunt, even when the terrain is only the fringed bottom of a sofa.

When a domestic cat does his own coat grooming, he ingests a great deal of hair. After a while the hair accumulates in a mass in the digestive system and develops into a *hairball,* which can eventually cause a serious blockage in the stomach or intestine. Some hairballs cannot be passed from the body normally and must be removed surgically, not without a great deal of discomfort and unpleasantness. Often a cat will regurgitate these hairballs and will have trouble keeping food down until the hair is all out of his stomach.

Brushing and combing your cat every day will definitely help prevent this problem.

Short-haired cats can be groomed daily with a hard-rubber, rectangular cat brush and a fine-toothed steel comb. If you massage the cat's coat with hands dampened with water you will loosen the dead hair and even pull some off. Using your fingertips, gently rub the skin both with and against the lay of the fur. Next, work the rubber brush through the coat with long, gentle strokes, taking as much dead and loose fur with you as possible. Be sure to stroke the entire body from shoulder to toe, from nose to tail. Ask a professional groomer or a pet-supply merchant about spray-on protein conditioners. They deepen coat color, add body and life to the coat and eliminate dry flakes. There are special products for light-colored coats and dark-colored coats.

It is not difficult to recognize hair that is no longer alive. It is rough-looking and quite dull in appearance. It sometimes has a snowy appearance at the tips of the follicles. Remove all fur fitting this description if it will comb or brush out. Do not force it. Next, work the coat with the fine-toothed comb in much the same manner. This too will remove dead and dull hair and, in addition, will massage the skin and bring a natural luster back to the fur.

Although the long-haired cat does not shed any more individual hairs than the short-haired cat does, the quantity is greater simply because of the length. Mats, tangles and hidden parasites are the dangers of the long coat and must be prevented by daily grooming if the cat is to be spared pain, poor health and a snarly, rag-like appearance. Begin grooming both long-haired and short-haired cats when they are kittens so that they will become easily accustomed to the routine. (See Chapter 2.)

You will need several combs and a brush. The most important comb is a medium-toothed steel comb with long, tapered teeth. The tips must be smooth and round to avoid hurting the skin or tearing out healthy hair. The teeth must be set widely apart to accommodate the long, abundant fur on the back, sides and underbody. A fine-toothed comb is suggested for the legs and neck, as well as for loose fur and small tangles. An extra-fine-toothed comb is needed for facial hair and long tufts between the toes. It is also good for removing debris and visible parasites such as fleas.

Comb the coat daily to prevent tangles, knots or mats. The degree of knotting depends on the type, texture and length of the cat's fur. Fine hair will knot more readily than coarse hair. Remove knots or mats very gently and with patience. You can remove mats by first using a liquid tangle-removing product and a de-matting tool, such as a seam ripper. Your thumb and index finger are the best de-matting tools available. If the cat's coat is badly matted all over, the body and leg fur may have to be clipped. If you are inexperienced, do not attempt this yourself. See a professional groomer or a veterinarian. The cat may have to be tranquilized. De-matting of a badly matted coat may cause the cat much unnecessary pain and result in an aversion to all future grooming procedures.

Assuming the combing goes well, you are now ready to brush your long-haired cat. Using a soft, natural-bristle brush only (never nylon), gently stroke with the lay of the fur, using short movements from the shoulder to the haunch to the tail. Brush downward and sideward along each leg. Do not forget to comb and brush the under-coat on the stomach, flanks, chest, backs of ears and behind all four legs. These areas can be very troublesome if neglected.

Combing and brushing your cat every day is a loving gesture and gives you an opportunity to express your affection in a very tangible way. Hugs, caresses and gentle talking are altogether proper and should enhance your pet's receptivity to the grooming. It is always best to start these hygienic habits in kittenhood because some cats absolutely refuse to allow you to groom them later in life. Even if groomed from kittenhood, some cats will suddenly decide they no longer want to participate. You must, unfortunately, force the issue and make it clear that they are going to be combed and brushed, no matter what. It's too important to neglect.

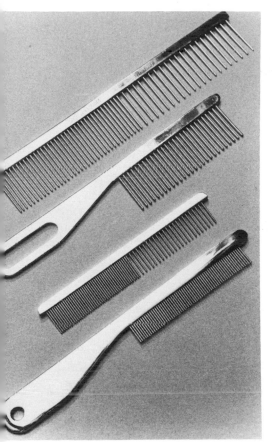 

Combs. (Top) Half fine/half medium Belgian comb with tapered teeth. This is used for lifting long coats. (Second from top) Medium Belgium comb with a handle. (Third from top) Smaller-sized half fine/half medium Belgium comb with blunt teeth for short coats. Blunt teeth are important for all short-coated cats. (Bottom) Fine-toothed comb with handle. This can be used for both short- and long-haired cats. It is especially useful for combing out the area around the head of long-haired cats.

Brushes. (Top) Soft-bristle toothbrush is used on long-haired cats, especially Persians and Himalayans, to scrub the facial area if there is eyestain. (Second from top) Soft brush to put powder into light-colored, long-haired coat. (Third from top) Natural-bristle brush. Tufts of bristles that are graduated in length penetrate coat more efficiently. This is recommended for short- and long-coated cats. (Bottom) Soft brush to remove powder from light-colored, long-haired cats.

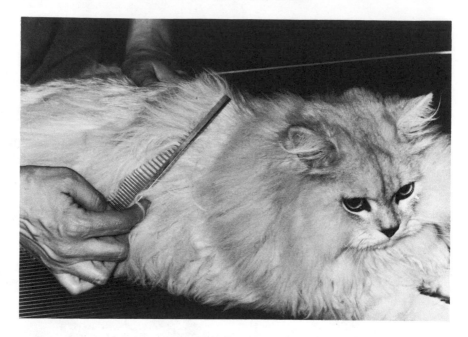

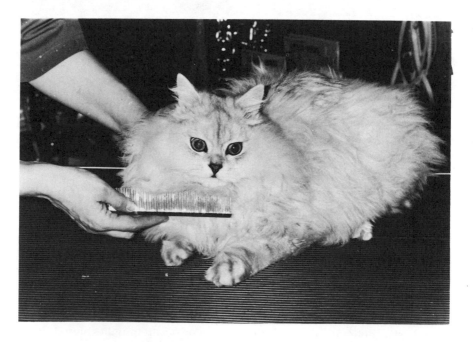

Combing the long-haired cat.

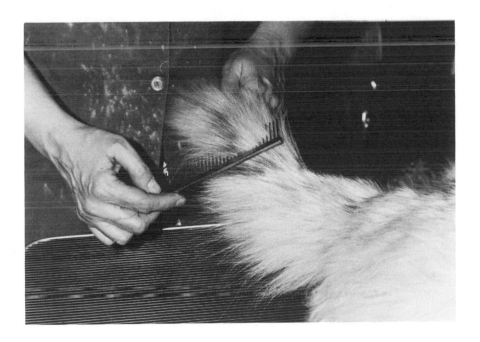

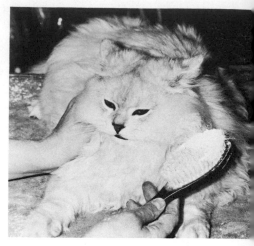

Dry-bathing the light-colored, long-haired cat. Sprinkle cornstarch or commercially prepared dry-cleaning powder throughout the cat's fur by parting the coat in many places. Shake the cornstarch on all parts of the body except the head. Dip a soft brush into the powder and brush it onto the head furnishings. Avoid getting the cornstarch or powder into the cat's eyes, nose or ears.

Shedding

Long fur on the carpet or short hairs on the couch are the merit badges for loving toleration by loyal pet owners. Our cats wear sumptuous fur coats. Shed fur, however, is simply dead hair that clings to carpeting, upholstery fabric and good clothing. Pet hair looks like dandruff on coat collars and gives the impression that your carpeting is under a blanket of snow. It dulls the most vivid colors and acts as a magnet for dirt and dust. Flying fur and dander make some people cough and sneeze while others become teary-eyed and itchy-skinned. Because cats are members of the family, we accept shedding with a resigned grin.

The process of casting off one layer of hair and replacing it with another is termed *molting*. To molt is to replace hair, skin, horns, feathers or scales after shedding the older covering. It is common throughout the animal kingdom. With fur-covered animals such as cats, nature's purpose is to replace the heavy winter coat with a lighter summer one. As the weather becomes colder, a heavier coat is once again grown. It is all a matter of insulation.

Shedding the winter coat begins in the spring, and under normal conditions takes approximately three weeks. Shedding the summer coat and replacing it with the heavier winter *pelage* occurs in autumn, preparing the animal for cold weather. Some breeds molt just once a

After one heavy application, confine the cat for fifteen or twenty minutes to allow the excess body oil and dirt to be absorbed by the powder. Using a clean, soft brush, remove the now-dirty cornstarch. There are commercially prepared dry shampoos available for cats of every coat color and length.

year in a long cycle that achieves the same effect. It is commonly accepted that molting is influenced by the length of time spent outdoors exposed to the natural sequences of light and darkness. Shedding and regrowth begin in spring as the days get longer and again in late summer as they shorten. In the natural state, animals are never exposed to any strong light other than the sun, and their coats conform to seasonal variation of daylight. It is suspected that abnormal shedding cycles may be caused by a cat's indoor life, which involves arrhythmic exposure to light and darkness. Pets exposed to prolonged periods of electric lighting may have extended molting cycles and shed continuously.

Nothing will prevent your cat from shedding. All you can do is try to reduce its impact. Cats require a well-balanced diet, as found in premium commercial cat food. If your cat is shedding excessively, perhaps a change of diet is called for. If the cat is fed home-cooked meals, a high-quality vitamin and mineral supplement is necessary along with a commercial coat conditioner or a teaspoonful a day of animal fat (cooked or raw). These supplements may be necessary even if your cat is being fed an acceptable diet. Regular combing and brushing helps rid the animal of dead hair and loose dander. A bath is also helpful. If the cat likes to sleep on a hot radiator, shoo her off. Artificial heat can enhance the shedding process.

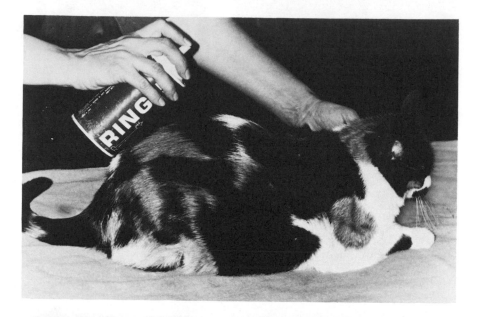

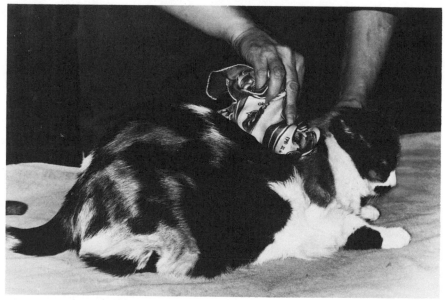

Making a short-haired cat look pretty. After combing and brushing, spray a protein conditioner on the coat. These products are readily available in pet supply stores. After one light spraying, take a silk scarf, chamois cloth, piece of black velvet, or terrycloth towel and rub over the coat. This will produce a lustrous sheen and make any cat look glamorous.

Mats, Knots and Tangles

The outer layer of the cat hair follicle is formed by overlapping scales. These scales protect the inner structure. However, the ends of the scales protrude and form microscopic barbs. When there is a lack of oil on the surface of the hair shaft, these barbs tend to lock into one another and create the mats, tangles and knots that are so troublesome. Mats are also formed by an accumulation of static electricity along the barbed edges.

Commercially prepared tangle removers are usually formulated with oils that are antistatic in nature while they add body to the hair. They also help repair the damaged hair caused by the tangles while helping to reduce the incidence of matting. The manufacturer's directions should be followed for good results. Be sure to drench the matted surfaces with the tangle-removing liquid. Use the fluid as a lubricant for the locked barbs by rubbing it in thoroughly. Allow the product to remain on the coat until the hair is damp or almost dry; then begin detangling with a tool, or your thumb and index finger. It is best to remove tangles and mats before bathing the animal.

Watch for matting during periods of damp weather. If the cat gets out in the rain or snow, its long hair is quite likely to mat. Wet hair will tangle if not cared for properly.

The Bath

One would imagine cats to be the least likely candidates for a bath, what with their image as the most fastidious of all the household pets. However, city dust and country dirt, not to mention soot, oil residues and other grime, can accumulate on fur faster and thicker than a raspy little tongue can wipe them away. An occasional cat bath is not only an aesthetic consideration but one of health as well. A now-and-again bath plus daily brushing and combing helps to prevent those unhealthy hairballs from forming along the cat's digestive tract.

Ideally, bathing a cat should begin early in his life so your pet will adapt to and accept the experience with ease and security. Most cats do not enjoy getting wet and will resist unless they've been exposed to the experience early in life. When a cat becomes attached to one or two humans in his life, he will generally allow them to do *most* things necessary for his well-being, such as administering medicine and taking him to the vet. A cat that is not given many tactile expressions of affection may resist being bathed by scratching, yowling and perhaps even biting. If the cat is really dirty and resists too much, a veterinarian may have to do the bathing. One alternative to wet bathing is to use a dry shampoo product sold in pet supply stores.

For a truly grimy cat who merely complains about being bathed, it is advised that you tough it out and insist that the animal accept the inevitable. The most experienced cat fanciers start bathing their felines at an early age. Show cats are almost always bathed two to three weeks before each event. That is in part why show animals look so magnificent.

If your white Persian looks like stale bread or your short-haired tabby with its broad tiger stripes resembles the inside of a vacuum cleaner bag, it's time for a dunk and a scrub. The cat will agree only *after* the bath. He may or may not cooperate. It will take two of you to accomplish a bath, especially if it is a first-time experience. The following materials are helpful in bathing a cat successfully:

A sink or small plastic tub
A small window screen
Cat shampoo (There are many kinds, designed for specific purposes that are self-explanatory. You may get tearless shampoo, medicated shampoo, protein-enriched conditioner shampoo, flea and tick shampoo, color shampoo or whitener shampoo.)

A plastic cup
A portable spray hose (optional)
A detangling liquid (for cats with matted fur)
Mineral oil
Absorbent cotton
A stainless steel cat comb (half fine/half medium is recommended)
A natural-bristle brush (some prefer a rubber cat brush for short-haired cats)

An electric hair dryer (type used by humans)
Three or four large towels
Cat carrier (for confinement during drying process)

If you have never bathed a cat before, or if your cat has yet to have its first bath, then it is best to get help. Ask someone whom the cat knows to assist you. Only experienced cat owners should try to give baths without another person there to hold the unwilling bather.

The kitchen or bathroom sink is the ideal tub for a cat bath because of the height. Set up the small window screen inside the sink so that it leans against one edge in a slant. The cat will be placed on it during the bath so that he can keep his balance by digging into the mesh with his nails. A folded towel placed on the bottom of the sink will serve the same purpose, as will a placemat, but the screen is best.

Place the cat on a counter and hold him with one hand on the back of his neck. Comb and brush out loose or dead hair and tangled mats. For stubborn mats use a detangling liquid. (Ring 5, St. Aubrey, Lambert Kay, Hagen, Oster, and Holiday are the top brand names for all grooming products. Detanglers come in both liquid and spray. Follow the directions on the package.)

Many authorities recommend that you place a few drops of mineral oil in the cat's eyes to prevent them from burning if the shampoo gets in. You may also loosely stuff a wad of absorbent cotton in each ear canal to prevent water from running in. Many experienced groomers prefer to use a tearless shampoo, and place their thumbs in the cats' ears and fold the tips over instead of adding cotton. Use your own judgment.

Fill the sink a third full with tepid water and add a small quantity of cat shampoo. Adding shampoo to the water helps to wet down the cat easily by getting the soap directly to the skin. Cat hair tends to resist moisture. Place the cat in the sink and allow him to stand on the screening for traction. One person should hold him while the other works with the shampoo and water. Use the plastic cup to pour the slightly soapy water over the cat. If there are no fleas to deal with, do not wet the head until last. However, wet the head *first* if the animal is infested with any form of parasite. Otherwise, when the body be-

Once the body, legs and tail are lathered, you may wet the head and use a tearless shampoo for that area.

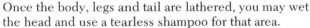

comes wet the fleas will scurry to the head area, where it becomes difficult to get them out.

If there are no parasites, start from back to front because wetting the head is frightening to the cat. Talk in a quiet, reassuring tone of voice as you work. Hopefully, the cat will be calmed by the time you are ready for the head. With the hair wet, apply the cat shampoo of your choice, rubbing it in with your fingertips. Get all the way down to the skin and clean the body with a massaging action, much as you would shampoo your own head. Once the body, legs and tail are lathered, you may wet the head; use a tearless shampoo for that area, no matter what kind of product you are using for the rest of the body.

Work up a good lather, getting it deep into the coat and onto the skin. Massage the shampoo into the shoulders, down the back and legs, between the toes, up and on the underbody and, finally, along the tail. Gently scrub the head and the ears. Carefully scrub around the eyes, under the chin and down the neck into the front bib. When a cat stands in bath water with a little shampoo added to it, the paws are automatically being softened and cleaned, especially between the toes. This produces cleaner paws. If the paws are sore or afflicted with an irritation or a fungus, use a medicated cat shampoo in the bath water.

You are now ready to rinse the shampoo out of the body. A hand spray or the type of portable showering device that connects to a

Rinsing the bath water off the cat is best accomplished with a sink hose, but a plastic cup will do the job, too.

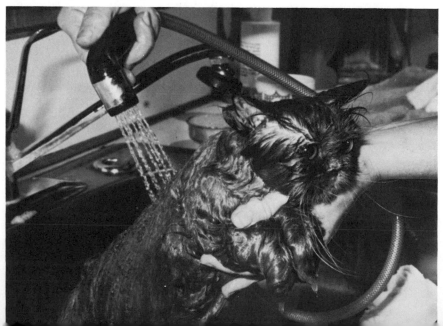

faucet is the most thorough way to rinse, because the force of the spray effectively carries away the soap, dirt and scurf (dead and scaly skin). A plastic cup will also do the job but will require more effort. Do not use a shower or spray on the cat's head or face. Use the cup out of consideration.

Rinse from head to tail. Start at the head and go down the back to the sides of the body, and then the legs, so all the soapy, dirty water runs off the cat and does not simply pour onto another part of the body.

If the cat is very dirty, a second shampoo is desirable and should be given immediately. Do not shampoo twice unless it is absolutely necessary. Never keep a cat in water longer than necessary. He will become very fussy and try to bolt. He could also fall victim to a chill, a serious medical problem.

Rinse the cat thoroughly. Failure to remove all the shampoo will result in a dull, soapy residue. Empty the sink and refill it with clear, tepid water. Rinse the cat once more until you see clear water coming off the body. Take a large towel and blot the body dry to get rid of the excess moisture. Using a second towel, remove the cat from the sink and towel-dry him instantly so he does not get chilled. With your fingers and the towel, gently squeeze the water out of the coat. Try not to create tangles during any part of the drying process. Continue to towel-dry until the cat is no longer dripping wet.

Dry the cat with a portable hair dryer set on a low-heat temperature. Brush or comb the fur as you work with the dryer.

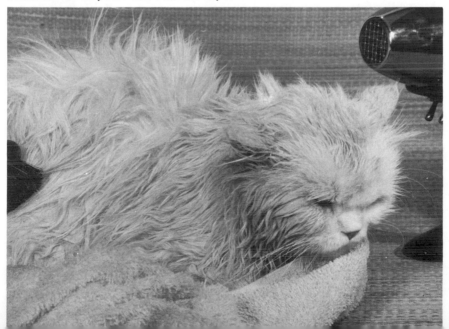

It is now time to use the portable hair dryer. Use it with the blower on but with the heat set on low. The "high" setting is too hot for cats. Never blow unheated air on the cat. This is especially important in the winter. For short-haired cats use a soft, natural-bristle brush or rubber brush as you work with the dryer. The drying motion requires short, quick strokes with the brush and the dryer. For long-haired cats, apply a fluff-dry technique. Do not let the warm air blow on the coat without using a natural-bristle brush or comb. Brush or comb the fur with long flowing strokes in upward motions. This has the effect of lifting the hair and allowing the underside of the follicles to dry from the flow of warm air. It also creates a very fluffy coat. Try to avoid blowing air directly into the cat's face or ears or it will instinctively bolt.

Do not allow the cat to roam around the apartment or house while it is still damp. This will only get him dirty all over again. Line the bottom of your cat carrier with a clean towel and place your pet inside until he is completely dry. Remember, long-haired cats will need more drying time than short-haired cats. Keep the carrier in a warm, safe area free from drafts and chills. This is very important.

It is now time to give your small clean friend a treat of some kind for putting up with a disagreeable experience. Indulge him with his favorite snack and thank him for his forbearance. Then complete the grooming process.

NAILS

Feline claws are unique because they are retractable and do not show in their usual, retracted position. When cats walk, only the very tips occasionally come in contact with the ground. The claws are formidable weapons and are extended when the cat prepares to fight, run or climb. The claws are also unsheathed when the animal is frightened or panicked. Of course, unsheathed claws are necessary for catching prey animals. Tree climbing, jumping, escape maneuvers, playing, fighting, mating, and many other activities also involve the retractability of the claws. They are *indispensable,* and this author is firmly against declawing, the surgical removal of the nails by a veterinarian to avoid scratching problems.

When a cat scratches on a scratching post or on your furniture, she is obeying an important impulse to remove the outer layer of

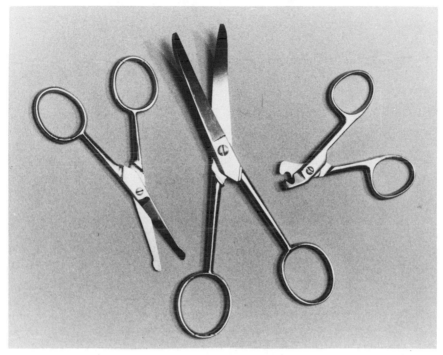

Scissors. (Left) Five-inch scissors with ball tips. Primarily used for trimming tips of ears and other fine-haired areas. (Center) Seven-inch blunt-edged, curved scissors for trimming body fur. Especially good for nervous or fidgety cats. (Right) Nail trimmer, used for all cats.

tissue and make room for the continuously growing nail underneath. You can avoid much of the damage to yourself and your possessions by keeping the nails trimmed. Your cat's nails should be trimmed at least once a week and after every bath.

The trick to trimming is to put gentle pressure on the nails so that they extend out of the skin covering. Place the cat's paw on your open palm. Select the nail that needs trimming and press your thumb against the corresponding toe. The nail will appear. Nail trimmers for cats are specially designed and *nothing else* should be used. These vital tools are readily available in a pet supply store. If the nails are ¼ inch past the pink area, they should be clipped. Most cat nails are white or buff-colored at the tips and pink as they get closer to the base. The pink area is called the *quick;* it indicates where the nerve

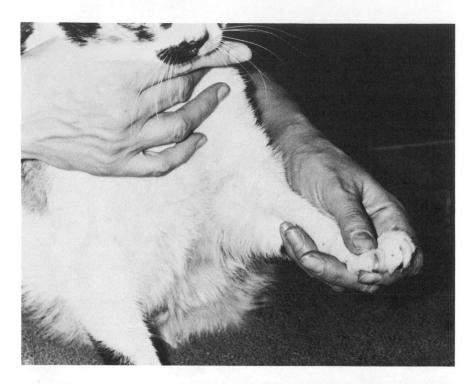

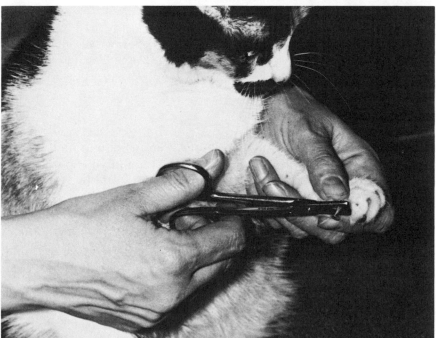

To make the cat's nails appear for trimming, press your thumb against each toe. To avoid hurting the cat, always trim the nail where it begins to curve.

endings are located and where the blood vessels begin. You must never clip the nails at the quick. If you do, you will cause pain and slight bleeding, and possibly infection. In dark-haired cats, some or all of the nails may be black or darker than usual. This will make it difficult to avoid the quick. If you trim the nail just at the curve, you will avoid any problems. If the procedure is too nerve-wracking for you, take the cat to a groomer or veterinarian and observe the professional's technique.

Once the nails have been clipped with the cutting tool, it is a good idea to smooth down the sharp edges as you would when cutting your own nails, with an emery board and nail buffer. Some cat owners use the emery board exclusively as a way of keeping the nails in trim. Although this procedure is time consuming, it does work.

EAR CARE

Cats should have their ears routinely cleaned with a few drops of light mineral oil or a feline ear-cleaning product prepared specifically for this purpose. Be sure that the animal does not suffer from ear mites, which are common in kittens and some grown cats. A constant wiping or scratching at the ears is a sure sign of mites, as is a chronic shaking of the head. Look inside the ear for redness due to inflammation and a black caking or crusting material. If you see these symptoms, take your cat to a veterinarian as soon as possible.

Moisten the inside of the ear with a few drops of mineral oil or feline ear solution. Experienced cat owners then swab out the liquid with a Q-tip, but a finger-held cotton ball is suggested for the novice. Do not enter the ear canal too deeply with either material for fear of damaging the delicate hearing mechanism.

If your cat does not accept ear cleaning very well, have someone help you. Wrap the cat's body in a towel so that all four paws are restrained and have your assistant hold her firmly. Only the head should extend out of the towel. Proceed with the ear cleaning. If there is a great accumulation of ear wax, do not attempt to clean it out yourself unless you are very experienced. Occasional ear cleaning is more for the sake of hygiene than good looks. It helps prevent costly and persistent ear conditions.

* * *

EYES

With the exception of tear staining, eye care is not really a grooming matter. Healthy eyes are bright and lustrous. When something is medically wrong, the eyes become watery, inflamed and even infected. The *haw* or third lid closes laterally in some types of eye problems and makes the eye appear covered with a translucent film. Medicated eye solution for cats or boric acid solution can be dropped or wiped into the eyes, but a visit to the veterinarian is the best thing.

Long-haired breeds, particularly those with short, snub noses (Persian types), tend to weep frequently, possibly because the tear ducts are compressed. The discharge of tears eventually causes eye-stain, a dark brownish look to the fur on the inner side of the eyes. When the tears overflow, they eventually cake on the facial hair. With such cats, daily care is absolutely necessary. You may clean the area below the eye with a commercial feline eye solution available in pet supply stores. This will remove any dirt that may be the cause of the tearing. Wash the stained area with a cotton ball soaked with warm water and dry the area thoroughly with a dry cotton ball. Stubborn stains can be covered with a commercial eyestain remover, white powder or a silicone chalk stick.

TEETH

As with human beings, a cat's teeth are most affected by the quality of the diet. Tartar accumulations can be retarded by introducing a small quantity of dry, hard food into the diet. The abrasion against the teeth and gums caused by chewing helps.

Bad breath and tooth discoloration are almost always due to tartar buildup. A washcloth, cotton ball or even a toothbrush can be used to clean away the food debris that becomes trapped between the teeth and eventually turns to tartar. Clean your cat's teeth once a week or as needed. Use tepid water or a solution of baking soda mixed with water. Simply wipe the teeth (provided your cat will tolerate it). If there is already a tartar buildup, see your veterinarian.

* * *

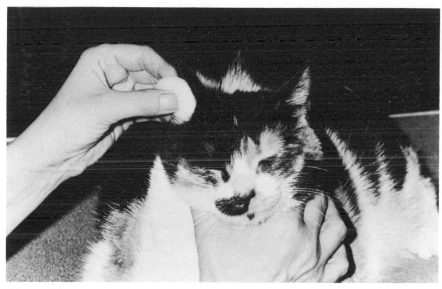

Cleaning your cat's ears periodically is important. It should be done before each bath.

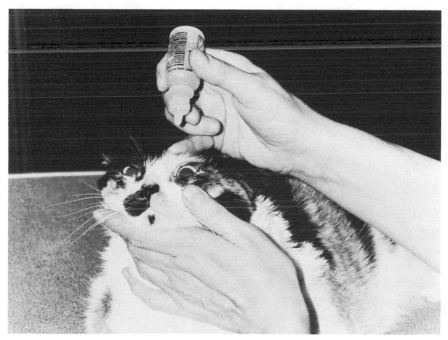

When mucus or foreign material accumulates in the cat's eyes, it is important to rinse them with a medicated eye solution. This will give the added effect of a clear and gleaming face.

ON PHOTOGRAPHING YOUR CAT

Now that you have your furry friend looking good, it is only reasonable to photograph her before the carpet dust and food bowl spoil the effect. Next to children, there is no subject more photographed than family pets, and for good reason. The color snaps of the cats in our lives forever fix in time where and when we were and, most importantly, what a joy it was to share our lives. A snapshot of your cat is like a time machine, a way to capture a moment, a split second of life, so that you may have it forever.

Because we are not discussing professional photography, the type of equipment you use is a matter of personal taste and economy. Although it is safe to say that the more expensive cameras offer the best opportunities, any pro will tell you that it isn't the equipment but the person operating it that determines the quality of the picture. No one can teach another person about aesthetics and artistic judgment. However, when photographing pets there are some guidelines that help.

The first and foremost rule has to do with patience. Be ready, and then wait. You may use every gimmick in the book, but if the cat doesn't want to cooperate you might as well pack it in unless you can wait until the animal stops fussing. When you and the cat are ready, be prepared to take a whole series of pictures. You may get only one good picture out of several rolls of film, but it will have been worth it. Most great animal photos are the result of patience and many rolls of film.

Photographing the cat at home is most important. She will probably be more relaxed and likely to do the familiar things you want to capture on film. Props and backgrounds are important to a good cat photo. If the background is too busy, the cat will fade into it and will be somewhat lost in the resulting picture.

When using a flash attachment for shooting indoor pictures, never aim the light directly into the cat's face. This will result in a flared distortion in the animal's eyes. In color film this is seen as solid red in the eye socket. A *fairly* reliable technique for avoiding this is to diffuse the light source. Cut a piece of thick plastic material (not Saran Wrap–type) to cover the light source of your flash unit. Rub it firmly with coarse steel wool so that it scratches many times in one direction. Tape the plastic over the flash. In many cases this will disperse the intense light enough to avoid the problem known as "red eye."

There are three types of photographs to try for with your cat: the *set-up shot,* the *posed portrait,* and the *candid shot.*

The *set-up* is usually contrived but always endearing. It almost always involves the use of props and some form of scenery. The best example is a kitten in a bowl or in someone's hat. After setting up your equipment, whatever it may be, simply place the cat in the container, return to your photographing location swiftly, and take a series of shots as the cat tries to leave the container. You may use all manner of props, such as a rubber mouse, a ball or a mechanical toy. You can tape some objects to the ground, sprinkle a bit of catnip on them and stand back. If you are not working with a flash, a cat and a mirror can make an engaging photo. Food-connected props can be quite successful. A kitten licking at a dish of cream has marvelous possibilities. A small kitten inside a large (and empty) food bowl is great fun. Smear butter on the cat's paws or lips and photograph the action.

The Set-Up Shot.

Team your cat up with someone else for a good set-up. Cats and kids are wonderful together, as are cats and other animals. Two, three or more cats together are always interesting to photograph. Set-up shots are good indoors but can be even better outside, provided there is no danger to the cat.

Posed portraits are the most difficult of all cat photographs to get. They require some sort of setting with a well-thought-out backdrop. You will need either good lighting on the subject or a flash unit that is extended from the camera with a special hook-up. Do not aim a flash directly into a cat's eyes.

Place the cat on a table that has been covered with some material. A backdrop of some kind is desirable, although a smooth, solid-color wall will do just fine. Obviously, the table covering and the wall should contrast or harmonize with the color of the cat. White cats against red, blue, or even brown backdrops stand out quite well, while lighter backgrounds should be used for darker-colored cats.

Have an assistant help you get the cat's attention while you shoot pictures. While standing off to the side, the assistant can talk to the cat, crinkle paper, hold a stringed toy up high or console the animal. Do not bother placing the animal in any position. It has to be up to the cat to pose in a natural, comfortable manner. Be patient and don't set up a session when you are pressed for time. Don't be afraid to allow the animal to control the situation. You will be rewarded.

Candid shots are the most fun and are either the easiest or the most difficult to take, depending on whom you ask. Many instant-type cameras now come with a zoom feature that enables you to get tightly framed shots without having to get too close to the animal. The closer you get to the cat, the more inhibiting the situation becomes for her. The object is to capture the cat in the middle of her normal daily routine. Set up the proper lighting conditions so that they conform to

The Posed Portrait.

the needs of your camera, then quietly and unobtrusively follow the cat around. Feeding, playing, rubbing, scratching, yawning, napping are but a few of the endearing activities you can capture on film. They are probably the most important pictures of your cat that you will take.

If the background is distracting, shoot from a high angle and use the grass or floor for a background. When outdoors it is extremely effective to shoot from a very low angle, using the sky for a background. Of course this works best when the cat has placed herself on

The Candid Shot.

a high perch of some kind such as a fence, table or tree.

When photographing cats, texture is an important consideration. Your cat is a soft, furry creature that almost resembles a stuffed toy. Therefore, think of photographing her against an interesting texture, such as a tree trunk, a velvet pillow, snow, icicles, ceramics of all sorts, driftwood, polished silver. Color snapshots are a joy, but do not underestimate the value of a well-composed black-and-white photograph. Good hunting.

7

Medic Alert and Other Emergencies

Despite their fastidious habits, their personal hygiene, their finicky selection of food (and their alleged nine lives), cats can and do get sick. They can also get themselves in trouble with the greatest of ease. Although *The Good Cat Book* is not a medical manual, it would be quite irresponsible for a cat care book not to touch upon medical considerations. This chapter is designed to alert the cat owner to the health hazards, along with the other types of emergencies that may require explanation. In most medical and emergency situations, the cat's human family can do much to save the day—and the cat's life. In many instances the services of a veterinarian are absolutely essential. When to treat the problem at home and when to see the vet are what this chapter is all about. You will be given important information about first aid, major cat ailments, immunizations, internal and external parasites, medical symptoms to watch for, home nursing, poisonous plants, and what to do when you lose your cat. We will also touch upon the catastrophe that results when cat meets bird.

Every cat owner sooner or later will require the services of a veterinarian. It is always best to know which one you will be using before your cat becomes sick, so choose a veterinarian prior to choosing your pet. It's that important.

163

Because most people find a veterinarian by word of mouth, you should speak to pet owners and get a consensus about the best ones. Price is no small matter and is something for you to discuss with the animal doctor of your choice. Cleanliness is another major factor. When you enter a vet's office, observe whether it is neat and clean. Are members of the staff (including the doctor) wearing clean gowns, uniforms or work clothes? Are the floors swept and mopped? Are animal toileting accidents cleaned up instantly? In my opinion, a good veterinarian doesn't have to like animals; he or she need only respect them. You do have a right to expect an animal doctor to be skilled and knowledgeable about current standards, practices and advances in modern veterinary medicine. Your veterinarian should be concerned with your cat's state of health in a caring manner. He or she must be sensitive to an animal's fears, pain and suffering, and have a humane approach to animals and their care.

In addition to any immediate or emergency medical care, cats require a physical examination by a veterinarian at least once a year —more often for older cats. Vaccinations must also be boosted from time to time, usually once a year.

WHEN TO SEE THE VETERINARIAN

Although some illnesses more or less take care of themselves, others become worse with time. If you can recognize the signs of illness and learn to discern what you can and cannot do at home, it may save you and your cat much grief. Early treatment of important symptoms can help prevent them from becoming serious or life threatening.

When something is wrong medically, your cat protects himself by curtailing all of his activity, or at least most of it. He is "not himself." He's simply not fun to be with, acts withdrawn and quiet, ignores his food and sleeps as much as possible. He may even look for warmth under blankets and other soft materials. His appetite may increase with some illnesses. Understanding medical symptoms requires that you know what is normal for your cat. Sudden changes in behavior are an indication that you should observe the cat closely for a day or longer.

Vomiting or diarrhea is not necessarily important enough to send you rushing to the vet, unless the condition continues for several days.

If blood is present, high fever, obvious pain, or continuing lethargy, see your veterinarian quickly.

Indications of pain require immediate veterinary attention. These include low, throaty cries that are impossible to mistake, limping, stiffness, refusal to move, pulsating or other unusual signs in the abdomen.

Taking Your Cat's Temperature

One of the most significant indications of illness is an abnormal temperature reading, and every cat owner should know how to get a reading. A rectal thermometer from any pharmacy will do, although you can get special ones for cats from a pet supply store.

If you have never taken a thermometer reading before, it is wise to have help. Have one person wrap the animal in a soft towel so that the paws cannot flail wildly. Have your assistant hold the cat in his or her lap, with one hand on the back of the head and the other against the small of the back. Place petroleum jelly (e.g., Vaseline) or mineral oil on the bulb end of the thermometer and insert it into the rectum. It takes at least thirty seconds to get an accurate temperature reading. Most animals tolerate thermometers fairly well if they are consoled

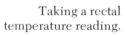

Taking a rectal
temperature reading.

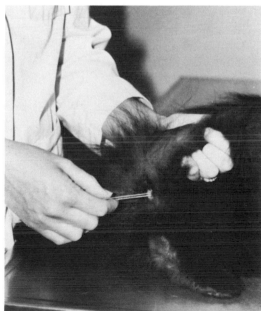

with gentle assurance. The average cat's normal body temperature is 100.5°F., but it may vary slightly lower or higher. The upper limit of a normal temperature is 102.5°F. Higher readings may indicate an infection that requires medical attention. Temperatures slightly above normal could merely indicate that your cat is nervous or physically drained. Take the temperature one hour later. If it is still higher than normal, something is probably wrong.

A temperature lower than normal by more than a degree may also signal a problem. Shock or loss of blood will cause this as well as a simple nap. Recheck the temperature one hour later. If it is still low, see your veterinarian.

Medical Symptoms

It is not always easy to know when to take your cat to a veterinarian. In addition to annual checkups and vaccinations, your cat may need medical diagnosis and treatment for any of dozens of ailments that befall the average pet and range from significant to serious. To help you decide when to call and ask for help or information, here is a list of symptoms. If your cat has one or more of these symptoms, call your vet and ask for an opinion.

Depression
Low, throaty crying
Bladder enlargement
Cloudy urine
Pink urine
Red urine
Extremely yellow urine
Constant straining to urinate
    resulting in small dribbles both
    in and out of the litter box
Inability to urinate
Constant leaking of urine
Abdominal enlargement
Abdominal soreness
Pale gums
Change in eating habits
    Difficulty eating
    Increased appetite

Poor or no appetite
Indications of poor vision
Bad breath
Vomiting (excessive)
Excessive thirst
Inability to move
Nasal discharge
Sneezing (excessive)
Drooling
Loss of haircoat
Trembling
Lumps
Hacking or coughing
Hoarseness
Unusual head shaking
Loss of breath or abnormal
    breathing
Diarrhea (excessive)

VACCINATION: PREVENTING MAJOR DISEASES

Kittens, and mature and older cats as well, are always vulnerable to five communicable diseases unless immunized through vaccination. Prevention of these serious cat diseases is far more fruitful and certainly less expensive than attempting a cure. (Rabies, of course, cannot be cured.) The five diseases are the three feline viral diseases (rhinotracheitis, calicivirus, pneumonitis), plus panleukopenia and rabies. Because cats may roam, come in contact with other cats, or have diseases brought to them by humans, they are exposed to a great many health hazards. Special protection must therefore be provided through the concern and efforts of individual pet owners. Specific preventive measures such as periodic health examinations and improved vaccines are available to protect against most of the dangerous diseases affecting cats.

Vaccination introduces a virus into the cat's body that causes antibodies to be formed against it. The virus is first passed through the bodies of other animals in a series of laboratory techniques called "attenuation" (weakening). By the time it is in its refined state, the virus will no longer cause the fully developed disease, but rather a mild, modified version that will create an immunity in an animal injected in the appropriate manner.

The proper age for vaccinations varies with the individual animal and the type of product used. The final decision should be left to your veterinarian. If you are given a kitten or buy one that has "had his shots," it is important to determine *which* shots were given and when. A newly purchased kitten will rarely have been given more than temporary disease protection. It is also important to remember that every animal is different and that no two cats will develop the same degree of active immunity following vaccination. A vaccine will seldom confer lifelong immunity. For this reason it is imperative that annual booster shots be administered by your vet. Veterinarians vary in the type of vaccine administered, the manner in which it is introduced into the animal's body, and the timing of the series. Each veterinarian chooses a vaccine that is effective for the prevailing conditions in his or her section of the country. It is a matter of regional conditions and the doctor's personal preferences.

Feline Respiratory Disease

This is not actually one disease, but a generic term for several different ones, all of which produce similar signs in the cat. Typical infections produce an unsightly and debilitating condition. All feline respiratory diseases are characterized by sneezing, tearing, inflammation of the eyes and nose, and ocular (eye) and nasal discharge. (These may also be symptoms of other illnesses as well.) Affected cats lose weight and become vulnerable to additional infections. Death can occur, especially among young kittens, pregnant females, and older cats. The various types of feline respiratory disease result from infection by different microorganisms. Each disease has unique characteristics.

Rhinotracheitis (FVR) is an acute respiratory disease of cats caused by a herpes virus. From 30 to 40 percent of feline respiratory disease is attributable to it. The first evidence of illness includes sneezing, elevated body temperature, drooling, and depression. Other signs are heavy discharge from the eyes and nose, ulcerated tongue, rough and soiled haircoat, failure to eat, and mouth breathing due to plugged nasal passage. If uncomplicated, the disease may run its course in one to two weeks. Rhinotracheitis has a 50 percent death rate among kittens, but few grown cats die from the infection.

Another acute respiratory disease is *calicivirus* (FC I) infection. This illness not only infects the respiratory tract, but also membranes of the mouth, causing painful tongue ulcers. Mild salivation and nasal discharge may occur. Because of the painful oral ulcers, affected cats often refuse to eat. Generally these conditions persist for two to three days; then the animals usually recover without treatment.

Another respiratory disease is *feline pneumonitis* (FPN), which is more related to a bacteria than to a virus. The first sign of the disease is a slight rise in body temperature. This is followed by watering of the eyes, then a slight discharge from the nose. Sneezing and coughing, although rare, may occur. Frequently the disease persists for extended periods and recurrent infections are common. Few kittens or cats die from it.

According to Norden Laboratories (a manufacturer of respiratory disease vaccine), all of these diseases may occur simultaneously, complicating diagnosis and making recovery even more difficult. Of the three diseases, only pneumonitis can be treated once infection has

The *otoscope* magnifies and lights the ear canal, allowing the veterinarian to check for mites or infections. It is an essential part of a complete check-up.

The *ophthalmoscope* magnifies and lights the inner parts of the eyes, including the retina, cornea, anterior chamber, iris, etc. No eye examination is complete without the use of this instrument.

developed. Since rhinotracheitis and calicivirus are viral diseases, they do not respond to antibiotics. Fortunately, however, cats may be immunized against all three diseases. Consult your veterinarian about immunization.

Panleukopenia (FPL)

This dreaded disease is also know as *feline distemper* or *feline infectious enteritis.* It is the most widespread and devastating disease affecting cats. It results in a high death rate, particularly among kittens and older cats. Older cats that do recover may never quite regain their health. Cats become infected by either direct or indirect contact with the disease. Studies have shown that households inhabited by sick animals can remain infective for over a year.

Temperature increases to 102.6° or even up to 103.8°F. are common a few days before such outward signs as loss of appetite and lethargy appear. This usually is followed by thirst, yet a hesitancy to drink; vomiting of watery, yellow liquid; and either diarrhea (sometimes bloody) or constipation. As the disease progresses, the animal becomes dehydrated. Panleukopenia is carried by the air and may be caught by a cat's breathing it in from infected cats. Infected cats also spread it through their excrement, urine and nasal discharges. One cat easily infects many others. All cats should be vaccinated for this disease starting as kittens in their eighth week and again in their twelfth. Annual booster shots are administered by most veterinarians.

Rabies

Despite the fact that this nightmarish disease is associated primarily with dogs, most mammals are susceptible. In our time rabies has become extremely rare in dogs and cats. But because there is no cure once it has been contracted, vaccination is extremely important.

According to the American Veterinary Medical Association, rabies is transmitted by animals by a bite from a rabid animal. The wound is contaminated with the virus, found in the saliva of the infected animal. Usually the signs of rabies develop within two weeks to three months after the bite. However, if the bite is on the head or face and is of a severe nature, symptoms may manifest themselves in as few as ten days. With slight wounds, the period from the time of a bite until symptoms of rabies occur is longer and has been known, though rarely, to have covered a year or more.

There are two types of rabies—"dumb" and "furious" rabies. Furious rabies in cats begins with a change in normal behavior. Friendly animals often become aggressive; timid creatures may become bold. Some will snap and bite constantly. Most cats will run away to hide. Sometimes there is a frothing at the mouth, giving the impression that the cat is "mad."

Dumb rabies differs in that there is no raving or "mad" period. Paralysis, usually of the lower jaw, is the first recognizable symptom. This soon spreads to the limbs and vital organs, resulting very shortly in death.

Veterinary medical scientists have developed safe and effective vaccines that give your pet maximum protection against rabies. Have your cat vaccinated as directed by your veterinarian.

If you are bitten by an animal that is even possibly rabid, consult a physician as quickly as possible for care of the wound. Thoroughly cleanse the wound with soap and irrigate with profuse quantities of running warm water. The animal that bit you, if available, must be taken to a veterinary hospital or confined under the observation of a public health official, where it can be kept alive for full development of symptoms. The bitten person can obtain a series of injections that usually prevent the disease if the shots are started in time.

SERIOUS ILLNESSES FOR WHICH THERE ARE NO VACCINES

Unfortunately, even though feline veterinary science has made remarkable gains in the last several years, there are still a variety of cat diseases for which no vaccines have been developed. Many of these diseases are serious and even fatal. Others are treatable.

Feline Leukemia (FeLV)

This disease is now known to be caused by a virus. The virus causes leukemia (cancer of white blood cells) and lymphosarcoma (cancer of lymph tissue cells) in cats. Significantly, it is transmitted contagiously among cats in a manner similar to other respiratory viruses. According to Professor Edward A. Hoover, Department of Veterinary Pathobiology at Ohio State University, saliva appears to be the most important vehicle for virus transmission from cat to cat, and infection involves relatively close contact. The virus does not remain infectious long outside of the cat's body and is killed by drying, detergents, and disinfectants.

In a paper for the Morris Animal Foundation, Professor Hoover states,

> After cats are exposed to Feline Leukemia Virus (FeLV), either of two outcomes is possible. First, the cat may be able to control the infection and produce antibody to the virus. These cats successfully develop immunity to the leukemia virus and do not get leukemia or other diseases caused by FeLV.
>
> The second possibility after a cat is exposed to FeLV is that the cat's immune system will be overcome by the virus and will not be able to limit its growth. In this event, FeLV will establish an active and persistent infection in the cat's body. FeLV infection, once established, usually persists for life.

Such cats may not show any signs of illness for years, but the virus will be present in their saliva, urine or feces, and thereby infect other cats.

A cat infected with feline leukemia virus can also develop other forms of leukemia, and other diseases creating such conditions as anemia, a panleukopenia-like disease, intestinal and kidney disorders, reproductive disorders, and various secondary infections due to impairment of the cat's immune system. Often lethargy, paleness of the mucous membranes, and loss of weight are the chief signs. Blood counts, x rays, and other laboratory tests are required to establish a correct diagnosis.

The percentage of cats that recover from this disease is small. Currently, there are no successful treatments for elimination of FeLV infection or the leukemia it causes. Infected cats must be identified and removed from contact with other cats. One focus of current research is the development of a vaccine. Early medical attention and treatment are essential.

Anemia

Signs of anemia are fever, depression, loss of appetite, weakness, emaciation and jaundice. The disease can be induced through a microscopic parasite that attacks red blood cells, destroying them, and causing internal bleeding and infection. It may also result from internal or external parasite attack. Anemia results from the loss of healthy red blood cells.

Reasonably healthy cats are able to rid themselves of this disease when they are treated by a veterinarian. Cat owners must be vigilant and watch for symptoms of anemia so the disease does not pass from a latent form to an active state.

Feline Infectious Peritonitis (FIP)

This is a disease of cats that is difficult (sometimes impossible) to diagnose, much less treat. FIP causes an inflammation of the lining of the abdomen. It was first reported in 1966. Knowledge is still incomplete.

The disease can be spread from one cat to another, but the mode of transmission is still unknown. Peritonitis is probably caused by a virus and is seen mostly in young cats. It may take as long as five months for symptoms to appear after exposure to the virus. Loss of appetite, high fever, weakness, and inflammation of the linings of the chest and abdominal cavities are the principal symptoms. Sometimes fluid accumulates in the abdominal and chest cavities. The disease is considered fatal. Research on it is presently being conducted in the United States.

Tumors

Cats, like all mammals, are vulnerable to a wide variety of benign and malignant tumors. In a paper for the Morris Animal Foundation, Elizabeth M. Hodgkins, DVM, Resident, Oncology Services, University of California, tells us that a tumor is a disorderly, uncontrolled growth of cells, which may be benign or malignant in nature. Tumors have many different appearances and cause various symptoms, depending on the tissues involved. Unfortunately, the majority of tumors seen in the cat are malignant; they require prompt diagnosis and treatment as soon as they are discovered. Cats are subject to skin tumors, mammary tumors, and oral tumors.

When unchecked, such tumors invariably prove fatal. Thus, the cat owner must be observant and suspicious of any and all unusual growths, swellings, rashes, discharges or behavior changes observed in his or her animal. Even young cats, especially the purebred varieties, frequently develop cancer. All white and white-faced cats are

especially predisposed to the development of "squamous cell carci-
noma" of the face, nose, eyes and ears. Sunlight plays a role in initi-
ating this form of skin cancer. Self-education by the owner, and early
detection and treatment are of extreme importance in avoiding the
life-threatening stages.

Common signs of cancerous tumors include:

Abnormal swellings
Chronic bleeding or discharge
Pigment change
Prolonged lameness
Bad odors
Persistent sores
Difficulty eating and swallowing
Weight loss
Fatigue

Possible treatments include surgery, radiation therapy, hyperthermia
(mild heating of the tumor with radio waves), and chemotherapy (administration of anti-cancer drugs). Some tumors do not respond to
treatments, while others respond exceptionally well.

Feline Urologic Syndrome (FUS)

Although many cat owners refer to this disease by such names as
cystitis and urinary obstruction, FUS is not a series of interchangeable
terms. A *syndrome* is a group of symptoms of several interconnected
illnesses that may appear individually or in various combinations
within the same patient. FUS comprises *cystitis, urolithiasis, urethral
obstruction* and *uremia.*

Cystitis refers to an inflammation of the bladder. It causes damage to the interior of the bladder and creates mucus, blood and other
organic bits and pieces that combine into an accumulation. *Urolithiasis* has to do with urine that is concentrated and retained for a
long period in the bladder. The accumulation of material from the
cystitis combines with tiny stones or sandy particles called *struvite.*
The bladder becomes inflamed and the combined stones, sand, mucus
and blood create "plugs." *Urethral blockage* occurs when the "plugs"
build up in the urethral passage, slowing the outward flow of urine or
stopping it altogether. *Uremia* is the last phase of FUS. When the cat
cannot urinate, the kidneys cease to function; poisonous wastes normally excreted in the urine are retained in the body. Uremic poisoning is the lethal result unless the cat's blockage is relieved swiftly. In

some extreme cases the bladder ruptures, causing death before uremic poisoning occurs.

There is much speculation and controversy about the actual cause of FUS and how to prevent its occurrence. Of the many possibilities under investigation are such nutritional factors as dry food, vitamin deficiency, excessive mineral intake, diets creating crystals because of alkaline urine, and low water consumption. Some observers believe it only occurs in castrated male cats, while others attribute the cause to the long, narrow urethra in males. There are theories having to do with metabolic disorders, kidney malformations and various infections. What makes the cause extremely difficult to identify is that all of these factors can and do play a part in the syndrome, either as secondary complications or as aggravators of the primary problem.

An extremely interesting research project that may have promise is being conducted by Catherine G. Fabricant, Senior Research Associate, New York State College of Veterinary Medicine, Cornell University. Ms. Fabricant has been working on the hypothesis that FUS may be the result of cell-associated herpes virus, which may be acquired prenatally, soon after birth, or early in life. Her contention is that once acquired, the herpes viruses persist for life, usually without apparent disease; however, they can be activated by stress or other factors and cause clinical disease. Not all researchers accept her findings, and some are pursuing other theories.

Early signs of trouble are irritability and restlessness, blood in the urine (light pink to red), frequent trips to the litter box, straining while in the squatting position (sometimes mistaken for constipation), and urinating outside of the litter box in various parts of the home. These are the signs that tell you to see a veterinarian as quickly as possible. Cats already in an advanced stage may cry in pain, strain constantly, display an enlarged abdomen, and vomit and drool. This indicates an emergency situation and time is of the essence. The veterinarian will have to relieve the obstruction as the first order of business. Most cats suffering from FUS not only survive, but respond well to treatment, although there is a small percentage of deaths. In chronic, recurring cases, surgery may be recommended.

Feline Skin Diseases

The most frequently seen skin ailments in cats must be treated properly so that they do not develop into serious infections or affect general health. *Bacterial skin diseases* are most frequently seen in *abscesses* on the body and *acne* localized on and around the cat's chin. An abscess is a pocket of infection that contains pus. These infected areas are surrounded by a membrane, much like a thick-walled balloon filled with water. These infections are almost always the result of puncture wounds, scratches or bites. Most of them are the result of cat fights. The winner has abscesses on the head while the loser has them on the rear. They often require surgical and medical treatment.

Feline acne can develop in a cat at any time during its life span, even in old age. It results from the inability of some cats to clean themselves properly under the chin. The symptoms are the appearance of blackheads and pimples, hair loss, and occasionally red skin and swelling. It does not seem to bother the cat. Gentle cleansing of the area removes many of the symptoms and can help prevent recurrences. This should be done on a regular basis with mild soap and water. Treatment is necessary when a cat starts to scratch the affected area. Most veterinarians prescribe an antibiotic for two to three weeks, with various other topical preparations. The problem tends to be a recurring one.

One of the worst feline skin disorders is *ringworm*, which, of course, is not a worm or any kind of parasite at all. It is a fungal skin disease that causes lesions on the cat (or human), characterized by a round, hairless area with or without scales and crust. Usually the head and extremities are affected. The initial lesions may produce others, accompanied by broken or discolored hairs, discolored or red skin, and episodes of itchiness. As the fungus grows, it spreads out many times in circular patches on the skin surface, which is why it is so named. Ringworm is highly contagious for any mammal, including humans. Veterinary treatment and environmental management are absolutely essential.

There is a dermatological syndrome known as *eczema*, which is not one specific skin disease but several. It is characterized by skin lesions with red bumps and scabs. They may be visible or may be found only by touching them. They may irritate and cause scratching, licking and hair loss, and they may exude fluids. Although eczema usually involves the back, it can spread over the surface of the entire body. Many skin diseases of undetermined cause may be attributed to eczema. More than a few laboratory tests may be necessary for a veterinarian to make a proper diagnosis and treatment.

INTERNAL PARASITES

For the squeamish this is one of the least pleasant subjects to confront. It is difficult for many humans to fathom that there are wormlike organisms of every size and shape that live within and feed off the bodies of their cats. Worms vary in kind, size, effect, and seriousness to the health of the animal. Although all worms can do harm to a cat's body, few create permanent or irreparable damage if detected and treated early enough. Many of these organisms ingest blood from the host animal, causing blood loss and damaged tissue.

Sometimes parasites produce infection or inflammation, in addition to toxic substances that harm the body. Parasitic infestation may lower the host's resistance to disease, carry disease to many parts of the body, or rob the host of vital nutrients from its daily ration.

Internal parasites are among the most common ailments of cats and other animals. Almost all kittens get them, and adult cats get them at one time or another. They must be identified in the most specific sense by a veterinarian and then treated medically according to type. Over-the-counter worm remedies cannot possibly be effective unless the type of worm infestation has been accurately identified by laboratory analysis.

All worms produce symptoms that alert the cat owner to the condition. Many of these symptoms are similar, though different internal parasites may be involved. Early signs are lethargy, appetite loss, diarrhea, bloody stool. The signs of heavy infestation are loss of weight, bloated stomach, dehydration (loss of fluid), dry and thinning coat, constant drowsiness, and anemia.

If your cat shows any signs of infestation, take a stool sample to your veterinarian for a laboratory analysis. Sometimes worms do not appear in one stool but may show up in others. Collect small specimens from one to five separate stools (collected every other day) and take the material to a veterinarian for microscopic examination. Consult your veterinarian for the proper procedure.

Ascarids (Roundworms)

No internal parasite is more common in cats than these. The adult worm lives in the intestine; its eggs pass from there to the stool and then out of the body. Cats may become reinfected by ingesting contaminated soil or feces, or eating prey animals that are contaminated. Ingested larvae travel through the body to the intestine and grow there to full maturity. Once again eggs are deposited in the intestine and the cycle continues.

Human infestation is possible and is particularly harmful to small children who may be contaminated as a result of handling infested pets. A child would have to ingest infested feces or rub it into an open body wound to become infected, however. It is an extremely rare occurrence.

Hookworms

These are common intestinal parasites more often found in dogs. Cats seem to have more resistance to them. Because hookworms can cause anemia, to which kittens are especially susceptible, one must treat this parasite seriously. Infection can result from skin contact with the worm eggs or by ingesting them from a contaminated environment. Adult hookworms thrive in the cat's small intestine; it is there that the female worm deposits thousands of eggs daily, many of which are passed on through the stool. The adults "hook" themselves onto the wall of the host animal's intestine and take "blood meals." The result can be anemia due to severe blood loss and diarrhea due to intestinal inflammation. In the young, weak or malnourished cat, hookworms can cause sudden collapse and death. Watch for weight loss, diarrhea or bloody stools. The eggs are microscopic in size and cannot be specifically identified without a laboratory stool analysis.

Heartworms

It was thought that only dogs were vulnerable to these lethal parasites. Recently, however, they have been reported in cats as well. Heartworms infect cats through the bite of a mosquito that has previously bitten an infected dog or cat. The worms are injected under the cat's skin by the mosquito; from there they eventually reach the heart and develop into adult worms. It takes six months for the worms to become adults after they are injected into the cat. The mature worm settles in the right side of the heart and in the pulmonary vessels of the lungs. This causes the heart to work much harder to pump blood to the lungs. As the heart weakens, every other organ in the body becomes affected because of insufficient blood flow. The immature heartworms *(microfilaria)* can only be detected through laboratory analysis of blood samples. Delayed treatment results in heart failure —with or without permanent damage to the liver and kidneys—leading to death. Treatment involves destruction of adult heartworms and elimination of the microfilaria from the blood. Hospitalization is almost always necessary.

Protozoans (Coccidia and Toxoplasmosis)

Diarrhea is the primary symptom of these intestinal parasites, which are extremely persistent. Coccidia produce a bloody diarrhea; several stool samples are needed for laboratory analysis in order to identify these parasites properly. They are microscopic and are transmitted through the feces of other animals. Good sanitation is important to prevent them from spreading, and veterinary treatment is vital.

It is seldom that a case of toxoplasmosis in cats reaches the veterinarian's office because of its rarity. It is of concern primarily because of its disastrous effects on pregnant women and their fetuses. Toxoplasmosis can cause pregnant women to miscarry or cause brain damage in a human fetus. Symptoms in the cat are fever, diarrhea, listlessness, difficulty in breathing and lack of appetite. This parasitic protozoan can be passed on to the cat through contaminated raw meat.

Treatment is not always successful. Cats, like other animals and humans, may excrete the organism in their feces while affected by the disease. Pregnant women should have their cats' blood tested by a veterinarian for toxoplasmosis early in their first trimester. If the cats test positive, the attending obstetrician must be informed immediately. Avoid contact with cat litter, feces, urine or saliva throughout pregnancy.

Strongyloides

These small roundworms (only ⅟₁₆ inch long) are found in cats, dogs and other mammals, including humans. They reside in the lining of the intestine. Eggs are deposited and hatch while still in the intestine. The immature worms are passed in the feces and can reinfect the host animal or others by being ingested through the mouth or the skin. Stool sample analysis is required for proper identification and treatment. Strongyloides cause loss of appetite, coughing, discharge from the eyes, and diarrhea. The disease also reduces resistance to infection.

Tapeworms (Cestodes)

There are many types of tapeworms found in infected cats. The head or *scolex* attaches itself to the intestinal lining, while the long body of segments (proglottids) remains free of the lining. Often the bottom segments break off and are passed in the feces, leaving the head still attached to produce new segments. These parasites are quite contagious.

Infection by tapeworm sometimes takes a long time to detect. It can begin with digestive upsets, irregular appetite, weight loss, stomach discomfort and poor coat condition. Diagnosis is made by examination of the fecal matter. Look for segments of the body in the cat's stool, bed or anal area. At first the segments are light-colored and about a quarter-inch in length. When dry, they shrivel and turn brownish in color and granular in shape, like tiny grains of rice.

The most common tapeworm harbored by cats is *Taenia taeniaeformis*, which is passed on to them by an intermediate host, in this case rats and mice. Another form of tapeworm often seen in cats is *Dipylidium caninum;* its intermediate hosts are fleas and lice. Treatment by a veterinarian is essential.

Other internal parasites that infect cats include *whipworms, threadworms, eye worms, stomach worms, lungworms,* and *flukes.* They must all be specifically identified by laboratory analysis and treated individually by a veterinarian. Each parasite requires a different medication and treatment appropriate to its unique characteristics. Your veterinarian is the only person qualified to make these determinations.

EXTERNAL PARASITES

Almost all cats at one time or another serve as hosts for external parasites, and these parasites are a serious threat to the well-being of your pet. These tiny, sometimes microscopic creatures feed off the bodies of their host animals. They damage the body's tissue, causing irritation and possible secondary infections. Others take blood meals from the host, creating a potential for anemia. External parasites can carry bacterial and viral infections with them. The most common external parasites are fleas, lice, ticks and mites. The annoyance, irritation, and debilitating effects of this kind of parasitic infestation can be serious and, for any responsible pet owner, the symptoms should not be taken lightly. These parasites are the enemy of you and your cat. They must be detected by their early signs and eradicated from the pet's body and the immediate environment. This involves medical attention, sanitation, fumigation, and specially prescribed grooming procedures.

Fleas

The many species of fleas are all capable of attacking most warm-blooded animals, including humans. They are small insects without wings and are black or brown in color. They invade the haircoat of cats and kittens and move rapidly. They are capable of jumping from eighteen to thirty-six inches. They live from blood meals taken from host animals, the haircoats of which provide a warm, compatible environment. Flea-infested cats become restless, may lose weight, and can damage their coats by biting and scratching. The flea bites can also become inflamed. Some animals develop allergic reactions to the bites of fleas and suffer with severe dermatitis. This reaction is caused by the flea's saliva, which is introduced into the skin while the flea is sucking blood.

The adult flea has a life span of up to one year; it lays its eggs in the environment where the host animal lives—in cracks, crevices, carpeting, and so on. The eggs hatch into larvae, which remain in the environment for up to two hundred days. The larvae eventually develop into adults, which infest the animal and begin the cycle again. The longer part of the flea's life cycle takes place in the environment and not on the cat.

While killing the fleas on the cat's body is important, the main problem is dealing with the steady supply of new fleas being hatched from eggs in the environment. The problem must be attacked on two fronts. First, remove the parasites from the cat with the help of bathing-dipping and/or frequent application of a flea powder or spray formulated for this purpose. (Do not use these insecticides on kittens, pregnant or lactating cats, or sick cats.) Do not mix different types of powders, liquids, chemicals, and "flea collars" without advice from a veterinarian.

Second, treat your cat's environment. Spray or dust your cat's sleeping area with products your veterinarian suggests. Aerosol fog-

gers are very effective. Spray deep into the crevices and bedding where the animal sleeps, eats and plays. Spray in and around the carpeting, and vacuum the entire home at least once a day during this fumigation period. Get rid of the vacuum cleaner bags. Flea eggs and larvae thrive in such bags and can soon regain a foothold in your house.

One of the most popular methods of flea control is the flea collar. Flea collars contain a slow-release chemical insecticide that spreads over the cat's fur and kills fleas after contact. Be cautious of allergic reactions in your cat to the chemical released by the collar. Some cats react strongly; some can tolerate such collars, but for only a limited time. Many experts advise cat owners to wait twenty-four hours after releasing the chemical in the collar before placing it around the cat's neck. Consult your veterinarian, but also keep a close watch on your cat. Never place a flea collar around the neck of a kitten unless the package tells you it was designed for that purpose.

Lice

No one loves a louse. Unlike the flea, there isn't even a hint of humor connected with this unmentionable insect. One never hears a pet owner confess to lice. Fleas, ticks, mites, even houseflies are discussed. But it's as if it were un-American to own a cat beleaguered by lice. It is thought that only neglected or homeless cats are ever infected by lice. Not true.

There are two forms of lice: those that bite and those that suck. The biters penetrate the skin of the host animal and feed on dead tissue, body secretions and hair. The suckers live off the animal's blood. The principal difference between lice and fleas is that lice remain in one spot and dig in. They are very small and extremely difficult to see. The services and advice of a veterinarian are important for their elimination and the correction of any resulting diseases.

Ticks

The most common tick is the American dog tick, which is of the "hard tick" variety. It can live in your house with great success by infiltrating cracks, bedding, carpeting and walls. Ticks infect dogs and cats at all times of the year, but are seen mostly in spring, summer and fall. Ticks exist in three stages after eggs are laid on the host: larval, nymphal, and adult. They may live up to a year in each stage. The adults lie in wait on a blade of grass or the twig of a bush and leap onto their victims as they brush past. Once an infestation exists in the human abode, an exterminator is necessary to get rid of them.

The female tick deposits eggs on the ground or in the cracks and crevices of buildings, doghouses or cat beds. They attach themselves to the skin of the host animal and feed on the animal's blood. Not only does the host animal lose blood, but it also experiences irritation from the bite along with possible infection. Some ticks produce a toxic chemical capable of producing paralysis and death. Severe anemia may occur in a heavily infested animal.

Ticks may be removed with tweezers, forceps, or the human hand (gloved or covered with Saran Wrap to avoid contamination of the fingers). Medicated baths and insecticidal sprays and powders help rid the cat's body of this terrible parasite. Long-haired cats that are allowed outdoors have the highest susceptibility to tick infestation. The favorite hiding places for ticks on the cat's body are on the abdominal region, the neck, the armpits, between the toes, in the anal region, and on the face and neck of some cats. When an attached tick is pulled away from the cat's skin, a small amount of tissue will also be pulled away. This causes a slight wound and scab. An antiseptic or antibacterial medication applied topically is important to prevent infection. Bacitracin is recommended, although any antiseptic will do.

Mange

Mange is caused by another type of external parasite, the mite. Fortunately, mange is rare in the well-fed, well-kept cat. The type of mange that only affects cats is called *notoedric mange;* it is a highly contagious skin disease, caused by a mite that burrows into the skin and causes intense scratching. The inflammation caused by the mites together with that caused by the scratching leads to crusted, thickened skin. Hair loss occurs in the infected areas.

Although it is rare, cats can also be infected by "red mange," or *demodectic mange.* In the early stages, this variety of mange is indicated by small areas of hair loss accompanied by a red, irritated appearance. It should be emphasized that mite-caused mange is more serious than a simple skin irritation or abrasion; do not consider it merely a source of discomfort for your cat. Both of these kinds of mange are serious skin diseases that can lead to complications, such as severe skin infections. Veterinarians usually treat mange by clipping, medicated baths, or sprays as well as oral medication or injections. Medical attention is essential.

Ear Mites

Ear mites can be a source of severe annoyance and disease. Cats that are constantly scratching or twitching their ears may be harboring these pests. Often an animal may be seriously infected with the pests before there is any outward sign of the parasites' presence, so it is a good idea to have your cat's ears examined by a veterinarian from time to time and during your cat's annual physical. If the inner ear has been invaded by the mites, deafness may result. Kittens often acquire the pests from their mothers. Consult a veterinarian and do not attempt to treat your cat for ear mites at home.

FIRST AID

Rendering medical treatment to a pet is a poor idea if you're not a veterinarian. But, as in human medicine, emergencies require quick, resourceful action and you may not have time to get professional help for those first, livesaving procedures. First aid is exactly what the term implies. The following procedures are of a temporary nature so that life can be saved, irreparable damage avoided, and the animal spared as much pain as possible.

The following first aid procedures have been adapted from the very best concise first aid booklet for animals, the *Angell Memorial Guide to Animal First Aid.** We are grateful to the American Humane Education Society, a division of the Massachusetts Society for the Prevention of Cruelty to Animals, for their gracious consent to use the material.

First aid is your first line of defense when your cat is injured or in some life-threatening situation requiring immediate medical attention. A sensible first aid kit can make the difference between life and death. The following list will cover most emergencies. (Or you may prefer to purchase a preassembled kit designed for pet owners and breeders. Write to: PET AID, Remac Pharmaceutical, P.O. Box 339, Wilmington, MA 01887.)

* Copies of *Angell Memorial Guide to Animal First Aid* may be obtained by writing to American Humane Education Society, 450 Salem End Road, Framingham, MA 01701. A nominal fee is charged. You may also write for their book list.

FIRST AID KIT

Tincture of Merthiolate or Mercurochrome
Bacitracin
First Aid Antiseptic Skin Ointment for dogs and cats
(Lambert Kay)
Antiseptic powder or spray
Aromatic spirits of ammonia
Mineral oil
Kaopectate
Tongue depressors
Sterile gauze bandage—1" and 2"
Ipecac (to induce vomiting)
Activated charcoal (for poisoning)
Eye ointment
Styptic powder (to stop minor bleeding)
Vaseline
Scissors
Tweezers
Absorbent cotton balls
Cotton applicators
Large and small gauze pads
Hydrogen peroxide (3% solution)
Adhesive tape
Rectal thermometer

Be Prepared. Many communities have emergency veterinary services available twenty-four hours a day; ask your veterinarian or your local veterinary medical association about this. Learn whom to contact and keep the phone number handy. Read and learn the following first aid and emergency treatment procedures beforehand so you are familiar with the signs of conditions. Practice the techniques described so that you feel comfortable when administering first aid.

When Your Cat Is Injured. Be careful when approaching an injured animal. An animal that is frightened or in pain may try to bite or scratch you, so protect yourself for the animal's safety—as well as your own.

Restraint. A cat can be restrained by wrapping her in a blanket, towel or coat. Then place the animal on her chest in a box to keep her quiet. If you *are* bitten by a sick or injured animal, contact your physician as soon as possible. Indeed, it is well to get medical advice if you are bitten by any animal, even if it appears healthy.

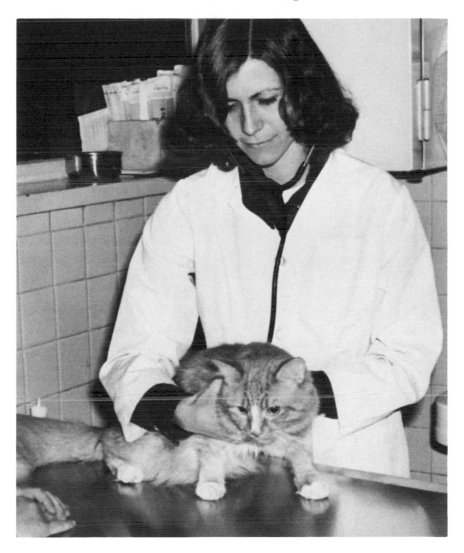

Transport. An injured animal will assume the least painful position by himself, so do not change his position any more than necessary. Any animal that cannot stand should be carried on a stretcher made from a board or other stiff, flat object. Slide the stretcher carefully under the animal or grasp the loose skin along his backbone to pull him onto the stretcher. If it seems best to secure the animal, do not strap him so tightly that you interfere with his breathing—you could aggravate internal injuries as well. If no board is available, two or more people can transport an injured cat on a blanket lifted as flat as possible by the four corners.

If you must move an animal by yourself, lift him with as little movement of the spine as possible. Place one arm under the rump and hind legs. Try to prevent the middle from sagging. With your other hand, try to keep the neck and head from flopping. Move slowly and carefully—rough handling or transport may worsen an animal's condition and increase the risk of shock.

Bite Wound

Signs. Open wounds, punctures, hair loss, salivating, pus or blood matted in the hair, sore swellings, elevated temperature.

Treatment. Clip the hair from around the wound, taking care not to cut the skin, then clean the wound with mild soap and water. Apply a bandage only to stop bleeding. Most bite wounds will become infected without professional treatment and may form an abscess, which can be a serious complication. Bites may cause internal damage, which is not readily visible. For severe abdominal wounds, apply a wide bandage to hold the internal organs in, if necessary; lightly wrap the trunk from the shoulders to the pelvis.

Bleeding, External

Signs. Slow, steady flow of dark red blood indicates an injured vein. Fast, pulsing flow of bright red blood indicates an injured artery.

Treatment. Apply a pressure bandage to the wound. If bleeding continues, do not remove the bandage; instead apply an additional bandage and more pressure. As a last resort to control bleeding, if there is going to be a delay in reaching a veterinarian, a tourniquet can be applied. This technique is primarily to control severe arterial bleeding from the legs or tail, when loss of blood may cause fatal shock. Apply the tourniquet between the cut and the heart and loosen every three to five minutes to allow some bleeding to take place, then re-tighten. In less severe injuries, cutting off the blood supply with a tourniquet may cause more damage than the loss of blood, so only use this method with great care.

Bleeding, Internal

Signs. White, pale or gray gums; coughing blood; bleeding from nose, mouth, or rectum or blood in the urine, collapse; rapid and weak pulse.

Treatment. It is impossible for you to know the extent of the injuries or even of the bleeding. Keep the animal as quiet as possible and transport her at once with great care and with minimal movement.

Fractures, Dislocations, Sprains

Signs. Reluctance to stand on one leg, limping, intense pain, bone appearing to "bend" where it shouldn't, joint bending in an abnormal way, swelling, bone protruding from skin.

Treatment. Apply a splint only if the lower part of a limb is dangling loosely; this will prevent the broken bone from causing further damage to surrounding tissue. If the animal will lie quietly and there will be little delay in reaching a veterinarian, do not apply a splint. A break in the upper part of a limb, or in the trunk or skull, is difficult to recognize and usually does not require splinting before transport to a veterinarian. If a splint is needed, use a straight, rigid object such as a smooth stick, narrow board, pole or rolled newspaper long enough to hold the limb still. If possible, the splint should be narrower than the limb. Padding should be placed between the splint and the limb. Tie the splint to the leg at multiple points, from the toes to the upper leg, securing the splint well both above and below the break. [A cat's rear legs are not straight, so you will not be able to use a straight splint on the entire leg. If absolutely necessary to splint the hind leg, do so with great care.] Do not tie the area of the break to the splint. Sometimes a break will cause paralysis in the animal. If that happens, transport it on a stretcher. It is important to realize that it is difficult for a layperson to determine whether an injury is a fracture, a sprain or a dislocation. Dislocations can be replaced more easily and will heal more rapidly if action is taken within twenty-four hours of the injury.

Burns

A burn may seem innocuous but produce serious damage to the skin that may not become evident for several days. An animal's heavy coat may mask the true extent of a burn until skin and hair slough off. Chewing on electric cords may cause mouth burns or worse (see "Electrical Shock," page 199).

Signs. Hair loss, swelling or red skin, blistering or even no sign at all, at first.

Treatment. For thermal burn from hot liquids or direct fire or heat, apply ice or cold water compresses to the affected area for twenty minutes to reduce swelling and blistering.

Clip the hair from the burn area to prevent contamination and to inspect the skin for damage.

For acid or alkali burns, immediately flush the skin with large amounts of water.

Convulsions

The most common causes of convulsions are trauma, epilepsy, lead poisoning, metabolic imbalance and distemper in dogs.

Signs. Shaking, falling over, legs thrashing, racing blindly, bumping into objects, vocalizing uncontrollably, salivating, urinating.

Treatment. Most convulsions last two or three minutes. If possible, confine the animal until the seizure passes to prevent him from hurting himself, but otherwise do not handle the animal. If the convulsion lasts more than five minutes or if the animal has more than one seizure within an hour, take the animal to a veterinarian. Any convulsion should be reported to a veterinarian.

Eye Injury

Eye injuries are frequently caused by a blow to the head, fighting with other animals, and foreign objects embedded in the eye (see "Foreign Objects," page 192).

Signs. Tearing, pawing at the side of the face, swelling of the membrane inside the eyelids (conjunctiva), third eyelid more prominent, bloodshot eyes, squinting or eye swollen or held shut.

Treatment. For swelling of the conjunctiva or eyelid, apply an ice pack (ice wrapped in a towel) to the closed eye. If the eye is out of the socket and if it will take over half an hour to reach the veterinarian, try to replace the eye by pulling the eyelids open as far as possible and gently pushing the eye back into the socket. Whether or not you are able to replace the eye in its socket, apply a salt solution (one teaspoon salt dissolved in one pint of warm water) to the eye as frequently as needed to keep it moist until you can get the animal to a veterinarian. There is no first aid you can administer for punctures or scratches of the eyeball. The animal must be taken to a veterinarian for treatment.

Drowning

Many animals, including cats, can swim, but can drown due to exhaustion or panic, so they should be watched carefully when in the water.

Signs. Unusual amounts of splashing or sinking.

Treatment. Hold the animal up by her hind legs at the hocks (the crook of the legs below the thighs) to allow water to drain from the lungs; gently swing to increase water flow from the lungs. Check for foreign objects in the throat. Lay the cat on her side and begin artificial respiration or mouth-to-nose resuscitation. Keep the animal warm (see "First Aid Techniques," page 199).

Heatstroke

Fat or old animals or animals having chronic heart or lung disease are most susceptible, as are short-faced cats, to heatstroke, but this is one condition that is easily avoided. NEVER leave an animal in a car in warm weather, even with the windows open. Animals prone to heatstroke should be exercised only during the cool part of the day in summer. All animals need free access to shade and water in warm weather.

Signs. Rapid breathing, loud panting, weakness, staggering, collapse or unconsciousness usually brought on by overexposure to the sun, overexercising in hot weather, or being left in a hot car.

Treatment. Place the animal in a cool shady spot with fresh air. Reduce body temperature by gently hosing the animal or soaking him in a partly filled tub of cool water. Use a rectal thermometer to monitor the animal's temperature; do not allow it to go below 103° F. If these measures do not bring immediate improvement, take the animal to a veterinarian without delay.

Difficulty in Delivering Young

Familiarize yourself with what takes place during a normal birth so you can more readily recognize a problem if it develops. The length of gestation for cats averages fifty-nine to sixty-four days from conception to delivery.

Signs. Female in labor for more than six hours before young are born, interval of several hours between births, young lodged in birth canal, mother refuses to open membrane sac containing young, newborn does not start breathing.

Treatment. Continuous labor or straining for six hours indicates a problem delivery and the animal should be taken to a veterinarian. If a newborn is partially visible but becomes lodged in the birth canal, try to reach as much of the young animal as possible and pull gently but firmly down from the base of the mother's tail and out. If this cannot be done with ease, a veterinarian may have to remove the young. If the mother does not remove the sac, quickly open and remove it to prevent suffocation. Dry the animal and remove the mucus from its mouth.

Foreign Objects

These objects may include bone, large chunk of food, string, toy or part of toy, ball, baby bottle nipple, cloth object (sock, stocking, etc.), broom straw, pin or needle with thread, fish hook, porcupine quills, shot or bullet, thorn, bee sting, splinter, glass.

Signs. Internal foreign object: Coughing, choking, inability to breathe, pawing at the mouth, foaming or salivating, shaking head, vomiting (when object is lodged in the stomach or digestive tract). Even a small object can block the intestine or air passage. External foreign object: Object or puncture usually visible, swelling, tenderness, limping, bleeding.

Treatment. Check the tongue, roof of the mouth, teeth, and gums. Hold the animal's tongue with a handkerchief to make looking down the throat easier; use your fingers, pliers or tweezers to remove the object. If you cannot reach it, hold the animal upside down by her hocks and shake her. A sharp blow on the back of the neck or between the shoulders will sometimes dislodge a blunt object from the throat. As a last resort, use a modified *Heimlich Maneuver.* Place your hands on either side of the animal's rib cage, then give the animal a very quick, firm squeeze to rapidly compress the lungs. This may force the object to pop out of the air passage. Squeezing too hard may break the animal's ribs and cause internal damage; compressing too slowly may let the air pass the object.

A foreign object embedded in the tissue should be removed, if possible, and the wound cleaned with soapy water and an antiseptic. A fish hook should be removed by cutting off the barb or eye of the hook with wire cutters and carefully working the hook out. NEVER pull the hook back through the skin without removing the barb. A pin or needle that is not easily removed should be left for a veterinarian to remove under anesthesia.

A foreign object such as a grass burr may be flushed from the surface of the eyeball with water or removed from the conjunctiva with a moistened Q-Tip unless it is embedded in the eye. If it is not easily removed, leave the object for your veterinarian to remove.

Thorns and splinters of glass or wood may become embedded in the foot. You can remove these yourself. Check the pads and skin between the toes; remove the objects; then clean the wound with soapy water and an antiseptic. Watch for signs of infection, which may result from any foreign object.

Poisoning

Poison may be inhaled, swallowed or absorbed through the skin.

Signs. Sudden onset of severe illness: retching, abdominal tenderness, trembling, convulsions, vomiting, diarrhea, dilated or pinpoint pupils, salivation, labored breathing, uncontrolled bleeding, weakness, collapse.

Treatment. Numerous substances are poisonous to animals and only the most common are listed here. However, in any case of suspected poisoning, do the following:

1. Try to determine what the poison was, when it was ingested and the amount swallowed.
2. Call your veterinarian or nearest poison control center. Remind your veterinarian of the animal's age, any medical problems, if it is taking medication and whether or not it has vomited since swallowing the poison.
3. If possible, bring the material in its container (or at least the label) to the veterinarian with the animal.

Vomiting may be brought on by one of the following methods, listed in order of effectiveness: syrup of ipecac (½ tsp. for a cat); 1 tsp. of equal parts hydrogen peroxide and water; ¼ tsp. of salt on the back of the tongue. DO NOT INDUCE VOMITING if you suspect that the poison is a strong acid or alkali, strychnine, a petroleum distillate; if the animal is unconscious; or if the signs of poisoning are already apparent. Milk or water may be given in most cases to wash the esophagus and to delay the absorption of the poison.

If the toxin is on the skin, flush the area with copious amounts of water, then gently lather the skin with a mild soap and water. DO NOT USE turpentine or other poisonous substances to remove paint, tar, asphalt or oil. Paint, tar and other similar materials adhering to the coat or skin can be removed before they harden by rubbing vegetable or mineral oil into the fur or on the skin to loosen the material. Cornmeal or flour can then be used to absorb the substance before brushing it out of the fur or wiping it off the skin. Follow with additional treatments and a bath in mild soapy water. Materials such as dried paint can be clipped from the haircoat.

COMMON HOUSEHOLD POISONS

POISON	COMMON SOURCES	FIRST AID
Lead	linoleum, lead paint chips, plaster, putty, varnish, ceramic glazes, golf balls, pesticides	Induce vomiting. Usually a progressive poisoning.
Ethylene glycol	car antifreeze, Sterno, windshield de-icer	Give vodka in milk
Petroleum distillates	paint and paint thinner, paint remover, kerosene, gasoline, benzene, furniture polish, floor wax, lighter fluid, motor or fuel oil	Corrosive. DO NOT induce vomiting. Give milk or water to wash esophagus.
	turpentine	Induce vomiting. Give milk or water.
	carbon tetrachloride	Induce vomiting. DO NOT give milk, fats or oils, ONLY water.
Arsenic	paint, herbicides, pesticides	Induce vomiting. Give milk or water.
Red Squill Warfarin (d-Con) ANTU Thallium Sodium Fluoroacetate (1080)	rodenticides, pesticides	Induce vomiting. Give milk or water.
Metaldehyde	snail bait	Induce vomiting. Give milk or water.
Chlorinated hydrocarbons	insecticides, pesticides, weed killers, such as chlordane, lindane, methoxychlor, heptachlor, toxaphene	Induce vomiting. DO NOT give milk, fats or oil, ONLY water.
Organophosphates	insecticides, pesticides, malathion, dichlorvos, fenthion, ronnel, parathion	Induce vomiting. Give milk or water.
Weak alkalis	soap, laundry detergent, shampoo	Induce vomiting. Give milk or water.
Strong alkalis	lye, caustic soda, drain cleaners, ammonia, grease solvents, washing powders, some metal cleaners and polishes	Corrosive. DO NOT induce vomiting. Give milk or water to wash esophagus.

POISON	COMMON SOURCES	FIRST AID
Weak acids including oxalic acid	household chlorine bleach, some disinfectants, some metal cleaners and polishes	Induce vomiting. Give milk or water.
Strong acids	some metal cleaners and polishes, sulfuric acid in car batteries (Lysol and some pine oil products should be treated as strong acids)	DO NOT induce vomiting. Give milk or water to wash esophagus.
Copper sulfate	toilet bowl cleaners (dilute)	Induce vomiting. Give milk or water.
	toilet bowl cleaners (undilute)	DO NOT induce vomiting. Give milk or water.
Phenol (carbolic acid)	household disinfectants and antiseptics, hexachlorophene, Lysol and pine oil products, fungicides, herbicides, tar, creosote	Induce vomiting. Give milk or water. Cats are particularly sensitive to phenol.
Phosphorus	non-safety matches, fireworks, striking surface of match boxes	Induce vomiting. DO NOT give milk, fats or oil, ONLY water.
Naphthalene	moth flakes and balls, insect repellents	Induce vomiting. DO NOT give milk, fats or oil, ONLY water.
Human medication	aspirin, amphetamines, barbiturates, iodine, paregoric	Induce vomiting. Give milk or water.
Other household products	aniline dyes in leather polish, dyes in some crayons, ink and glues, nail polish remover, nicotine in cigarette filters and tobacco	Induce vomiting. Give milk or water.

COMMON POISONOUS PLANTS

House Plants

NAME	POISONOUS PARTS
Alocasia	All
Avocado	Leaves, stems
Bird of paradise	All
Caladium	All
Dumb cane	All
Elephant ear	All
Holly	Berries, leaves
Ivy	All
Mistletoe	Berries
Philodendron	All
Poinsettia	All
Skunk cabbage	All
Snow-on-the-mountain	All
Wild call	All

Garden Plants and Shrubbery

Amaryllis	Bulb
Azalea	All
Bayonet	Root
Black-eyed Susan	All
Black locust	Leaves, stem, seeds
Bleeding heart	All
Boxwood	All
Burning bush	Leaves, fruit
Buttercup	All
Cactus, candelabra	All
Castor bean	All parts, beans most toxic
Cherry laurel	All
Chinaberry	All
Christmas rose	All
Cornflower	All
Crocus, autumn	All
Crown-of-thorns	All
Cyclamen	Tuber (a swollen underground stem)
Daffodil	Bulb
Daphne	All
Death camas	Bulb
Delphinium	All
Euonymus	All
Flax	All

NAME	POISONOUS PARTS
Four o'clock	Root, seeds
Foxglove	Leaves, seeds
Golden glow	All
Hyacinth	Bulb
Hydrangea	All
Ivy	Leaves, berries
Iris	Bulb
Jessamine	Flowers
Jerusalem cherry	All
Jonquil	Bulb
Lantana	All
Larkspur	All
Laurel	All
Lily, climbing or glory	All
Lily, spider	Bulb
Lily-of-the-valley	All
Lupine	All
Mock orange	Fruit
Monkshood	All
Mountain laurel	All
Narcissus	Bulb
Oleander	All
Oleander, yellow tree	Nuts
Peony	Roots
Pimpernel	All
Poinciana	All
Poppy	All
Privet, common	All
Rhododendron	All
Rosary pea	All
Scotch broom	Seeds
Snowdrops	All
Star of Bethlehem	Bulb
Sweetpea	Stem
Tobacco (nicotiana)	All
Tulip	Bulb
Tung tree	Nuts
Virginia creeper	All
Wisteria	Seeds
Yew	All

Garden Fruits and Vegetables

Apricot	Pits
Cherry	Leaves, bark of tree
Cherry, ground	Foliage, sprouts

(continued)

NAME	POISONOUS PARTS
Eggplant	Foliage, sprouts
Elderberry	Leaves, bark of shrub, opening buds, young shoots
Peach	Leaves, pits, bark of tree
Potato	Foliage, sprouts
Rhubarb	Leaves
Tomato	Leaves, sprouts

Wild Plants

NAME	POISONOUS PARTS
Arrowgrass	All
Baneberry	Root, stem, berries
Beargrass	All
Bittersweet	Leaves, unripe fruit, stem
Bloodroot	Roots, stem, juice of stem
Bluebonnet	All
Buckeyes (horse chestnuts)	All
Buttercup	All
Cherries, most wild varieties	Berry
Corydalis	All
Dicentra (bleeding heart)	All
Hellebore	All
Hemlock, poison	All
Hemlock, water	All
Horsebeans	All
Horsebrush	All
Horse chestnuts (buckeyes)	All
Iris, wild	All
Java beans	All
Jimson weed	All
Laurel	All
Locoweed	All
Mushrooms (toadstools)	All
Nightshade	All
Pokeweed	All
Staggerweeds	All
Tansy mustard	Flower

Shock

Shock is usually brought on by trauma, massive blood loss, or severe fright. Rough handling, especially of an injured animal while it is being transported, may also cause shock.

Signs. Pale gums, rapid shallow breathing, rapid or weak pulse, subnormal body temperature, nervousness or prostration, "dazed" appearance.

Treatment. Keep the animal quiet and comfortable and avoid noises that might prompt him to move. Cover him with a blanket to keep him warm. It is vital to get an animal in shock to a veterinarian immediately since he may need intravenous fluids, a blood transfusion, or drugs to survive.

Electrical Shock

Electrical shock most frequently occurs from an animal's gnawing through the insulation of a live wire.

Signs. Burns on the lips and gums where the animal contacted the wires, difficulty breathing, unconsciousness.

Treatment. Use caution to avoid electrical shock yourself. Unplug the cord if possible, then follow the treatment suggested for Shock. Give artificial respiration or mouth-to-nose resuscitation if the animal is not breathing. Though some animals suffer only a mouth burn, others may develop pulmonary edema (the lungs filling with fluid). Any animal that has suffered an electrical shock should be observed for several hours since the onset of severe symptoms may be delayed.

Urinary Obstruction

This condition is common in male cats and is sometimes mistaken for constipation.

Signs. Squatting or straining to urinate, but little or no urine produced; blood in the urine; licking the genital area; frequent trips to the litter box.

Treatment. There is no first aid for this problem that can be administered at home. The animal must be taken to a veterinarian at once to avoid death from uremic poisoning.

First Aid Techniques

First aid techniques are precisely what the name implies. They are life-saving, emergency measures that are applied as quickly as possible. They are not replacements for veterinary care, and any animal requiring first aid should be seen immediately by a veterinarian.

Pressure Bandage. (For limbs.) Apply a thick folded cloth to the wound and press firmly. To maintain pressure, a cloth, tie or other material should be wrapped around the limb, over the wound. If the bandage must remain on the animal more than thirty minutes, the entire limb, including the toes, should be wrapped.

Tourniquet. A tourniquet should be used only when a pressure bandage does not control severe bleeding. Use a cord, tie, stocking, or similar material between the wound and the heart. It is easiest to apply the tourniquet above a joint to prevent it from slipping. Watch for a slowing of the bleeding to determine how tight to tie the tourniquet. DO NOT expect the bleeding to cease entirely. Release every three to five minutes to allow some blood flow.

Artificial Respiration. If the animal is not breathing, give artificial respiration or mouth-to-nose resuscitation. For artificial respiration, place your hands on either side of the animal's chest. Press firmly with the top hand and release so that air is expelled and then inhaled.

Mouth-to-nose resuscitation may also be used to revive an animal that is not breathing. Close the animal's mouth. After taking a deep breath, place your mouth over the animal's nose, exhale, then allow the air to escape. Continue until the animal begins breathing on its own.

Using either method, give a cat about ten to fifteen breaths per minute.

HOME NURSING FOR YOUR CAT

After a prolonged illness involving a stay at the animal hospital, your cat will need looking after and special medical attention at home. This is especially true for surgery, broken limbs and extensive medical tests. You will need to know how to give the patient pills or liquid medication. Force feeding may be necessary or perhaps home care of splints or casts.

In order to facilitate healing after an operation, do not allow the cat to drink or eat for a short period of time. Your veterinarian will be more specific. Because of the excitement of coming home, your cat may become ravenous and eat or drink too much. This, in turn, could make him vomit, and the violent muscular contractions can exacerbate the cat's illness or injury.

Make certain that the cat's normal sleeping quarters are clean, dry and warm (depending on the weather). Keep other pets, children and visitors away. Maintain a quiet, sedate atmosphere. Watch the cat at specific intervals. Look for signs of reversals such as vomiting,

When administering a pill you must tilt the cat's head back. Place your index finger on the left corner of the mouth and your thumb on the right corner. Gently press the corners of the mouth. The use of both hands is necessary to accomplish this procedure.

depression, bleeding, wet bandages, chewing at the stitches or cast. Call the veterinarian if any of these signs occur.

Provide the exact diet prescribed by the veterinarian with no deviations. Keep all bandages, splints or casts dry. Do not allow the cat to become excited or too active. Keep the bedding clean and fresh.

Administering Pills

Some cats simply lick the pill, capsule or tablet right out of your hand. Most do not. Breaking up the pill and sprinkling it over the food is not efficient because it may not get eaten. Also, if it has a bitter taste, the cat may then reject it forever. The trick is to take the choice away from the cat by placing the medicine at the back of the throat and getting him to swallow. With a bit of practice (and luck) the cat will become accustomed to the procedure and even look forward to it.

Place the cat on your lap and gently talk to him as you rub his back. Get him in the mood. Press your left forearm gently but firmly against the cat's back. (Reverse these directions if you are right-handed.) Place your left hand on the cat's head so that the index finger rests on the left corner of the cat's mouth and the thumb on the right corner. Tilt the cat's head upward so that it is at a right angle to the ceiling. Take the pill in your right hand, holding it between the thumb and first finger. Press the corners of the cat's mouth, forcing him to open wide. Press gently downward on his lower front teeth with the second finger of your right hand to open his mouth still further. Try to place the pill as far back onto the tongue as possible. Close the cat's mouth and hold it shut with your left hand, but keep the chin pointing upward. Pet the cat's throat to get him to swallow. It works every time. You may also butter the pill. Or you may use a pill delivery device, for sale or given free in many veterinarians' offices, that resembles a plastic hypodermic syringe without the needle. Follow the directions on the package.

How to Administer Liquid Medicine

A plastic medicine dropper is the important tool needed for this purpose. Follow the directions given for administering pills (above).

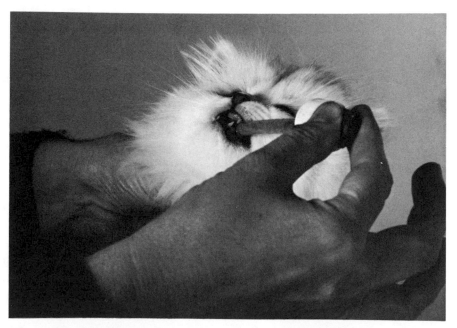

When administering liquid medicine a plastic dropper is the most useful tool available.

Fill the plastic dropper with the prescribed amount of fluid. (Never use a glass dropper.) Slip the end of the dropper between the cat's rear teeth and then squeeze the rubber bulb. The contents should squirt onto the back of the tongue. It is important to tilt the cat's head upward until she has swallowed the liquid. It is not necessary to hold the jaws shut as in giving a pill. Rub the cat's throat and she will swallow the liquid. Be careful not to let the cat bite the dropper in two or swallow the entire dropper by accident. In that event it is imperative to hold the cat upside down by the hind legs and shake the object out of the throat. (See "Foreign Objects," page 192.)

Force Feeding

This is an unpleasant but at times essential task. Reduce the food to a purée or paste in a blender, or use a commercially prepared strained baby food. The technique is similar to that used in administering a pill. Place a quantity of the food on the index finger of your right hand. Open the cat's mouth with your left hand. Open the mouth even wider with the second finger of the right hand. Smear the food onto the roof of the cat's mouth, withdrawing your finger quickly. As you pull the finger out, allow the food to scrape against the back of the cat's front teeth. This gives him no alternative but to lick and swallow. Allow for a slight rest period between servings to avoid overstressing the sick animal.

WHEN YOU LOSE YOUR CAT

Cats are naturally curious. They explore, wander, and can get themselves in bad trouble. There are several ways to prevent this. If your cat does become lost, don't despair. There is a network of good cat lovers out there who can help you.

Prevention

When a cat turns up missing, one of three things has happened: It has strayed away from home and is lost, exploring, or involved sexually; it has been harmed, either by an automobile or another animal; or it has been stolen. These calamities are almost always the result of a cat's being allowed out on its own, without restraint. The only other possibility is the cat's darting out of an open door.

Prevention, of course, is the best way to avoid this most awful of situations. This author does not believe a cat should be allowed out of its home on its own under any circumstances. It is pointless to place a cat in the backyard and expect it to stay. Hopping up on a fence that seems a formidable obstacle for humans is easy for a full-grown cat. There is no way to train a cat to stay out of trouble when out wandering about. And even an altered cat will roam around what it considers its territory. If you feel your cat needs fresh air, it is suggested that you teach it to walk with you on a leash and harness. (See Chapter 5.) Assuming you are reading this before your cat is lost, it is a good idea to take many good snapshots of your pet that can be used for identification purposes, should the need arise.

There is no greater assistance in recovering a lost pet (especially if it has been stolen) than having it tattooed and listed with a major registering organization. "I.D. Pet," the largest such organization with the highest recovery rate, is based in Noroton Heights, Connecticut.* This is an international system of animal identification, registration, and recovery assistance. It operates through a network of authorized agents who, for a fee, tattoo the animal with a coded combination of letters and numbers. Their identification code always begins with the prefix x. Once tattooed, the pet is registered (for an additional fee) at the Connecticut-based service center for the life of the animal and/or the owner. Pets that have already been tattooed with Social Security numbers, CFA numbers, or family names are also accepted for registration. The recovery rate for lost or stolen pets is excellent.

After the cat is tattooed and registered, the owner receives an ID tag for the animal's collar that states on one side: "Please call I.D. PET. Toll free: 800-243-9147. Connecticut call collect: 1-327-3157." On the other side: "Warning! I am tattoo registered. If found, phone collect." Of course, cats are usually tattooed inside the ear. The tattoo is painless in its application and does not spoil the coat in any way. It is accepted by the AKC and the CFA for show animals. The five-minute procedure is so gentle that it does not require any form of anesthesia.

The tattoo, collar tag and warning decal (all included) tell a potential thief that what he is about to steal can always be positively, individually identified by police and that the evidence stands up in a court of law. Few wish to risk being caught with readily identifiable

* Write or call: I.D. Pet, Inc., P.O. Box 2244, Noroton Heights, CN 06820; toll-free: (800) 243-9147.

property. Many tattooed animals are released by petnappers upon discovery of a tattoo. Of course lost cats are somewhat easier to recover from shelters, pounds and SPCA-type agencies when the animal is tattooed with an identification number *that has been registered.* This is an important way to prevent the permanent loss of your cat.

How to Recover a Lost or Stolen Cat

There is a certain amount of telephone work that should be done first thing. Contact your city pound or shelter and give them your name, address and phone number. Describe your pet and make them aware of your loss. Others to contact are all humane groups in your area, plus any of those people who devote time to rescuing animals. These members of the so-called "underground humane movement" are the ones who take out small classified ads in local newspapers offering free cats, dogs, puppies and kittens.

Organize the children in your immediate vicinity to spread out and ask their friends and neighbors to look for the cat. Make sure they have a well-made poster to give away. Posters are easily duplicated these days at a duplicating center. Keep the material on the poster brief with only the essential information. You may draw a pen-and-ink sketch of the cat or use one of your clear, sharp photos. In either case, tape the illustration to the center of the original and have it duplicated. It is safer not to list your address. Here is a good sample poster:

LOST CAT

On or about _____*(date)*_____ our cat disappeared
from the vicinity of _____*(approximate location)*_____
(He *or* She) answers to the name

_____

The cat is (*state sex*), (*state age*), and is a (*state breed or breed mix*).
(*Give a brief description including color, special markings, and tags or collars.*)
REWARD IS OFFERED
Please contact: (*Telephone number only*)
(*Drawing or photo of cat*)

The posters must be widely distributed on walls and poles throughout your vicinity. Put them in store windows, supermarket bulletin boards, veterinarian waiting rooms, animal shelters, and so on. The greater the distribution of your poster, the greater is your chance for recovery. Many cats who wander away are rescued by kindly animal lovers who make some efforts themselves to find the proper owner. Your posters, along with newspaper ads and local radio announcements, can help to get you and the person who has found your pet together. If your cat has been tattooed and registered, call the registry immediately for their valuable assistance.

Do not be shocked if you receive a telephone call from someone who asks for a ransom for your pet. This is a fairly common criminal practice. Unfortunately, not everyone who asks for the ransom actually has your pet. The caller may be taking advantage of your advertising. Petnappers prey on your fear and anxiety. Try to remain calm. Do not allow yourself to become hysterical. That is the state they want you to be in, so they can ask for a large amount of money. Don't be afraid to bargain and dicker over the price of the "reward," which is how they will refer to the ransom. Pay the ransom, but do not turn over the money unless you actually have your hands on your cat. Make a mental note of the thief's description, and the license plate if he or she leaves in a car or taxi. Report the incident to the police immediately, offering them all your information.

WHEN CAT MEETS BIRD

As discussed in Chapter 3, the cat is born with certain predatory responses that can never be eliminated, no matter how many years she spends as a domesticated animal. Unfortunately, the fluttering motion of a sick or old bird will attract the attention of any cat and turn her into an instant hunter. To a cat, a bird is nothing more than dinner and a floor show. As has been pointed out earlier, it is not meanness of spirit or cruel glee that compels the cat to behave this way. It is the genetically organized response to prey animals that automatically locks into gear when it is elicited. For this reason cat owners owe it to the larger world to keep their pets indoors if they live in a heavily populated bird refuge or waystation. Do not set up feeders or birdhouses on your property if you have a cat wandering freely about the place. Placing a bell and collar around the cat's neck

When cat meets bird . . . watch out.

does not really work. The cat will soon learn how to move without ringing the bell and the collar could always snag on a bush and choke her. The alternative is to live bird-free—or keep the cat indoors.

The Injured Bird

In the interest of fair play and humane attitudes, it would be nice for all cat owners to know what to do for an injured bird . . . especially if it was their pet that did the deed.

Very young birds sometimes fall out of their nests. Of course it is good for humans to intervene and save the chick from predators such as cats. But the ideal way to solve the problem is to place the little one back in its nest. Only the mother and father know how to feed and care for the young so that they have a decent chance of surviving. If you cannot find the nest, place the chick on a high tree branch as close to the nest as you can guess. The parents will find the youngster by its chirp.

Most birds die of various diseases, old age or unfortunate natural circumstances. Occasionally a house cat will snag a healthy one on the rise and bring it down with its teeth and claws. If you are fortunate enough to get there in time, shoo the cat away from the bird with great authority. If the bird is still moving, pick it up with both hands, grasping it firmly around the entire body. Allow the head to protrude between the thumb and index finger of the hand it is resting on, while the other hand rests firmly atop the body. Be gentle and do not squeeze the bird. It is bound to be under great stress.

Spread your fingers apart and try to determine the extent of the injury. If there are no broken bones (there probably won't be), and if there is no apparent sign of injury, open your hands and encourage the bird to fly away. With luck, it will.

If there is evidence of injury, such as bleeding from a wound caused by the cat, carry the bird indoors. Clean the wound with soap and tepid water. If the bleeding continues, apply baking soda or corn-starch directly to the source of the bleeding. Press the powder into the opening and hold it there for a short time. Call a veterinarian. If you cannot see the vet for several hours or a day or two, it is essential to keep the bird warm and feed it or it will probably die.

Place the bird in a carton tufted with some soft material. Cover the top with a window screen held in place by a heavy object. Be certain the bird and the cat cannot see each other. Rig a heating pad alongside the box or inside so that you can achieve a temperature of 80° F. This can also be accomplished with a bright light bulb, although it is best to keep the bird in a dark environment. Darkness will relax the animal. Do not allow the bird to become overheated.

Birds must eat constantly to survive. They are either seed eaters or insect eaters. This translates into grains or meat in the human kitchen. Seed eaters may eat dry cereal, wheat germ, shelled nuts, seeds, non-citrus fruits or berries. Insect eaters may take a bit of raw or cooked hamburger, strained baby food (beef), chicken, hard boiled egg or canned pet food. Meal worms are ideal if you can get them.

After a decent-sized meal, leave the bird in its box and allow it to sleep for as long as it can. Watch for continuous bleeding and repeat the above procedures for bleeding as required. Have the bird treated by a veterinarian as soon as possible. If you do these things, the bird just might survive and you can walk tall with your head upright and you will win accolades from bird lovers. Of course, the cat may be in the doghouse for quite a while.

8

Cats and Kids

Do you remember your first cat? Was your front tooth under a pillow then or was the world wobbling as you stood on your two feet for the first time? If you had a cat, then you remember. Those were the giggle years. If you had a cat. From Dr. Dentons to training bras, from pediatrician to orthodontist, your cat walked you through that half-forgotten dream and, like Alice's looking-glass, you stepped through, looked around, and discovered yourself. Whatever happened to your favorite doll or cap pistol and your lucky socks? And did that cat really love you as much as you remember? Yes, he did. That is one of the silver strands connecting then and now. Growing was a pain and a song and a blush and a reassuring meow from down below. By the time the dream was mostly over, you had to stoop down from a greater distance to pet the dear old boy, that furry Peter Pan of a cat. You had grown tall. Your cat had kept the faith through the whole business and accepted your giggling madness, your teary-eyed explosions, your march from the potty to the executive washroom. Where is that old guy now, anyway? In a shoe box, beneath the tree out back, or did he blow away like childhood itself? It's a delicious chocolate of a memory and more precious than the discovery of ice cream. If you had a cat.

WHAT TO TELL A CHILD ABOUT CATS

Children are suspicious of or frightened by the unknown. By teaching them the following facts about cats, you can help assure that they will understand cat behavior, which in turn will promote a happy relationship between child and pet.

Cats are meat-eating hunters. In the wild they are the most powerful and skilled of all the animals that hunt. They hunt alone. All cats resemble each other in looks and in many of the ways they behave. The lion, tiger, cheetah and ordinary house cat are related and part of the same family. There are about forty different species of cats, which is a pretty small number compared to mice. There are over a thousand different kinds of rodents.

Cats are called meat-eaters or *carnivores*. In order to eat they must hunt other types of animals, catch them and devour them. That is why they have such sharp claws and teeth that are excellent for cutting and tearing. Cat claws are long, curved and sharp. When they are scraped on tree trunks or other rough surfaces (like your furniture), the claws stay sharp and polished. There are eighteen claws on four paws (five on each front paw, four on each back paw), and they can be pulled in or retracted into a sort of pocket or sheath at the tip of the toes. When the claws are pulled in behind the toes you cannot hear a cat walk, because of the pads on each paw. This is good for hunting silently. When cats jump from high places, the pads soften their landing.

Other parts of their bodies also help them hunt. Their whiskers act like feelers for measuring and getting into small places in the dark. Their ears can move in different directions so they can catch every sound. They have strong muscles for jumping and running and a tail to balance their weight when they leap.

Cats can hear sounds that may be too high-pitched for humans to hear. They also see better in the dark than humans. Although a cat cannot see anything in total darkness, there is almost always some light. The stars and the moon provide a little light, which the cat can use. Its pupils open very wide to catch the light.

Cats have about five hundred muscles that they can control. There are very strong muscles in the jaws, which help them catch and eat food. There are small muscles that pull the claws in and out of their sheaths. There are very large muscles in their legs, thighs, chest and stomach. It is from all these muscles that the cat derives its great strength. When a cat falls, she can twist and land on her feet because of a very flexible backbone. This is what allows it to turn and twist so easily. Of course, if the cat fell from a great height she could not survive.

The domestic cat that we live with today is thought to be related to the bush cat of Africa, which looks like a tabby cat except that its stripes run from back to belly. Our house cat is not a wild species that somehow became tamed. It has several wild ancestors but is not directly descended from any single one of them. It is merely a cousin to the large and small wild cats that live in the jungles, plains and deserts of the wild regions of the world.

In order to have kittens, adult male and female cats come together to mate. The tomcat makes a singing sound to the female and tries to attract her attention. She may purr at first but hiss and spit a second later. When cats mate it looks unfriendly, but it sounds worse than it really is.

Cats are classified as mammals, which means that they are warm-blooded and are born alive, not hatched from eggs. Kittens, like all mammals, feed from their mother's breast by sucking milk.

While the kittens are still inside their mother they are covered with protective tissues called birth membranes. When they are born, the membranes are still wrapped around them like slippery Saran Wrap bags. The mother cat must break open the membranes with her teeth and lick them away from the kittens' bodies so they can breathe. She then licks the babies dry so that they do not catch a chill. After kittens are born, the placenta that protected and nourished the kittens inside the mother must be ejected from the birth canal. This is normal and it is also normal for the mother to eat it. It is a rich source of protein and other nutrients.

The kittens are blind, deaf and totally helpless when they are born. Mother cat keeps them warm by curling her body around them. When she does this they already know to drink milk from her breasts. After three weeks the kittens can see, hear and move about. After four to eight weeks they begin to take solid food in addition to breast milk, and by eight to ten weeks they stop drinking mother's milk altogether. This is called weaning.

When a cat licks her own fur she is grooming or cleaning herself. Cats lick themselves often throughout their lives. This cleans the fur and removes dead hair. When a cat washes herself she uses her tongue and her paws. She first licks all around her mouth; then she licks her paws and uses both tongue and paw to wash her face. Slowly and carefully she washes her entire body.

Cats and kittens love to play and have fun. Much of their time is spent this way. However, play is their way of going to school and learning how to hunt and chase and fight. Do not be surprised if a sweet-natured cat suddenly turns hunter in the house and captures a mouse. The cat may toy with it for a while and then kill it because that is what cats were born to do. They are not mean and cruel, only natural. It is the way of nature.

LIVING WITH CHILDREN AND CATS

When a kitten moves into a house with its new family, it should not be younger than eight weeks. The children must be made to understand that this is a young baby and needs gentle, loving care. It is all right to pet and stroke the kitten, but he must not be squeezed, pulled, treated like a stuffed toy or subjected to loud noises.

The newcomer must be allowed to explore the new home without children interfering with that activity. A cat bed should be provided with something soft inside. This area must be off-limits to the children so that the little cat can rest as much as he needs to without being disturbed.

Playtime is a very important part of the kitten's development. Opportunities to play must be allowed on the animal's terms—that is, when he wants to. The kids cannot be allowed to force the cat to play when *they* want him to. If they join in the cat's play period, they mustn't overexcite the little animal or he will become frightened. Children have to be guided in how to behave with their new pet. They will take their cues from how their parents behave.

From the beginning the child can be shown how to hold the cat properly so that the pet not only feels safe but also feels wanted and loved. (See Chapter 2.). Explaining the nature of cats to your child will help establish respect and, one hopes, affection for the animal. It is a good idea to read aloud "What to Tell a Child About Cats" from this chapter.

Tell your child that as a larger, older member of the family he or she may take on some of the responsibilities for the kitten's well-being. This affords the child an opportunity to develop self-esteem through accomplishment. Nothing helps develop a relationship between a child and a pet better. You may point out to the child that care-taking efforts place him or her in a position similar to that of a parent.

Every member of your family should take a dominant position over the family pet, including the children. This does not, of course, mean that a child should be allowed to abuse the animal physically or mentally. Children past six years of age can assume some of the responsibilities for the cat's care, which has the effect of dominance. It is good for the mental health of both child and animal.

Although a cat must be dealt with gently, eventually it must be taught what it can and cannot do. A mother cat will immediately discipline a kitten when it becomes necessary. Likewise, everything should be done to encourage a child to take a leadership position. From the attitude of being the cat's leader and surrogate parent, your child will develop a caring and responsible view toward the family pet. A sensitive and meaningful relationship will grow between the two. It may be extremely valuable to the child and to the cat as well. The principal difference between a pet and a child is that the animal instinctively understands and accepts the world as it is. The child must take half a lifetime to perceive its own world so that it might gain some form of mastery over it and at the same time live in harmony with it.

Some parents will not allow a child to have a pet unless they make an unworkable bargain that the child assume full responsibility for the totally dependent animal. Conversely, some parents are fearful of the child's assuming any of the cat chores for fear of the animal's harming the child or the child's harming the cat.

In reality neither of these viewpoints is correct. There are some aspects of cat care that should always be handled by an adult, exclusively. However, many activities connected with the cat's health and happiness can and should be the sole province of the young member(s) of the household.

Among the jobs a child can handle are feeding the cat, cleaning its bowls and living areas, daily brushing, baths, litter box maintenance. Training and discipline matters are best left to the adults in the house. Trips to the veterinarian, and home nursing and medical procedures are necessities that can be accomplished by adults and children together.

One of the first questions that arises when a new cat joins the family is whether she may sleep with the children on the bed. For

many, sleeping with their cat is the most pleasant part of owning a pet. There are those who merely yield to their animal's wishes, but secretly agonize over the question. Whatever you decide, the time to choose is in the beginning, before the habit becomes patterned behavior.

Here is what you must consider. A cat in bed will certainly leave more than a few cat hairs on the blanket and perhaps a sprinkle of kitty litter on the bottom sheet. Whether cat tracks or fur on your child's bed is good hygiene or bad depends on the lifestyle of the animal and the diligence of the humans involved. But that has only to do with physical hygiene. Emotional and personal hygiene are also issues.

From a special perspective, one can view childhood as an ongoing process where the child slowly, sometimes painfully, learns to separate from the parents and become independent. Starting with infancy, children are continually learning to leave home and meet the world. However, this is a frightening challenge loaded with emotional ambivalence. Children, especially infants, will often become attached to a "huggy" or "lovey" as an object to cling to during the rough periods. Teddy bears and security blankets are fine for toddlers, but a cat is more acceptable for an older child.

If a youngster is lucky enough to have his or her own cat, sleeping with the animal should be permitted if that is what they themselves have worked out. Most cats will settle down at the foot of the bed and will not want to be held throughout the night, if at all. However, if both child and pet want to nest together, that is fine. A living, breathing teddy bear can do more for a child striving for independence than any parental strategy. A cat can be an object of affection without the child's losing ground in her or his striving for maturity. This is a more important form of hygiene than clean sheets.

Sleeping with a cat in the same bed is one of the more loving, deeply gratifying comforts in life. But the idea of cleanliness where we sleep is an important one. Is it clean, hygienic or even healthy to allow our pets in bed with us? In truth, it is not unless certain precautions are taken.

There is no avoiding some amount of superficial dirt on the animal's paws. This is easily removed with a slightly dampened towel before allowing the pet in bed. (Of course, cats crawl in and out of bed throughout the night, so your best hope is a clean floor.) Make it a habit to brush your cat's coat each night. This will remove most dirt and debris as well as making the animal feel loved and good. Check between toes and clean them out if necessary. It is a favorite hiding place for fleas and ticks.

Clip your cat's claws every week and check them constantly. There is nothing worse than sharp claws if the cat has bad dreams or gets rolled on. If you have recently sprayed or powdered your animal for fleas, do not allow her to sleep in the bed until the fumes of the insecticide have worn off. Many cats wear an all-year flea collar. Remove it before bedtime. This is especially important for children.

Some parasites (internal and external) can be transmitted to humans. Therefore, veterinary examinations become an absolute necessity for pets who sleep with children, as are baths, combings and brushings. There are several feline *zoonoses* (diseases that can be transmitted from animal to human), but they are uncommon and not a problem for the cat that enjoys reasonable veterinary scrutiny.

If your cat is indoors most of the time and has reasonable living habits along with a clean environment, then sharing the bed is a great idea. When the world closes in, pets and kids can cling to each other and set things right again.

*   *   *

KIDS AND CATS: RANDOM THOUGHTS
FROM EDA LESHAN

Everyone knows Eda LeShan from her dozen or more books, her articles in magazines, and from her many television appearances on such shows as *Dinah Shore, Dick Cavett, Mike Douglas, Phil Dona-hue, The Today Show, Good Morning America*, and *Not For Women Only.*

Mrs. LeShan has been an educator and family counselor for more than thirty years. In her books, articles, television appearances and lectures she has helped more people understand the delicate needs of children and adults than almost anyone else who comes to mind. Many consider her to possess a rare combination of intellectual attainment and personal warmth and sympathy for the collective flaws in our collective natures. Eda LeShan loves cats as she loves all of life. Here, then, are some recorded thoughts on cats from Eda LeShan.

One of the advantages for a child in having a cat is that it can give and receive unconditional love. You are loved because you exist and not because you achieve and not because you're a success or get good marks. In loving a cat there is the feeling "You and I love each other but we're still individuals." In other words you can love something or someone and still have very separate lives. The autonomy of a cat and its inner dignity may be a good lesson for all parents. I would like parents to notice that a happy cat is one that can be left alone when it wants that and not have to do what everyone else does, one that can make decisions for itself. Maybe the best parent educator would be a cat. I've spent thirty years of my life trying to teach parents how to behave with their children. Perhaps a cat could do it better.

As far as children being totally responsible for the cat is concerned, it cannot work. If you say something is forever to a child and it can't be changed, then he or she won't take any risks. What we have to teach children is that you don't really accomplish anything until you take risks. You must risk failure to achieve anything. When a family decides to have a cat, it's a risk that the whole family takes and they will have to see if they can work it out. If you make a lot of rules ahead of time you are bound to fail. You are going to have to be flexible enough to make changes as the members of the family learn and grow.

Parents have to realize that children can't be as responsible as adults; if they were, they would be grownups. When you tell a child that he or she must take all the responsibility for a pet, you are destroying the pleasure of having it because the child knows he or she is going to fail. You must tell a child that we're going to have to work this thing out as we go along, even if we end up screaming at each other. There will be times when the child fails in taking some responsibility and the parent fails in being reasonable about it, but they will fight it out and work it out. It doesn't have to be forever. Nobody should anticipate how he or she is going to feel. One should not be wallowing in guilt if one fails, but the risk is worth it. A family is a cooperative enterprise and the people in it ought to try to help each other. You ruin the relationship between an animal and a child if the only reason for having it is to teach responsibility. The relationship is for love and fun.

We are the only animal in the animal kingdom that has decided play is not important anymore. The greatest thing that pets can teach parents and children is that the only way they can become their own species is through play. Children use cats as the object for their own play. They not only use their pets for projecting inner feelings about themselves but for developing relationships. My daughter Wendy used to talk to her cat as if it were somebody in her class or another adult or someone in an imaginary relationship.

When a pet is hurt or lost or if it dies, it is not a negative experience for the child but rather a part of learning what it is to be human. Parents must help children live through their grief and mourning and allow it by living through it with them. It should be shared and not hidden or repressed. Don't tell a child to be brave about it by covering it up. Rather, a child should be told that this is worth crying about. It is one of the ways in which we learn about pain and gain something positive from a very negative experience. When it happens to people it is then a little better understood.

The more civilized life becomes, the more important animals become to human beings. Most of us are born with paranormal abilities, which are our instinctual, nonverbal, nonsensory parts of our personality, which very rapidly get pushed away by an ververbal, overtechnological society. One of the reasons why people get backaches and migraines and ulcers

and hit each other and all the horrible problems of life is that in
a sense they are only living out the intellectual part of
themselves. God knows, we do that with our children. The other
side of ourselves, the animal side, doesn't get a chance to live.
Animals and gardening are the vegetative part of our souls.
Everything about modern life has cut us in two. To watch a bird
take a bath or a dog run along a beach or to just sit and watch a
cat washing itself is to watch something eternal and natural. I
think these things are important for resuscitating our poor
beleaguered souls.

The more a child dislikes a cat, the more he or she is
repressing the catlike quality in him- or herself. If you can get a
child to openly talk about a cat he or she will express
apprehension about the cat's unpredictability, if it will purr or
scratch you. They find their parents unpredictable. They see this
in themselves and don't know if they are going to be
overwhelmed by the impulse to scratch or bite. A child's

relationship with an animal is a very good way of getting some information about what's bothering him or her.

Those poor kids in the ghetto, they should all have cats. They're less expensive than dogs and maybe they'll keep them from getting bitten by rodents. Most of them are just starving for some kind of relationship with someone who gives them something just because they are. They would get that from a cat.

If children abuse an animal for any reason—either because of rivalry between two kids trying to get it away from each other or in the expression of their own anger, which is being misdirected so that they are hurting the animal instead of a brother or sister or parent—then the animal has to be protected in exactly the same way you would protect a sibling. We are not allowed to do that. You must explain that "I wouldn't allow someone to hurt you and you must not hurt anyone else." There is no better way to know if a child is emotionally ill than if he or she hurts animals. It's a very serious indication of disturbance. And I think parents have to be pretty firm that they will not permit that. One of the great advantages with cats is that they won't put up with that. They give it right back. I guess, if you have a hostile child, you're better off with a cat than a dog. A cat will sure as hell protect itself and maybe that's a good thing for kids to find out. As far as the sibling business, if there are real problems then it isn't the animal that's the problem, it's the relationship, and parents better look to what's going on.

Cats are an introduction to the process of what it's like to be alive. If a family is open to its feelings, then it's a marvelous experience and teaches a great deal. The universals of birth and death and everything in between are lessons well taught by cats. It's something we all need in our lives.

FOLLOW THE BOUNCING BALL: KIDS AND CATS AT PLAY

We live in a time when every experience of childhood, we are told, is supposed to teach something or expand the mind. But your author remembers childhood as a time of bubble gum, baseball cards, spinning tops, yo-yos, pick-up-sticks, Simon Says, doggie fetch, pussycat pussycat, and "anyone 'round my base is it." There was only one rule during play and that was to have a good time. Play means

fun. And if people try to tell you that cats and kids cannot play together and have a great deal of fun, tell them they are crazy.

When children play with cats there are guidelines to make the
experience safe, loads of fun, and meaningful to their relationship.
There are only a few activities where the child and the animal can
interact on the same level. Usually, games that kids play with cats use
a special method. The child essentially stimulates or elicits certain
predictable responses from the cat through calculated actions. The
most obvious is the retrieval game. Here the youngster rolls a ball or
crumpled piece of paper to the opposite side of the room and gets the
cat's attention with a high-pitched tone of voice. The cat should respond and give chase. With the proper reward system, you have the
makings of years' worth of fun. The formula: Child elicits response
through specific action—cat behaves with predicted response
(maybe)—the cat is rewarded for that response.

Most other play activities may or may not involve direct contact
with the cat. Just follow the bouncing ball and see what happens.

Portrait of a Cat as a Young Puss

A sure winner for all kids from toddler to teenager is using the cat
as a subject for art work. Have the child place a large piece of paper
on the floor. With one hand try to hold the cat in position while tracing
an outline of the animal's outer lines with the other. Crayon or magic
marker is best. For the really young, you may do the tracing for him or
her and allow the child to fill it in with solid coloring. Older kids can
simply utilize the cat as a model and draw what they see of the cat
during her daily activities. Most children love to draw, color or paint
and there are many varied and creative ways to do it. Bear in mind
that it is not necessary for the drawing to resemble a cat in our terms.
It is only the vision and the creative spirit of the child that matters.
Do not interfere with the "right" way to draw or paint a cat. Any
choice the child makes is the "right" way.

Start a Cat Diary

From the first moment your child can put letters together to form
simple words, entice him or her to keep a diary of the cat's life. Use a
full-size notebook or drawing pad for words and illustrations. Start
with a birth record and put down all of the pet's essential information,
such as place of birth, breeder, date, city, and so on. Leave spaces for

photos and drawings. After each important event in the cat's life, take the time with your child for the two of you to remember the events of the day and record them (in the child's own handwriting, of course). Write the event and the date it happened on the page and then ask your child about his or her feelings regarding the event. Make it clear that the child may make an entry at any time about anything involving the cat. If your child cannot write, then you can take dictation. Be sure to take down descriptions exactly as your child gives them. You will adore having a record of the child's speech patterns later in life. You will also be amazed at the insights of a very young mind. You may illustrate the pages with the child's own drawings, or photos or illustrations cut from magazines, newspapers or greeting cards.

The Young Cat Writer

Using the same techniques, encourage the child to create her or his own storybook, using the cat as the central character. An interesting technique is to have the child tell the story of your family from the point of view of the cat. You may learn some startling things about what your kids are thinking and feeling.

Create Your Cat's Family Tree

This is only possible when the cat's pedigree is available (if it has a pedigree). Draw a big tree, with your cat as the center of attraction in the trunk just before the branches begin. On the extending branches paste colored drawings of the cat's relatives. Each cat drawing should have the cat's name printed on the body for identification. Wherever possible point out similar characteristics—same color coat, personality traits, eyes, and so on.

Fun and Games

Here are a series of activities that you can involve your kids and cats in. And, if you're feeling young enough, you can join right in. There's no age limit in playing with cats.

Cat's in the Bag. All you really need is a large paper bag. Open it wide and lay it on its side, forming a cave opening. Inside, at the very back, place a food treat, some catnip or a yeast tablet. Step aside and watch the cat entertain the family.

Feathers. Many florist shops sell peacock feathers. They are long, elegant and delightful in and of themselves. Your child will love having several. Have the child sitting on the couch. Call the cat. When he gets within reach, gently entice him with the tip of the feather. Allow the feather to sway and move up and down, side to side and in circles. Tickle the cat under the chin. You will be delighted at the cat's response. It almost always works.

Your Move. Anyone who has ever lived with cats knows that almost any and all movement captures their attention. When you pull a long string across the floor and move it from side to side, it resembles the movements of a snake. Any cat worth its weight will pounce on it. Rope, cord, plastic bag ties, chain, leashes are all correct for this kind of fun. Don't forget to put these toys away when not in use. They are unsafe when unsupervised.

Fetch. Ping-Pong balls, rubber balls, crumpled sheets of paper all make excellent toys for your cat to retrieve. This game will require a bit of positive reinforcement. Before you do anything, give the cat a food treat or a yeast pill. This is to get him in the proper frame of mind. Next, roll the ball across the floor and say, "Herbert, fetch." If the cat runs after the ball (and he might), allow him to do what he wants after he catches up to the toy. Immediately reward him with a food treat or a yeast pill. Repeat the action. Do this five or six times. Eventually the cat will give chase at the first roll of the ball.

Musical Cats. A kitten on the keys is truly an amusing interlude. If you are lucky enough to have a cat, a kid, and a piano, then you must try this. Place the cat on one end of the keyboard and try playing a simple tune on the middle or opposing end. Within a few seconds you should have a feline accompanist.

Cat Tote. Take an old pair of long pants, short pants or jeans.Cut off the legs a few inches below the crotch. Sew the legs shut. Work a piece of clothesline, long thin material, or even an old belt (adult's) through the belt loops, with enough length to loop into a shoulder strap. If the pants are large enough, you now have a shoulder bag large enough to cart the cat around the house from room to room.

Rules of the Game

It is a losing proposition to compete with a child's imagination when it comes to inventing games to play. Sometimes it only takes a very general suggestion, such as "Why don't you play with the cat?" and the child is off and running, turning boxes and kitchen utensils into cities, musical instruments or luxury liners. The cat can be an accomplice, a playmate, a part of the game. If the child is very young, an adult will have to supervise the play so that neither one abuses the other. Games that involve pulling, carrying, lifting or pushing the cat should be ruled out without question. Cats are very different from dogs in that they will hit back when hurt or made uncomfortable. Place the cat on a box and you may have a puppet show. Wrap a handkerchief around its body and you have a costume. Roll an empty sewing spool across the floor and you witness a hunt. It is only as limited as the imagination. Safety, kindness, gentle sense of humor, gratitude and respect are the guidelines for developing games that cats will play. When the cat calls it quits for the day, do not let the child pursue her. Everyone should rest at that point and recharge her or his batteries. If the play was good the cat will return eagerly for the next session. Cats and kids are a joy forever.

9

The Old Tiger Mews

Old folks are just bent kids.

—George Carlin

Okay, so he doesn't leap very far anymore and he's off by himself more than he used to be. His appetite has slackened and rainy days make him stiff and his old roar at the window has been replaced by a mew at the wall. That doesn't qualify him yet for a Viking funeral with his sword and shield in his paws as the burning boat drifts to the Hall of the Cat Gods. There are still a few more lives left for an old tiger and they should not be reduced to a Tom and Geriatric cartoon. Lest you forget, old cats are simply aging boys and girls and can still raise catnip hell if they want to, if they need to, if they are encouraged to.

Just because a cat is advancing to its brittle years doesn't mean you should start chiseling its name in stone. There are still a lot of good times up the road. Give a cheer for aging cats and thrice will they cheer back at you. An old cat is your merit badge for keeping your part of the bargain. It means you know a great deal about good cats and loving care. Excelsior!

CARING FOR THE AGING CAT

As cats get older, they go through physical, chemical and behavioral changes just as humans do. With some knowledge of these changes you can make their later years, and yours with them, much happier and healthier.

227

Stress

Nothing ages a cat faster and with more irreversible effects than stress. Physical and emotional stress not only hasten the aging process, but can actually deliver a death blow. There is only so much resistance to stress that a body can deliver before it begins to succumb. If an organ is stressed and therefore partially damaged, the life of the animal is considerably shortened. Illness produces physical stress. Anxiety in any form causes emotional stress.

Because older cats have more difficulty fighting disease, stress and stressful situations make them more susceptible. Much greater attention, therefore, must be paid to medical situations than with younger cats, and situations that upset the older cat must be avoided. Try to avoid long separations between the aging cat and her family. That may be the worst event in her life. She is certainly going to be upset, anxiety-ridden and frightened. The emotional stress involved in such a situation can be extremely debilitating and cause serious illness.

Aging cats must not be exposed to other cats who are sick. They must not be moved from one home to another, especially to a strange, temporary home. It is an extremely emotional situation for an older cat when her territory and position are challenged by another cat. This happens when the owner decides to introduce another pet into the household at this late time. It is not only unfair, but also indicates a lack of knowledge of your cat. Do not adopt a kitten or young adult if your old cat has always lived alone or hasn't shared the territory for a very long time. It is unkind to do so and somewhat dangerous from a medical point of view.

Food

A cat is considered aged (senescent) by the time she is nine. High-quality, nourishing food becomes extremely important and enhances the longevity of the animal. A number of feline diseases and disorders affect the cat's digestive processes. These include kidney disease, tumors, growths and arthritis. These illnesses create such symptoms as increased thirst, loss of appetite, constipation, diarrhea, diminished sense of taste or smell, stiffness when moving, sudden loss of lifelong house training. These are serious symptoms in the aging cat and must be treated by a veterinarian as soon as possible.

Continued quality food intake and efficient digestion of that food are extremely important to older cats. An animal that won't eat or rest deteriorates quickly. It is important to note that older cats do not require as much food as younger ones. Their metabolic rate is lower. But because the animal is more visible at home (and more of an object of concern), the tendency is to give her what she insists on and consequently to overfeed her. Overweight in older cats is an important problem. The mammalian body normally loses about a third of its lean body mass, including skeletal muscles and all other cellular tissues, in extreme old age. However, it is too often replaced with stored fat and body water. Thus, vital organs and body chemical systems have as much or more work to contend with, yet possess less lean body mass with which to accomplish their various tasks. This produces a more subtle but equally fatal form of stress. Overweight cats, especially older cats, get that way by eating too much of the wrong food. Although some food reduction program is recommended, it is essential for a veterinarian to examine the cat and tailor the diet to the animal's specific needs and limitations.

At the other extreme, the aging cat may refuse food. As cats age they lose their sense of smell and, to some degree, their sense of taste. This is dangerous because they will not eat what they cannot smell. It is advisable to stimulate their olfactory sense by "hyping" the ration with food that is strong in odor or taste. A sprinkling of cooked fish flakes on top of or mixed into the normal ration smells delicious. Many cats enjoy the odor of garlic or onion or other spice. A strong, cooked meat aroma may be the answer to the problem.

Vitamin and mineral supplements are a good idea for older cats and should be recommended by a veterinarian. Because the age of the cat and its medical demands are variables, it is advised to seek a prescribed diet from your veterinarian. In general it is safe to say that you must not allow the cat to become addicted to one food exclusively. A combination of commercial products and home-cooked foods is highly desirable. Cooked fish, meat, vegetables, egg yolks (cooked), cheese and cereal are the kinds of food you may include in your older cat's diet. One teaspoon a day of oil, butter or animal fat is important for maintaining a healthy skin and haircoat.

Grooming

It is absolutely essential that your older cat be groomed every day. This means combing and/or brushing as described in Chapter 6.

As the cat ages, his ability to wash himself diminishes. It is a physical exertion for a cat to groom himself and grooming becomes less and less possible in old age. Long-haired cats, obviously, need grooming the most, but all cats require this attention. Dead hair and scurf (dead and scaly skin) must be removed and parasitic infestation avoided by daily combing and/or brushing. It is essential to avoid mats, tangles and knots in the aging long-haired cat, because removing them after they've formed can have a stressful effect and harm the animal.

Nail care is also important because the cat will not be using his favorite scratching post so often. The need to remove the outer sheath continues, but the cat is less capable of doing it for himself as he ages. Clipping his nails as often as necessary will prevent them from growing too long and too sharp and will help the cat to avoid hooking them into the carpeting.

Bathing an older cat is just not worth it if it is too stressful. This really depends on whether the cat enjoys the bath or hates it (many hate baths their entire lives). Remember the axiom, Do nothing that causes an old cat anxiety. There are commercially prepared "dry shampoos" if the old guy or gal is really a mess, and you can "sponge bathe" too. A warm washcloth around the face and body (especially after a sloppy meal) once or twice a week is all the cat really needs. If you must give the cat a bath and if he doesn't mind, be certain the bathing area is warm (no drafts) and that the cat is dried thoroughly with a blow dryer as described in Chapter 6.

One of the primary advantages in the daily grooming of older cats is that you can routinely check for new growths, warts or lumps. Many of these will be fat deposits. Others may be cysts or benign tumors that can be removed with no harmful effects. Malignancies, if caught in time, are also usually treatable.

Medical Attention

Preventive medicine becomes most important as cats get older. Do not wait for sickness to hit because it can be devastating. Complete physical examinations including laboratory testing of blood, urine and feces should be done every six months once the cat reaches nine or ten years of age. Behavioral or physical changes require veterinary investigation as soon as possible to keep minor symptoms from developing into major diseases. Do not allow the cat to fall behind on his vaccination boosters. It is more important at this phase of life than before.

Geriatric cats (past their prime) require more frequent screening and laboratory tests. Early detection can help to spot diseases such as diabetes, heart and renal dysfunction, prostate problems and other diseases. Geriatric pets benefit greatly from a planned program of health care. There are three stages of pet development. Stage one is a period of growth from the time a kitten is born until its biological systems are developed. Stage two is the mature period, which includes the animal's most active years and lasts until the body begins to show signs of deterioration. Stage three is the golden years of maturity, which can be the best in pet and owner relationships. Cats will remain self-sufficient (up to a point) if provided with added warmth and adequate diet (reduced by several calories per pound of body weight). Proper diet, moderate exercise and a little extra consideration can help make your pet's golden years the best.

Take more time to prevent dental problems than before. Although cats seldom develop cavities, the tartar buildup can cause infection of the gums, which will result in loose teeth and eventually lost teeth. The pain involved will stop the cat from eating at a time when nutrition is of vital importance. Owners can reduce much of the tartar with their fingers once or twice a week. Watch your older cat for infections or inflammations of the mouth and throat. These may be caused by jagged teeth or tartar buildup. Regular dental care from your veterinarian is necessary.

Digestive problems in older cats are quite common. Diarrhea and constipation are the most common symptoms, but refusal to eat is also a great problem. If the cat does not drink enough, the stool tends to harden and the bowel movements slow down considerably. Ask your vet about laxatives and high-fiber foods. Hairballs are also a factor and require special medications. Diabetes mellitus sometimes occurs in older cats and is manifested by increased drinking of water and weight loss. There are many possible problems connected with the lungs, heart, blood, nervous system, reproductive system, skin, eyes, ears, nose, kidneys and urinary system. Careful observation for changes in the older cat can be extremely useful in preventing serious illness.

Today, animals can enjoy most of the same high-caliber medical services that are available to their human families. With the proper medication and medical treatment, both humans and animals can live more comfortable and longer lives. This, of course, is contingent upon following the advice of the physician or veterinarian along with the faithful administration of the recommended treatments and medica-

ON DEATH AND DYING

We live in a time when death is almost a taboo subject. We are shielded from this very natural, inevitable phenomenon. The death of pets is an exception to this, and although heartbreaking, can reconnect us with the process and allow us to consider it directly and with dignity.

When a dear old friend is incurably ill and in pain it is time to consider the ultimate act of love. To mercifully, gently and caringly say goodbye to an old cat is human and humane. Putting an end to your old, sick cat's life is to free him from his mortal burden of labored agony.

Euthanasia is the most difficult of decisions and need not be borne alone. The guidance and counsel of your veterinarian is not only available but necessary for making the correct decision. It is a matter for your entire family to be made aware of, so that they might participate in that most awful of realities.

The cycle of life ultimately comes to an end. It is painful, but natural and certainly inevitable. By having the entire family participate in the decision, you allow them to prepare for their own emotions and expressions of grief and mourning. At that time it is important to avoid the use of euphemisms for the word "death." When dealing with children, the expression "put to sleep" is extremely harmful. It creates a frightening association with the idea of going to sleep for the night. It also implies, through a misuse of the language, that the pet didn't really die.

The concept of death is at first a frightening one to a child (and to many of us adults), but it needn't remain so. When a pet dies, a child will have many questions that must be answered. *Why did the cat die? Was it anyone's fault? What happens to the cat now? Do we all die? Who will take care of me when you die?* It is quite likely that you have never confronted these questions. The best way to handle the matter is to have an open discussion, with everyone in the family participating. This will prevent the buildup of nightmares and dark fantasies about the "forbidden" subject. The truth, as you know it, will always serve you and your family best. Never abandon it.

If your cat is to have any dignity in his death, the reality of his end must be met honestly and with as full an expression of your grief as possible. He is worth mourning for, crying over and then, when time permits, remembering with fondness and joy.

The Last Write

An Ohio newspaper, *The Columbus Dispatch*, runs a weekly column called *All About Cats*, written by Brunson Caito (*nom de plume* for Kathleen Brunson and Mary Caito). It is a happy feature that is a sort of gossip column about the doings of local cats in the Columbus vicinity. Several years ago the paper ran an item about the death of a local cat. There may be something to be learned from it.

The article was about a nineteen-year-old cat named Pinky. He was a free roamer most of his life and was the sire of many kittens in his time. He was one of Ohio's own. But after a long career, he fell victim to a serious illness. He was treated at the Ohio State University Veterinary Hospital. Pinky had many admirers; he enjoyed at least one visitor every day and was the hospital's first patient ever to receive a get-well card. He was a much-loved cat.

After his hospital stay he was placed in the care of a brother and sister who had promised their mother, Pinky's mistress, they would care for the old guy after she was gone. The brother lived in the town of Logan during the week (near his job in Columbus) and went to

New Straitsville each weekend. Litter boxes were set up in both towns for the aged cat, who traveled with him.

Every kindness imaginable was considered for Pinky. His family even set up three boxes as steps beside their beds because he was too weak to jump. That way he could sleep with those he loved. Time passed and the old tom died. All of his family and most of his friends said a fond farewell as he was placed to rest somewhere on a rugged hill in Ohio. "There will be a headstone on the grave of Pinky and flowers will grow there from spring to autumn."

The memory of Pinky and all the other dear little cats that ever raced across our lives will live as long as we do. Try to remember that when your next wonderful kitten climbs up your arm and licks the inside of your ear, waking you from a sound sleep.

PART TWO

A Who's Who of Uncommon Cats

Despite her buttered paws and pampered whiskers, the typical family feline is not a card-carrying member of the very elite Cat Fancy. Ask a family about their pussy-footed friend and they'll respond with a chuckle, "Scheherazade? Why, she's just a house cat." The truth of the matter is that while the larger percentage of cats are random-bred, there are millions of gorgeous members of the more fanciful breeds. Anyone owning a cat, even *le chat ordinaire*, ought to become more knowledgeable about the many intriguing pure breeds that exist. To understand pure breeds is to appreciate better those of unknown lineage.

All pure breeds of cat stem from the various old or ancient breeds, the natural or discovered types that breed true every time. From these older breeds were created mutations and hybrids, which, in turn, have become stabilized breeds themselves. Even the most ordinary domestic cats have been formalized into stable pure breeds called the American Shorthair and the British Shorthair.

The old and natural breeds to which I refer are the *Abyssinian* and *Egyptian Mau*, which come from Egypt; *Birman*, from Burma; *Japanese Bobtail*, from Japan; *Siamese*, probably from Siam; *Burmese*, from Siam; the *Korat*, definitely from Siam; *Persian*, probably from Persia; the *Turkish Angora*, from Turkey; the *Maine Coon Cat*, from New England; the *Manx*, from the Isle of Man; and the *Russian Blue*, from Russia.

Later we will introduce you to twenty-six pure breeds, although there are others in the United States and throughout the world. These are the breeds that are officially sanctioned for registration and competition by the Cat Fanciers' Association, Inc. (CFA). This association is the largest in the world. It registers more cats and more catteries, and sponsors more cat shows than any other similar organization. There are six other registry associations in the United States and one in Canada. They are listed at the end of this section.

The Cat Fanciers' Association was organized in 1906 with the following goals: improving the breeds of cats; registering pedigrees of

237

cats and kittens; developing rules for cat shows; issuing licenses for cat shows held under their rules; and promoting the interests of breeders and exhibitors of all cats. Later, a most important objective was added—the promotion of the welfare of all cats.

CFA held its first shows in 1906, one in Buffalo and one in Detroit. In 1909 it published its first Stud Book and Register in the *Cat Journal.* CFA has no individual memberships. Breeders and exhibitors who are members of local clubs (such as the Empire Cat Club of New York City) simply become affiliated with the larger association. In this respect it uses much the same system as the American Kennel Club. By 1978 a total of 608 clubs from the United States, Canada and Japan were affiliated with the Cat Fanciers' Association. Well over 250 shows sponsored by CFA are held every year throughout the United States, Canada, Hawaii and Japan. Whether one considers cat shows a sport, a hobby or an avocation, certainly CFA and the other registries are the hub around which it all revolves.

Although it is not within the purview of this book to write about the many fascinating aspects of showing cats and the Cat Fancy as a whole, it certainly bears mentioning to the novice cat owner who may become interested as a result of the new family pet.

The showing of cats begins with the acquisition of a purebred animal, one with a pedigree registered with any of the eight registry associations. A kitten of show quality always costs more money than those of house pet quality and is almost always obtained from a breeder who is an active member of the Cat Fancy. The purpose of a cat show is to determine the best specimens of the various breeds and varieties. Each registry association has developed a set of "show standards" for every breed by which to evaluate competing cats at a show. The "standard" is based on an aesthetic ideal created over the years by the many members of the cat clubs associated with each respective breed. In other words, each breed has a highly developed set of physical and aesthetic characteristics set down on paper by the various associations as a guide for cat show judges, breeders, and exhibitors. All cats that compete in shows are measured against the "standards" created for their breeds; winning or losing depends on how each cat compares to the abstract notion of the ideal cat of the breed.

Within the "standards," a point-scoring system has been created for each physical aspect of the cat. Various parts of the head earn a given number of points, as do the body, coat and color. These point earnings vary from breed to breed. It is important to understand that no cat wins a championship without having a harmony of components

Richard H. Gebhardt, distinguished cat show judge and breeder. Here he judges a Blue Point *Siamese*.

that approach the ideal of its breed. The cat is judged on the way the individual aesthetics of its physicality relate to one another. The whole must be greater than the sum of its beautiful parts.

According to the CFA Show Standards, a cat's "condition" mirrors the total cat. Diet, care, environment, and heredity all play vital roles in producing a well-conditioned cat; every facet of the cat reflects the results of these important factors. The show cat should be in prime physical condition. It should be faultlessly clean. Grooming should enhance the beauty of the cat, emphasizing the nature of the breed. Well-balanced temperamentally, the show cat should be receptive to the judging procedure. A calm, stable disposition both enhances the cat and allows the judge to evaluate and display the cat to its best advantage. General health and vigor are reflected by clear eyes, shining coat and alert appearance. In movement, the cat will exhibit the characteristic grace and beauty natural to its breed. As a cat on exhibit is handled, the judge uses his or her hands to evaluate the size and shape of the bone structure, the muscle tone, and the basic conformation of the cat.

There are two kinds of shows: the Specialty show and the All-Breed show. Specialty shows are limited to one breed or a category of breeds such as Short-haired cats. The All-Breed show includes any number of breeds and the competition is divided into various classes. The Novice Class is for unaltered cats that have yet to win a first-place

Grand Premier Michele Louise is the perfect show cat . . . aloof, splendidly arrogant, a one-of-a-kind White Spay *Persian*.

Persian Gothic. Grand Champion Frederick the Great and protégé sit in immutable splendor as the chaotic cat show unravels about them. "Fritz" has seen it all before.

ribbon. The Open Class is the next step up for unaltered cats working their way toward a championship. The Champion Class is for those cats that have won the title Champion (the qualifications for which vary from association to association).

The Grand Champion Class is for unaltered cats that have amassed a given number of points and wins in other shows and have also earned the title Champion. There are corresponding classes for altered cats called Premiership. Other classes for non-Championship competition at cat shows include Any Other Variety, for cats and kittens having failed to meet their own breed requirements in some way; Provisional Breed, whole cats and kittens of a breed not *fully* recognized by a particular registering association; Household Pet, for cats and kittens of random-bred lineage or pure-bred lineage with a disqualifying fault for Championship competition; Kitten Class, for young cats over four months but not older than eight months of age. Obviously there is much more involved in cat shows than can be discussed here. (See "Suggested Reading," page 335.)

The requirements and qualifications for entering and winning at cat shows vary because they are governed by eight different national organizations, each sanctioning its own individual shows. The confusion can be dealt with only by becoming familiar with the rules of each organization on a one-by-one basis. At the end of this section you will find the names and addresses of each organization so that you may write to any one or all for their rules and regulations.

For those who are intrigued with the idea of purebred cats, and who might wish someday to become involved with the Cat Fancy, we present the following, the Official Show Standards of the Cat Fanciers' Association. Here you will find the aesthetic ideals for the twenty-six cat breeds that are currently recognized for registration and competition by the CFA. For further elucidation we have added a photograph of each breed and an Author's Note offering a bit of the breed's history and behavioral characteristics. The author's statements are delineated from the official CFA Show Standards by italics and must be attributed to him personally. A glossary of terms follows the CFA standards. One last note. The CFA Show Standards change every year. Even new breeds are added occasionally. Though the standards may vary slightly from year to year the essential features of each breed remain constant. The novice fancier should consult a serious cat breeder or a registry organization for the most up-to-date breed standards.

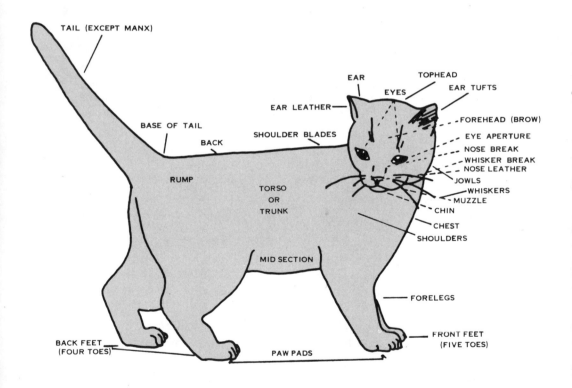

TAIL (EXCEPT MANX)

BASE OF TAIL

BACK

RUMP

SHOULDER BLADES

EAR LEATHER

EAR

EYES

TOPHEAD

EAR TUFTS

FOREHEAD (BROW)

EYE APERTURE

NOSE BREAK

WHISKER BREAK

NOSE LEATHER

JOWLS

WHISKERS

MUZZLE

CHIN

CHEST

SHOULDERS

TORSO
OR
TRUNK

MID SECTION

FORELEGS

BACK FEET
(FOUR TOES)

PAW PADS

FRONT FEET
(FIVE TOES)

Courtesy of the Cat Fanciers' Association, Inc. (CFA).

The Official Show Standards of the Cat Fanciers' Association, Inc.

ABYSSINIAN

AUTHOR'S NOTE—*The Abyssinian is probably an ancient breed but no one is certain. Everyone agrees that it came from Abyssinia (Ethiopia) or Egypt three or four thousand years ago. It may have descended from two small African wild cats. Some have written that it is descended from the ancient caffre cats or the sacred cats of Egypt. Any or all of the above possibilities could be true of these spirited, loving, perennially playful cats. An Aby was probably the first cat in history to appear in a painting, in an Egyptian tomb about four thousand years ago. Abyssinians were brought to the United States around the turn of the century.*

Point Score

Head (25)		Tail	5
Muzzle	6		
Skull	6	Coat (10)	
Ears	7	Texture	10
Eye shape	6		
		Color (35)	
Body (30)		Color	15
Torso	15	Ticking	15
Legs and feet	10	Eye color	5

GENERAL: The overall impression of the ideal Abyssinian would be a colorful cat of medium size giving the impression of eager activity and showing a lively interest in all surroundings. Lithe, hard and muscular. Sound health and general vigor. Well balanced temperamentally and physically; gentle and amenable to handling.

HEAD: A modified, slightly rounded wedge without flat planes; the brow, cheek and profile lines all showing a gentle contour. A slight rise from the bridge of the nose to the forehead, which should be of good size with width between the ears and flowing into the arched neck without a break.

MUZZLE: Not sharply pointed. Allowance to be made for jowls in adult males.

EARS: Alert, large, and moderately pointed; broad, and cupped at the base and set as though listening. Hair on ears very short and close-lying, preferably tipped with black or dark brown on a ruddy Abyssinian or chocolate brown on a red Abyssinian.

EYES: Almond-shaped, large, brilliant and expressive. Neither round nor Oriental. Eyes accentuated by dark lidskin, encircled by light-colored area.

BODY: Medium long, lithe and graceful, but showing well-developed muscular strength without coarseness. Abyssinian conformation strikes a medium between the extremes of the cobby and the svelte lengthy type. Proportion and general balance more to be desired than mere size.

Ruddy *Abyssinian,* male.

LEGS: Proportionately slim, fine boned.

PAWS: Small, oval and compact. When standing, giving the impression of being on tip-toe. Toes, five in front and four behind.

TAIL: Thick at base, fairly long and tapering.

COAT: Soft, silky, fine in texture, but dense and resilient to the touch with a lustrous sheen. Medium in length but long enough to accommodate two or three bands of ticking.

PENALIZE: Off-color pads. Long narrow head. Short round head. Barring on legs. Rings on tail. Coldness or grey tones in coat.

DISQUALIFY: White locket, or white anywhere other than nostril, chin, and upper throat area. Kinked or abnormal tail. Dark unbroken necklace. Grey-black hair with no ruddy undercoat. Any black hair on red Abyssinian. Incorrect number of toes.

Abyssinian Colors

RUDDY: Coat ruddy brown, ticked with various shades of darker brown or black; the extreme outer tip to be the darkest, with orange-brown undercoat, ruddy to the skin. Darker shading along spine allowed if fully ticked. Tail tipped with black and without rings. The undersides and forelegs (inside) to be a tint to harmonize with the main color. Preference given to *unmarked* orange-brown (burnt-sienna) color. *Nose Leather:* Tile red. *Paw Pads:* Black or brown, with black between toes and extending slightly beyond the paws. *Eye Color:* Gold or green, the more richness and depth of color the better.

RED: Warm, glowing red, distinctly ticked with chocolate brown. Deeper shades of red preferred. However, good ticking not to be sacrificed merely for depth of color. Ears and tail tipped with chocolate brown. *Nose Leather:* Rosy pink. *Paw Pads:* Pink, with chocolate brown between toes, extending slightly beyond paws. *Eye Color:* Gold or green, the more richness and depth of color the better.

AMERICAN SHORTHAIR

AUTHOR'S NOTE.—*No, the American Shorthair was not found here living with the Indians. It came over on the boat like millions of other immigrants. It is descended from the basic European working cat. However, the American Shorthair differs from all common cats in that it has been bred to meet breed standards that keep it strong, muscular, intelligent and lively.*

Point Score

Head (including size and shape of eyes, ear shape, and set and structure of nose)	30	Coat	15
		Color	20
		Eye color	10
Type (including shape, size, bone and length of tail)	25		

GENERAL: The American Shorthair is believed by some naturalists to be the original breed of domestic cat. It has for many, many centuries adapted itself willingly and cheerfully to the needs of man, but without allowing itself to become effete or its natural intelligence to diminish. Its disposition and habits are exemplary as a house pet, a pet and companion for children, but the feral instinct lies not too far beneath the surface and this breed of cat remains capable of self-sufficiency when the need arises. Its hunting instinct is so strong that it exercises the skill even when well provided with food. This is our only breed of true "working cat." The conformation of the breed is well adapted for this and reflects its refusal to surrender its natural functions. This is a cat lithe enough to stalk its prey, but powerful enough to make the kill easily. Its reflexes are under perfect control. Its legs are long enough to cope with any terrain and heavy and muscular enough for high leaps. The face is long enough to permit easy grasping by the teeth with jaws so powerful they can close against resistance. Its coat is dense enough to protect from moisture, cold and superficial skin injuries, but short enough and of sufficiently hard texture to resist matting or entanglement when slipping through heavy vegetation. No part of the anatomy is so exaggerated as to foster weakness. The general effect is that of the trained athlete, with all muscles rippling easily beneath the skin, the flesh lean and hard, and with great latent power held in reserve.

HEAD: Large, with full-cheeked face giving the impression of an oblong just slightly longer than wide.

NECK: Medium in length, muscular and strong.

NOSE: Medium in length, same width for entire length, with a gentle curve.

MUZZLE: Squared. Definite jowls in studs.

CHIN: Firm and well-developed, forming perpendicular line with upper lip.

EARS: Medium, slightly rounded at tips, set wide and not unduly open at base.

EYES: Round and wide with slight slant to outer aperture. Set well apart. Bright, clear and alert.

BODY: Medium to large, well-knit, powerful and hard with well-developed chest and heavy shoulders. No sacrifice of quality for the sake of mere size.

LEGS: Medium in length, firm-boned and heavily muscled, showing capability for easy jumping.

PAWS: Firm, full and rounded, with heavy pads. Toes: five in front, four behind.

TAIL: Medium long, heavy at base, tapering to an abrupt blunt end in appearance, but with normal tapering final vertebrae.

COAT: Short, thick, even and hard in texture. Somewhat heavier and thicker during the winter months.

PENALIZE: Excessive cobbiness or ranginess. Very short tail. Obesity or boniness.

DISQUALIFY: Deep nose break. Long or fluffy fur. Kinked or abnormal tail. Locket or button. Any appearance of hybridization with any other breed. Incorrect number of toes.

American Shorthair Colors

WHITE: Pure glistening white. *Nose Leather:* Pink. *Paw Pads:* Pink. *Eye Color:* Deep blue or brilliant gold. Odd-eyed whites shall have one blue and one gold eye with equal color depth.

BLACK: Dense coal black, sound from roots to tip of fur. Free from any tinge of rust on tips or smoke undercoat. *Nose Leather:* Black. *Paw Pads:* Black or brown. *Eye Color:* Brilliant gold.

BLUE: Blue, lighter shade preferred, one level tone from nose to tip of tail. Sound to the roots. A sound darker shade is more acceptable than an unsound lighter shade. *Nose Leather:* Blue. *Paw Pads:* Blue. *Eye Color:* Brilliant gold.

RED: Deep, rich, clear, brilliant red; without shading, markings, or ticking. Lips and chin the same color as coat. *Nose Leather:* Brick red. *Paw Pads:* Brick red. *Eye Color:* Brilliant gold.

CREAM: One level shade of buff cream, without markings. Sound to the roots. Lighter shades preferred. *Nose Leather:* Pink. *Paw Pads:* Pink. *Eye Color:* Brilliant gold.

CHINCHILLA: Undercoat pure white. Coat on back, flanks, head and tail sufficiently tipped with black to give the characteristic sparkling silver appearance. Legs may be slightly shaded with tipping. Chin and ear tufts, stomach and chest, pure white. Rims of eyes, lips and nose outlined with black. *Nose Leather:* Brick red. *Paw Pads:* Black. *Eye Color:* Green or blue-green.

SHADED SILVER: Undercoat white with a mantle of black tipping shading down from sides, face and tail from dark on the ridge to white on the chin, chest, stomach and under the tail. Legs to be the same tone as the face. The general effect to be much darker than a chinchilla. Rims of eyes, lips and nose outlined with black. *Nose Leather:* Brick red. *Paw Pads:* Black. *Eye Color:* Green or blue-green.

SHELL CAMEO (Red Chinchilla): Undercoat white, the coat on the back, flanks, head and tail to be sufficiently tipped with red to give the characteristic sparkling appearance. Face and legs may be very slightly shaded with tipping. Chin, ear tufts, stomach and chest white. *Nose Leather:* Rose. *Rims of Eyes:* Rose. *Paw Pads:* Rose. *Eye Color:* Brilliant gold.

SHADED CAMEO (Red Shaded): Undercoat white with a mantle of red tipping shading down the sides, face, and tail from dark on the ridge to white on the chin, chest, stomach, and under the tail. Legs to be the same tone as face. The general effect to be much redder than the Shell Cameo. *Nose Leather:* Rose. *Rims of Eyes:* Rose. *Paw Pads:* Rose. *Eye Color:* Brilliant gold.

BLACK SMOKE: White undercoat, deeply tipped with black. Cat in repose appears black. In motion the white undercoat is clearly apparent. Points and mask black with narrow band of white at base of hairs next to skin, which may be seen only when the fur is parted. *Nose Leather:* Black. *Paw Pads:* Black. *Eye Color:* Brilliant gold.

BLUE SMOKE: White undercoat, deeply tipped with blue. Cat in repose appears blue. In motion the white undercoat is clearly apparent. Points and mask blue, with narrow band of white at base of hairs next to skin, which may be seen only when fur is parted. *Nose Leather:* Blue. *Paw Pads:* Blue. *Eye Color:* Brilliant gold.

CAMEO SMOKE (Red Smoke): White undercoat, deeply tipped with red. Cat in repose appears red. In motion the white undercoat is clearly apparent. Points and mask red with narrow band of white at base of hairs next to skin, which may be seen only when fur is parted. *Nose Leather:* Rose. *Rims of Eyes:* Rose. *Paw Pads:* Rose. *Eye Color:* Brilliant gold.

TORTOISESHELL SMOKE: White undercoat deeply tipped with black with clearly defined, unbrindled patches of red- and cream-tipped hairs as in the pattern of the Tortoiseshell. Cat in repose appears Tortoiseshell. In motion, the white undercoat is clearly apparent. Face and ears Tortoiseshell pattern with narrow band of white at the base of the hairs next to the skin, which may be seen only when hair is parted. White ear tufts. *Eye Color:* Brilliant gold. Blaze of red or cream tipping on face is desirable.

CLASSIC TABBY PATTERN: Markings dense, clearly defined and broad. Legs evenly barred with bracelets coming up to meet the body markings. Tail evenly ringed. Several unbroken necklaces on neck and upper chest, the more the better. Frown marks on forehead form intricate letter "M." Unbroken line runs back from outer corner of eye. Swirls on cheeks. Vertical lines over back of head extend to shoulder markings, which are in the shape of a butterfly with both upper and lower wings distinctly outlined and marked with dots inside outline. Back markings consist of a vertical line down the spine from butterfly to tail with a vertical strip paralleling it on each side, the three stripes well separated by stripes of the ground color. Large solid blotch on each side to be encircled by one or more unbroken rings. Side markings should be the same on both sides. Double vertical row of buttons on chest and stomach.

MACKEREL TABBY PATTERN: Markings dense, clearly defined, and all narrow pencillings. Legs evenly barred with narrow bracelets coming up to meet the body markings. Tail barred. Necklaces on neck and chest distinct, like so many chains. Head barred with an "M" on

Silver Tabby
American Shorthair,
male.

the forehead. Unbroken lines running back from the eyes. Lines running down the head to meet the shoulders. Spine lines run together to form a narrow saddle. Narrow pencillings run around body.

PATCHED TABBY PATTERN: A Patched Tabby (Torbie) is an established silver, brown, or blue tabby with patches of red and/or cream.

BROWN PATCHED TABBY: Ground color brilliant coppery brown with classic or mackerel tabby markings of dense black with patches of red and/or cream clearly defined on both body and extremities; a blaze of red and/or cream on the face is desirable. Lips and chin the same shade as the rings around the eyes. *Eye Color:* Brilliant gold.

BLUE PATCHED TABBY: Ground color, including lips and chin, pale bluish ivory with classic or mackerel tabby markings of very deep blue affording a good contrast with ground color. Patches of cream clearly defined on both body and extremities; a blaze of cream on the face is desirable. Warm fawn overtones or patina over the whole. *Eye Color:* Brilliant gold.

SILVER PATCHED TABBY: Ground color, including lips and chin, pale silver with classic or mackerel tabby markings of dense black with patches of red and/or cream clearly defined on both body and extremities. A blaze of red and/or cream on the face is desirable. *Eye Color:* Brilliant gold or hazel.

SILVER TABBY: Ground color, including lips and chin, pale, clear silver. Markings dense black. *Nose Leather:* Brick red. *Paw Pads:* Black. *Eye Color:* Green or hazel.

RED TABBY: Ground color red. Markings deep rich red. Lips and chin red. *Nose Leather:* Brick red. *Paw Pads:* Brick red. *Eye Color:* Brilliant gold.

BROWN TABBY: Ground color brilliant coppery brown. Markings dense black. Lips and chin the same shades as the rings around the eyes. Back of leg black from paw to heel. *Nose Leather:* Brick red. *Paw Pads:* Black or brown. *Eye Color:* Brilliant gold.

BLUE TABBY: Ground color, including lips and chin, pale bluish ivory. Markings a very deep blue affording a good contrast with ground color. Warm fawn overtones or patina over the whole. *Nose Leather:* Old rose. *Paw Pads:* Rose. *Eye Color:* Brilliant gold.

CREAM TABBY: Ground color, including lips and chin, very pale cream. Markings of buff or cream sufficiently darker than the ground color to afford good contrast, but remaining within the dilute color range. *Nose Leather:* Pink. *Paw Pads:* Pink. *Eye Color:* Brilliant gold.

CAMEO TABBY: Ground color off-white. Markings red. *Nose Leather:* Rose. *Paw Pads:* Rose. *Eye Color:* Brilliant gold.

TORTOISESHELL: Black with unbrindled patches of red and cream. Patches clearly defined and well broken on both body and extremities. Blaze of red or cream on face is desirable. *Eye Color:* Brilliant gold.

CALICO: White with unbrindled patches of black and red. White predominant on underparts. *Eye Color:* Brilliant gold.

DILUTE CALICO: White with unbrindled patches of blue and cream. White predominant on underparts. *Eye Color:* Brilliant gold.

BLUE-CREAM: Blue with patches of solid cream. Patches clearly defined and well broken on both body and extremities. *Eye Color:* Brilliant gold.

BI-COLOR: White with unbrindled patches of black, or white with unbrindled patches of blue, or white with unbrindled patches of red, or white with unbrindled patches of cream. *Eye Color:* Gold, the more brilliant the better.

VAN BI-COLOR: Black and white, red and white, blue and white, cream and white. White cat with color confined to the extremities: head, tail, and legs. One or two small colored patches on body allowable.

VAN CALICO: White cat with unbrindled patches of black and red confined to the extremities: head, tail, and legs. One or two small colored patches on body allowable.

VAN BLUE-CREAM AND WHITE: White cat with unbrindled patches of blue and cream confined to the extremities: head, tail, and legs. One or two small colored patches on body allowable.

AMERICAN WIREHAIR

AUTHOR'S NOTE—*The spunky American Wirehair's origins can be traced to the very birthday of one cat, Council Rock Farm Adam of Hi-Fi, in 1966, in Verona, New York. He and his sister Tip-Toe were born with fur more like sheep wool than the traditional coats of their common cat parents. Since then they have been bred to type and have become an original American breed.*

Point Score

Head (including size and shape of eyes, ear shape and set)	25	Coat	45
		Color and eye color	10
Type (including shape, size, bone and length of tail)	20		

GENERAL: The American Wirehair is a spontaneous mutation. The coat, which is not only springy, dense, and resilient, but also coarse and hard to the touch, distinguishes the American Wirehair from all other breeds. It is characteristically active, agile, and keenly interested in its surroundings.

HEAD: In proportion to the body. Underlying bone structure is round with prominent cheekbones and well-developed muzzle and chin. There is a slight whisker break.

NOSE: In profile the nose shows a gentle concave curve.

MUZZLE: Well developed. Allowance for jowls in adult males.

CHIN: Firm and well developed with no apparent malocclusion.

EARS: Medium, slightly rounded at tips, set wide and not unduly open at the base.

EYES: Large, round, bright, and clear. Set well apart. Aperture has slight upward tilt.

BODY: Medium to large. Back level, shoulders and hips same width, torso well rounded and in proportion. Males larger than females.

Silver Mackerel Tabby *American Wirehair*, female.

LEGS: Medium in length and bone, well muscled and proportionate to body.

PAWS: Oval and compact.

TAIL: In proportion to body, tapering from the well-rounded rump to a rounded tip, neither blunt nor pointed.

COAT: Springy, tight, medium in length. Individual hairs are crimped, hooked, or bent, including hair within the ears. The overall appearance of wiring and the coarseness and resilience of the coat are more important than the crimping of each hair. The density of the wired coat leads to ringlet formation rather than waves. The coat, which is very dense, resilient, crimped, and coarse, is most desirable, as are curly whiskers.

PENALIZE: Deep nose break. Long or fluffy fur.

DISQUALIFY: Incorrect coat. Kinked or abnormal tail. Evidence of hybridization resulting in the colors chocolate, lavender, the Himalayan pattern, or these combinations with white.

American Wirehair Colors

White, Black, Blue, Red, Cream, Chinchilla, Shaded Silver, Shell Cameo, Shaded Cameo, Black Smoke, Blue Smoke, Cameo Smoke, Classic Tabby Pattern, Mackerel Tabby Pattern, Silver Tabby, Red Tabby, Brown Tabby, Blue Tabby, Cream Tabby, Cameo Tabby, Tortoiseshell, Calico, Dilute Calico, Blue-Cream, Bi-Color. *See American Shorthair for color definitions.*

OWC (OTHER WIREHAIR COLORS): Any other color or pattern with the exception of those showing evidence of hybridization resulting in the colors chocolate, lavender, the Himalayan pattern or these combinations with white, etc. *Eye Color:* Appropriate to the color of the cat.

BALINESE

AUTHOR'S NOTE—*The Balinese is also an American-created breed, but with a distinctly "foreign" background. In the early sixties they were considered mutant long-hair Siamese. They are now a recognized breed of their own, but they have not lost that gregarious Siamese character and gift of gab.*

Point Score

Head (20)		Legs and feet	5
Long flat profile	6	Tail	3
Wedge, fine muzzle, size	5		
Ears	4	Coat (20)	
Chin	3	Length	10
Width between eyes	2	Texture	10
Eyes (5)		Color (25)	
Shape, size, slant and		Body color	10
placement	5	Point color—matching	
		points of dense color,	
Body (30)		proper foot pads	
Structure and size, including		and nose leather	10
neck	12	Eye color	5
Muscle tone	10		

GENERAL: The ideal Balinese is a svelte, dainty cat with long, tapering lines, very lithe but strong and muscular. Excellent physical condition. Neither flabby nor bony. Not fat. Eyes clear. Because of the longer fur the Balinese appears to have softer lines and less extreme type than other breeds of cats with similar type.

HEAD: Long tapering wedge. Medium size in good proportion to body. The total wedge starts at the nose and flares out in straight lines to the tips of the ears forming a triangle, with no break at the whiskers. No less than the width of an eye between the eyes. When the whiskers and face hair are smoothed back, the underlying bone structure is apparent. Allowance must be made for jowls in the stud cat.

SKULL: Flat. In profile, a long straight line is seen from the top of the head to the tip of the nose. No bulge over the eyes. No dip in nose.

NOSE: Long and straight. A continuation of the forehead with no break.

MUZZLE: Fine, wedge-shaped.

CHIN AND JAW: Medium size. Tip of chin lines up with tip of nose in the same vertical plane. Neither receding nor excessively massive.

EARS: Strikingly large, pointed, wide at base, continuing the lines of the wedge.

EYES: Almond-shaped. Medium size. Neither protruding nor recessed. Slanted toward the nose in harmony with lines of wedge and ears. Uncrossed.

BODY: Medium size. Dainty, long, and svelte. A distinctive com-

Lilac Point *Balinese*, female (Ch. Gaynells Danae).

bination of fine bones and firm muscles. Shoulders and hips continue same sleek lines of tubular body. Hips never wider than shoulders. Abdomen tight.

NECK: Long and slender.

LEGS: Long and slim. Hind legs higher than front. In good proportion to body.

PAWS: Dainty, small, and oval. Toes, five in front and four behind.

TAIL: Bone structure long, thin, tapering to a fine point. Tail hair spreads out like a plume.

COAT: Long, fine, and silky without downy undercoat.

COLOR: *Body:* Even, with subtle shading when allowed. Allowance should be made for darker color in older cats as Balinese generally darken with age, but there must be definite contrast between body color and points. *Points:* Mask, ears, legs, feet, tail dense and clearly defined. All of the same shade. Mask covers entire face including whisker pads and is connected to ears by tracings. Mask should not extend over top of head. No ticking or white hairs in points.

PENALIZE: Lack of pigment in nose leather and/or paw pads in part or in total; crossed eyes.

DISQUALIFY: Any evidence of illness or poor health. Weak hind legs. Mouth breathing due to nasal obstruction or poor occlusion. Emaciation. Kink in tail. Eyes other than blue. White toes and/or feet. Incorrect number of toes. Definite double coat (*i.e.,* downy undercoat).

Balinese Colors

SEAL POINT: Body even pale fawn to cream, warm in tone, shading gradually into lighter color on the stomach and chest. Points deep seal brown. *Nose Leather:* Same color as points. *Paw Pads:* Same color as points. *Eye Color:* Deep vivid blue.

CHOCOLATE POINT: Body ivory with no shading. Points milk chocolate color, warm in tone. *Nose Leather:* Cinnamon-pink. *Paw Pads:* Cinnamon-pink. *Eye Color:* Deep vivid blue.

BLUE POINT: Body bluish white, cold in tone, shading gradually to white on stomach and chest. Points deep blue. *Nose Leather:* Slate-colored. *Paw Pads:* Slate-colored. *Eye Color:* Deep vivid blue.

LILAC POINT: Body glacial white with no shading. Points frosty grey with pinkish tone. *Nose Leather:* Lavender-pink. *Paw Pads:* Lavender-pink. *Eye Color:* Deep vivid blue.

Birman.

BIRMAN
(Sacred Cat of Burma)

AUTHOR'S NOTE—*The Birman comes to us from history and legend. They were the temple cats of Lao-Tsun and were much loved by the Buddhist priests. They have been called the Tibetan Temple Cats. Because two Europeans, August Pavie and Major Russell-Gordon, helped the priests escape Burma during a perilous time, they were given a pair of Birmans in 1919. The cats have been carefully nurtured in France since that time. They came to this country around 1960. The Birman is a unique, natural cat. It is not Siamese or Persian, although the color-points and long coat could lead one to think so. The white gloves on all four paws are a positive identification. The Birman is not just an object of beauty. It is very playful, intelligent and active, a family-loving cat.*

Point Score

Head (including size and shape of eyes, ear shape and set)	30	Coat	10
		Color	25
Type (including shape, size, bone and length of tail)	25	Eye color	10

HEAD: Skull strong, broad, and rounded. Forehead slopes back and is slightly convex. There is a slight flat spot just in front of the ears.

NOSE: Roman in shape, nostrils set low, length in proportion to size of head.

CHEEKS: Full. The fur is short in appearance about the face, but to the extreme outer area of the cheek, the fur is longer.

JAWS: Heavy.

CHIN: Full and well developed. Lower lip is strong, forming perpendicular lines with upper lip.

EARS: Medium in length. Almost as wide at the base as tall. Modified to a rounded point at the tip; set as much to the side as into the top of the head.

EYES: Almost round.

BODY: Long but stocky.

LEGS: Medium in length and heavy.

PAWS: Large, round and firm. Five toes in front, four behind.

TAIL: Medium in length, in pleasing proportion to the body.

COAT: Long, silken in texture, with heavy ruff around the neck, slightly curly on stomach. This fur is of such a texture that it does not mat.

COLOR: *Body:* Even, with subtle shading when allowed. Strong contrast between body color and points. *Points Except Paws:* Mask, ears, legs and tail dense and clearly defined, all of the same shade. Mask covers entire face including whisker pads and is connected to ears by tracings. No ticking or white hair in points. *Front Paws:* Front paws have white gloves ending in an even line across the paw at the third joint. *Back Paws:* White glove covers the entire paw and must end in a point, called the laces, that goes up the back of the hock.

PAW PADS: Pink preferred, but dark spot on toe pad acceptable because of the two colors in pattern.

EYES: Blue in color. The deeper blue the better. Almost round in shape.

PENALIZE: White that does not run across the front paws in an even line. Siamese-type head. White shading on stomach and chest.

DISQUALIFY: Lack of white gloves on any paw. Kinked or abnormal tail. Crossed eyes. Incorrect number of toes. Areas of pure white in the points, except paws.

Birman Colors

SEAL POINT: Body even pale fawn to cream, warm in tone, shading gradually to lighter color on the stomach and chest. Points, except for gloves, deep seal brown. Gloves pure white. *Nose Leather:* Same color as the points. *Paw Pads:* Pink. *Eye Color:* Blue, the deeper and more violet the better.

BLUE POINT: Body bluish white, cold in tone, shading gradually to almost white on stomach and chest. Points, except for gloves on paws, deep blue. Gloves pure white. *Nose Leather:* Slate-color. *Paw Pads:* Pink. *Eye Color:* Blue, the deeper and more violet the better.

CHOCOLATE POINT: Body ivory with no shading. Points, except for gloves on paws, milk chocolate color, warm in tone. Gloves pure white. *Nose Leather:* Cinnamon-pink. *Paw Pads:* Pink. *Eye Color:* Blue, the deeper and more violet the better.

LILAC POINT: Body a cold, glacial tone verging on white with no shading. Points, except for gloves, frosty grey with pinkish tone. Gloves pure white. *Nose Leather:* Lavender-pink. *Paw Pads:* Pink. *Eye Color:* Blue, the deeper and more violet the better.

Bombay (Grand Champion Shawnee Ai Ai of Sankachi). Courtesy of S. G. Sulloway and J. E. Kachler.

BOMBAY

AUTHOR'S NOTE—*The meeting of a Burmese and a black American Shorthair produced the first Bombay. This laconic lover was created in the fifties in America but it was named for the black leopards of India. Docile in manner, the Bombay is a soft-spoken, almost silent cat. It is always black with eyes that are always copper or gold.*

Point Score

Head and Ears (25)		Body	15
Roundness of head	7	Tail	5
Full face and proper profile	7		
Ears	7	Coat (20)	
Chin	4	Shortness	10
		Texture	5
Eyes (5)		Close-lying	5
Placement and shape	5	Color (30)	
		Body color	20
Body (20)		· Eye color	10

HEAD: The head should be pleasingly rounded with no sharp angles. The face should be full with considerable breadth between the eyes, tapering slightly to a short, well-developed muzzle. In profile there should be a visible nose break; however, it should not present a "pugged" or "snubbed" look.

EARS: The ears should be medium in size and set well apart on a rounded skull, alert, tilting slightly forward, broad at the base and with slightly rounded tips.

CHIN: The chin should be firm, neither receding nor protruding, reflecting a proper bite.

EYES: Set far apart with rounded aperture.

BODY: Medium in size, muscular in development, neither compact nor rangy. Allowance is to be made for larger size in males.

LEGS: In proportion to body and tail.

TAIL: Straight, medium in length; neither short nor "whippy."

COAT: Fine, short, satin-like texture; close-lying with a shimmering patent-leather sheen.

COLOR: The mature specimen should be black to the roots. Kitten coats should darken and become more sleek with age. *Nose Leather:* Black. *Paw Pads:* Black. *Eye Color:* Ranging from gold to copper, the greater the depth and brilliance the better.

DISQUALIFY: Kinked or abnormal tail. Lockets or spots. Incorrect number of toes. Nose leather or paw pads other than black. Green eyes. Improper bite. Extreme break that interferes with normal breathing and tearing of eyes.

BRITISH SHORTHAIR

AUTHOR'S NOTE—*The British Shorthair was created when the English began selectively breeding their pet cats in the nineteenth century. After World War I some Persian blood was added to create the luxurious, sophisticated cat we see today. The British Shorthair was given American citizenship in the seventies and we're happy to have it on these shores.*

Point Score

Head (25)

Muzzle and chin	5	Neck	5
Skull	5	Eye shape	5
Ears	5		

Body (35)   Color (20)
   Torso   20   Eye color   5
   Legs and paws   10   Coat color   15
   Tail   5

Coat (20)
   Texture, length and density   20

GENERAL: The British Shorthair cat is compact, well balanced and powerful, showing good depth of body, a full broad chest, short to medium strong legs, rounded paws, tail thick at base with a rounded tip. The head is round; round cheeks, firm chin, medium ears, large, round and well-opened eyes with a medium nose with a gentle dip. The coat is short and very dense.

HEAD: Round and massive. Round face with round underlying bone structure well set on a short, thick neck.

NOSE: Medium, broad. In profile there is a gentle dip.

CHIN: Firm and well developed. The distinctive muzzle is well developed with a definite stop beyond large round whisker pads.

EARS: Ear set is important, medium in size and set far enough apart that the inner base is perpendicular to the midline of the eye. Broad at base and rounded at the tips.

EYES: Large, round, well opened. Set wide apart and level.

BODY: Medium to large, well knit and powerful. Level back and a deep broad chest.

LEGS: Short to medium, well boned and strong.

PAWS: Round and firm. Toes: five in front and four behind.

TAIL: Short and thick, but in proportion to body length and rounded tip.

COAT: Short, very dense, well bodied, resilient and firm to the touch. Not double coated or woolly.

COLOR: For cats with special markings: 10 points for color and 10 points for markings. Shadow tabby markings in Solid Color, Smoke or Bi-Color kittens are not a fault.

PENALIZE: Definite nose stop. Overlong or light undercoat.*

DISQUALIFY: Incorrect eye color, green rims, tail defects. Long or fluffy coat, incorrect number of toes. Locket or button.*

---

* The above listed Penalties and Disqualifications apply to all British Shorthair cats. Additional penalties and disqualifications are listed under colors.

Silver spotted *British Shorthair*.

British Shorthair Colors

WHITE: Pure white, untipped with yellow. *Eye Color:* Deep sapphire blue, gold or copper. Odd-eyed whites shall have one deep sapphire blue and one gold with equal color depth. *Nose Leather:* Pink. *Paw Pads:* Pink.

BLACK: Jet black to roots, no rusty tinge, no white hair anywhere. *Eye Color:* Gold or copper with no trace of green. *Nose Leather:* Black. *Paw Pads:* Black or brown.

BLUE: Light to medium blue, lighter shade preferred, very level in color. Sound darker shade more acceptable than unsound lighter shade. No tabby markings or white anywhere. *Eye Color:* Gold or copper. *Nose Leather:* Blue. *Paw Pads:* Blue.

CREAM: Rich cream, lighter shades preferred, level in color, sound to the roots. No white anywhere. *Eye Color:* Gold or copper. *Nose Leather:* Pink. *Paw Pads:* Pink. *Disqualify:* Heavy tabby markings.

BLACK SMOKE: White or pale silver undercoat, deeply tipped with black. Cat in repose appears black; in motion the white or silver undercoat is clearly apparent. *Eye Color:* Gold or copper. *Nose Leather:* Black. *Paw Pads:* Black.

BLUE SMOKE: White or pale silver undercoat, deeply tipped with blue. Cat in repose appears blue; in motion the white or silver undercoat is clearly apparent. *Eye Color:* Gold or copper. *Nose Leather:* Blue. *Paw Pads:* Blue.

CLASSIC TABBY PATTERN: Markings dense, clearly defined, and broad. Legs evenly barred with bracelets coming up to meet the body markings. Tail evenly ringed. Several unbroken necklaces on neck and upper chest, the more the better. Frown marks on the forehead form an intricate letter M. An unbroken line runs back from the outer corner of the eye. Swirls on cheeks. Vertical lines over back of head extend to shoulder markings, which are in the shape of a butterfly with both upper and lower wings distinctly outlined and marked with dots inside outline. Back markings consist of a vertical stripe paralleling it on each side, the three stripes well separated by stripes of the ground color. Large solid blotch on each side to be encircled by one or more unbroken rings. Side markings should be the same on both sides. Double vertical row of buttons on chest and stomach.

MACKEREL TABBY PATTERN: Markings dense, clearly defined, and all narrow pencillings. Legs evenly barred with narrow bracelets coming up to meet the body markings. Tail barred. Necklaces on neck and chest distinct, like so many chains. Head barred with an M on the forehead. Unbroken lines back from the eyes. Lines running down the head to meet the shoulders. Spine lines run together to form a narrow saddle. Narrow pencillings run around body. *Penalize:* Brindling. *Disqualify:* White anywhere.

SILVER TABBY: Ground color, including lips and chin, pale clear silver. Markings dense black. *Eye Color:* Green or hazel. *Nose Leather:* Brick red. *Paw Pads:* Black.

RED TABBY: Ground color red, including lips and chin. Markings deep rich red. *Eye Color:* Gold or copper. *Nose Leather:* Brick red. *Paw Pads:* Brick red.

BROWN TABBY: Ground color brilliant coppery brown. Markings dense black. Lips and chin the same shade as the rings around the eyes. Back of leg black from paw to heel. *Eye Color:* Gold or copper. *Nose Leather:* Brick red. *Paw Pads:* Black or brown.

BLUE TABBY: Ground color, including lips and chin, pale bluish ivory. Markings a very deep blue affording a good contrast with ground color. Warm fawn overtones or patina over the whole. *Eye Color:* Gold or copper. *Nose Leather:* Old rose. *Paw Pads:* Rose.

CREAM TABBY: Ground color, including lips and chin, very pale cream. Markings of buff or cream sufficiently darker than the ground color to afford good contrast, but remaining within the dilute color range. *Eye Color:* Gold or copper. *Nose Leather:* Pink. *Paw Pads:* Pink.

SPOTTED TABBY PATTERN: Good, clear spotting is essential. The spots can be round, oblong, or rosette-shaped. Any of these are of equal merit but the spots, however shaped or placed, shall be distinct. *Head:* As Classic Tabby. *Body and Legs:* Good, clear spotting essential. *Tail:* Spots or broken rings desirable. *Color:* Silver with black spots, brown with black spots. Red with deep rich red spots. Any other recognized ground color acceptable with appropriate spotting. *Eye Color:* As for Classic Tabby. *Nose Leather and Paw Pads:* As for Classic Tabby. *Penalize:* Solid spine color line, brindling, markings not distinct and separate. *Disqualify:* White anywhere.

TORTOISESHELL: Black, red and cream, equally balanced, and each color to be as brilliant as possible. No white. Patches to be clear and defined, no blurring and no tabby or brindle markings. Legs, feet, tail, and ears to be as well patched as body and head. Red blaze desirable. *Eye Color:* Gold or copper. *Nose Leather:* Pink and/or black. *Paw Pads:* Pink and/or black. *Penalize:* Brindling, tabby markings, unbroken color on paws. Unequal balance of color. *Disqualify:* White anywhere.

TORTOISESHELL AND WHITE: Black, red, and cream on white, equally balanced. Colors to be brilliant and absolutely free from brindling or tabby markings. The tri-color patching should cover the top of the head, ears and cheeks, back and tail and part of the flanks. Patches to be clear and defined. White blaze desirable. *Eye Color:* Gold or copper. *Nose Leather:* Pink and/or black. *Paw Pads:* Pink and/or black. *Penalize:* Brindling, tabby markings, unbroken color on paws. Unequal balance of color. *Disqualify:* White predominating.

BLUE-CREAM: Blue and cream to be softly mingled. Not patched. *Eye Color:* Gold. *Nose Leather:* Blue and/or pink. *Paw Pads:* Blue and/or pink. *Penalize:* Tabby markings, unbroken color on paws. Solid patches of color. *Disqualify:* White anywhere.

BI-COLORS: Black and white, blue and white, red and white, cream and white. White blaze desirable. *Eye Color:* Gold or copper. *Penalize:* Brindling or tabby markings. *Disqualify:* White predominating.

BURMESE

AUTHOR'S NOTE—*Wong Mau of Burma was the mother of the entire American Burmese breed. She was brought to America in the thirties and mated with a Siamese for lack of another Burmese. The Cat-Book Poems, dating from the Ayudhya period of Siam (1350–1767), picture the Burmese on a page with the Siamese, the Korat, and a black cat with a white collar called the Singha-sep. The descendents of this historic line are all a gorgeous brown; they are gregarious and people-loving.*

Point Score

Head (25)			Legs and feet	5
Roundness of head	7		Tail	5
Breadth between eyes	4		Coat (10)	
Full face with proper profile	8		Short	4
Ear set and placement	6		Texture	4
Eyes (5)			Close lying	2
Placement and shape	5		Color (30)	
Body (30)			Body color	25
Torso	15		Eye color	5
Muscle tone	5			

GENERAL: The overall impression of the ideal Burmese would be a cat of medium size and rich solid color; with substantial bone structure, good muscular development and a surprising weight for its size. This, together with its expressive eyes and sweet face, presents a totally distinctive cat which is comparable to no other breed. Perfect physical condition, with excellent muscle tone. There should be no evidence of obesity, paunchiness, weakness, or apathy.

HEAD: Pleasingly rounded without flat planes whether viewed from front or side. Face full, with considerable breadth between the eyes, tapering slightly to a short, well-developed muzzle. In profile there should be a visible nose break.

EARS: Medium in size and set well apart on a rounded skull; alert, tilting slightly forward, broad at base with slightly rounded tips.

EYES: Set far apart and with rounded aperture.

Burmese, female.

BODY: Medium in size, muscular in development, and presenting a compact appearance. Allowance to be made for larger size in males. An ample, rounded chest, with back level from shoulder to tail.

LEGS: Well proportioned to body.

PAWS: Round. Toes: five in front and four behind.

TAIL: Straight, medium in length.

COAT: Fine, glossy, satin-like in texture; short and close lying.

COLOR: The mature specimen should be rich, warm sable brown; shading almost imperceptibly to a slightly lighter hue on the underparts, but otherwise without shadings or markings of any kind. *Nose Leather:* Brown. *Paw Pads:* Brown. *Eye Color:* Ranging from yellow to gold, the greater the depth and brilliance the better.

PENALIZE: Green eyes.

DISQUALIFY: Kinked or abnormal tail. Locket or button. Incorrect number of toes. Blue eyes.

*   *   *

COLORPOINT SHORTHAIR

AUTHOR'S NOTE—*To get a Colorpoint Shorthair one must cross-breed a Siamese with an American Shorthair of the desired color, say red or mackerel tabby. It takes several generations and a lot of know-how, but a Colorpoint is a stunning creature. Of course, once successful, two Colorpoints can be bred together to get offspring of the same color.*

Point Score

Head (20)		Muscle tone	10
Long flat profile	6	Legs and feet	5
Wedge, fine muzzle, size	5	Tail	3
Ears	4		
Chin	3	Coat (10)	
Width between eyes	2	Color (30)	
		Body color	10
Eyes (10)		Point color—matching points	
Shape, size, slant and		of dense color,	
placement	10	proper foot pads	
		and nose leather	10
Body (30)		Eye color	10
Structure and size,			
including neck	12		

GENERAL: A Colorpoint Shorthair is a separate breed. The type description and scale of points are the same as for the Siamese. A svelte, dainty cat with long tapering lines, very lithe, but muscular. Excellent physical condition. Eyes clear. Strong and supple. Neither flabby nor bony. Not fat.

HEAD: Long tapering wedge. Medium size in good proportion to body. The total wedge starts at the nose and flares out in straight lines to the tips of the ears forming a triangle, with no break at the whiskers. No less than the width of an eye between the eyes. When the whiskers are smoothed back, the underlying bone structure is apparent. Allowance must be made for jowls in the stud cat.

SKULL: Flat. In profile, a long straight line is seen from the top of the head to the tip of the nose. No bulge over eyes. No dip in nose.

NECK: Long and slender.

NOSE: Long and straight. A continuation of the forehead with no break.

MUZZLE: Fine, wedge-shaped.

EARS: Strikingly large, pointed, wide at base, continuing the lines of the wedge.

EYES: Almond-shaped. Medium size. Neither protruding nor recessed. Slanted toward the nose in harmony with lines of wedge and ears. Uncrossed.

CHIN AND JAW: Medium in size. Tip of chin lines up with tip of nose in the same vertical plane. Neither receding nor excessively massive.

BODY: Medium size. Dainty, long, and svelte. A distinctive combination of fine bones and firm muscles. Shoulders and hips continue same sleek lines of tubular body. Hips never wider than shoulders. Abdomen tight.

LEGS: Long and slim. Hind legs higher than front. In good proportion to body.

PAWS: Dainty, small, and oval. Toes: five in front and four behind.

TAIL: Long, thin, tapering to a fine point.

COAT: Short, fine-textured, glossy. Lying close to body.

COLOR: *Body:* Even, with subtle shading when allowed. Allowance should be made for darker color in older cats as Colorpoint Shorthairs generally darken with age, but there must be definite contrast between body color and points. *Points:* Mask, ears, feet, legs, and tail dense and clearly defined. All of the same shade. Mask covers entire face including whisker pads and is connected to ears by tracings. Mask should not extend over the top of the head. No ticking or white hairs in points.

PENALIZE: Lack of pigment in nose leather in part or in total.

DISQUALIFY: Any evidence of illness or poor health. Weak hind legs. Mouth breathing due to nasal obstruction or poor occlusion. Emaciation. Visible kink. Eyes other than blue. White toes and/or feet. Incorrect number of toes.

Colorpoint Shorthair Colors

RED POINT: Body clear white with any shading in the same tone as points. *Points:* Deep red, lack of barring desirable. *Nose Leather:* Flesh or coral pink. *Paw Pads:* Flesh or coral pink. *Eye Color:* Deep vivid blue.

CREAM POINT: Body clear white with any shading in the same tone as points. *Points:* Apricot, lack of barring desirable. *Nose Leather:* Flesh to coral pink. *Paw Pads:* Flesh to coral pink. *Eye Color:* Deep vivid blue.

Lynx Point *Colorpoint Shorthair*, female.

SEAL-LYNX POINT: Body cream or pale fawn, shading to lighter color on stomach and chest. Body shading may take form of ghost striping. *Points:* Seal brown bars, distinct and separated by lighter background color; ears seal brown with paler thumbprint in center. *Nose Leather:* Seal brown or pink edged in seal brown. *Paw Pads:* Seal brown. *Eye Color:* Deep vivid blue.

CHOCOLATE-LYNX POINT: Body ivory. Body shading may take form of ghost striping. *Points:* Warm milk-chocolate bars, distinct and separated by lighter background color; ears warm milk-chocolate with paler thumbprint in center. *Nose Leather:* Cinnamon or pink edged in cinnamon. *Paw Pads:* Cinnamon. *Eye Color:* Deep vivid blue.

BLUE-LYNX POINT: Body bluish white to platinum grey, cold in tone, shading to lighter color on stomach and chest. Body shading may take form of ghost striping. *Points:* Deep blue-grey bars, distinct and separated by lighter background color; ears deep blue-grey with paler thumbprint in center. *Nose Leather:* Slate-colored or pink edged in slate. *Paw Pads:* Slate-colored. *Eye Color:* Deep vivid blue.

LILAC-LYNX POINT: Body glacial white. Body shading may take form of ghost striping. *Points:* Frosty grey with pinkish tone bars, distinct and separated by lighter background color; ears frosty grey with pinkish tone, paler thumbprint in center. *Nose Leather:* Lavender-pink or pink edged in lavender-pink. *Paw Pads:* Lavender-pink. *Eye Color:* Deep vivid blue.

RED-LYNX POINT: Body white. Body shading may take form of ghost striping. *Points:* Deep red bars, distinct and separated by lighter background color; ears deep red, paler thumbprint in center. *Nose Leather:* Flesh or coral pink. *Paw Pads:* Flesh or coral pink. *Eye Color:* Deep vivid blue.

SEAL-TORTIE POINT: Body pale fawn to cream, shading to lighter color on stomach and chest. Body color is mottled with cream in older cats. *Points:* Seal brown, uniformly mottled with red and cream; a blaze is desirable. *Nose Leather:* Seal brown to match point color; flesh or coral pink mottling permitted where there is a blaze. *Paw Pads:* Seal brown to match point color; flesh or coral pink mottling permitted where the point color mottling extends into the paw pads. *Eye Color:* Deep vivid blue.

CHOCOLATE-CREAM POINT: Body ivory, mottled in older cats. *Points:* Warm milk-chocolate uniformly mottled with cream; a blaze is desirable. *Nose Leather:* Cinnamon; flesh or coral pink mottling permitted where there is a blaze. *Paw Pads:* Cinnamon; flesh or coral pink mottling permitted where the point color mottling extends into the paw pads. *Eye Color:* Deep vivid blue.

BLUE-CREAM POINT: Body bluish white to platinum grey, cold in tone, shading to lighter color on stomach and chest. Body color is mottled in older cats. *Points:* Deep blue-grey uniformly mottled with cream; a blaze is desirable. *Nose Leather:* Slate-colored; flesh or coral pink mottling permitted where there is a blaze. *Paw Pads:* Slate-colored; flesh or coral pink mottling permitted where the point color mottling extends into the paw pads. *Eye Color:* Deep vivid blue.

LILAC-CREAM POINT: Body glacial white, mottling if any in the shade of the points. *Points:* Frosty grey with pinkish tone, uniformly mottled with pale cream; a blaze is desirable. *Nose Leather:* Lavender-pink; flesh or coral pink mottling permitted where there is a blaze. *Paw Pads:* Lavender-pink; flesh or coral pink mottling permitted where the point color mottling extends into the paw pads. *Eye Color:* Deep vivid blue.

EGYPTIAN MAU

AUTHOR'S NOTE—*The Egyptian Mau is the sedate spotted cat from ancient Egypt. It shares in common with its more active Abyssinian cousin a birdlike quality of voice. Both cats also appear frequently in ancient paintings and religious symbols. The Egyptian retains a hint of the wild from which it most likely came. It has that supposedly typical catlike quality of aloof reserve, making close friends with only a special few; a rare cat indeed.*

Point Score

Head (20)		Coat (10)	
Muzzle	5	Texture and length	10
Skull	5		
Ears	5	Pattern (25)	
Eye shape	5		
		Color (20)	
Body (25)		Eye color	5
Torso	10	Coat color	15
Legs and feet	10		
Tail	5		

GENERAL: The Egyptian Mau is the only natural domesticated breed of spotted cat. The Mau conformation strikes a balance between the heftiness of the cobby and the sveltness of the Oriental types. Its overall impression should be one of an active, colorful cat of medium size, with well-developed muscles. Perfect physical condition with an alert appearance. Well balanced physically and temperamentally.

HEAD: A modified, slightly rounded wedge without flat planes, the brow, cheek and profile all showing a gentle contour. A slight rise from the bridge of the nose to the forehead, which then flows into the arched neck without a break. Allowance to be made for broad heads in adult males.

MUZZLE: Not pointed. Allowance to be made for jowls in adult males.

EARS: Alert, large, and moderately pointed, broad at base and upstanding, with ample width between ears. Hair on ears short and close lying. Inner ear a delicate, almost transparent, shell pink, and may be tufted.

EYES: Large and alert, almond-shaped, with slight slant toward the ears. Skull apertures neither round nor Oriental.

BODY: Medium long and graceful, showing well-developed muscular strength. General balance is more to be desired than size alone. Allowance to made for very muscular necks and shoulders in adult males.

LEGS AND FEET: In proportion to body. Hind legs proportionately longer, giving the appearance of being on tip-toe when standing upright. Feet small and dainty, slightly oval, almost round in shape. Toes: five in front and four behind.

Egyptian Mau.

TAIL: Medium long, thick at base, with slight taper.

COAT: Silky and fine in texture but dense and resilient to the touch with a lustrous sheen. Hair medium in length but long enough to accommodate two or more bands of ticking, separated by lighter bands.

PENALIZE: Short or round head. Pointed muzzle. Small ears. Small, round or Oriental eyes. Cobby or Oriental body. Short or whip tail. Spots on body which run together. Poor condition.

DISQUALIFY: Lack of spots. Wrong eye color. Tail kink.

Mau Pattern (Common to All Colors)

PATTERN: Good contrast between pale ground color and deeper markings. Forehead barred with characteristic "M" and frown marks, forming lines between the ears that continue down the back of the neck, ideally breaking into elongated spots along the spine. As the spinal lines reach the rear haunches, they meld together to form a dorsal stripe, which continues along the top of the tail to its tip. The tail is heavily banded and has a dark tip. The cheeks are barred with "mascara" lines; the first starts at the outer corner of the eye and continues along the contour of the cheek, with a second line, which starts at the center of the cheek and curves upward, almost meeting below the base of the ear. On the upper chest there are one or more necklaces, preferably broken in the center. The shoulder markings are a transition between stripes and spots. The upper front legs are heavily barred but do not necessarily match. Markings on the body are to be randomly spotted with variance in size and shape; round, evenly distributed spots are preferred. Spotting pattern on each side of the body may not match, but spots should not run together in a broken, mackerel pattern. Haunches and upper hind legs to be a transition of spots and stripes, breaking into bars on the thighs and back to elongated spots on the lower leg. Underside of body to have "vest button" spots, dark in color against the correspondingly pale ground color.

COLORS: All colors compete within one color class.

EYE COLOR: Light green "gooseberry green" preferred, amber cast acceptable. Allowance to be made for slow eye color development in young adults.

SILVER: Pale silver ground color across the head, shoulders, outer legs, back and tail. Underside fades to a brilliant pale silver. All markings charcoal color, showing good contrast against lighter ground colors. Back of ears greyish-pink and tipped in black. Nose, lips, and eyes outlined in black. Upper throat area, chin and around nostrils pale clear silver, appearing white. *Nose Leather:* Brick red. *Paw Pads:* Black, with black between the toes and extending beyond the paws of the hind legs.

BRONZE: Light bronze ground color across head, shoulders, outer legs, back and tail, being darkest on the saddle and lightening to a tawny buff on the sides. Underside fades to a creamy ivory. All markings dark brown, showing good contrast against the lighter ground color. Back of ears tawny pink and tipped in dark brown. Nose, lips, and eyes outlined in dark brown, with bridge of nose ocherous. Upper throat area, chin, and around nostrils pale creamy white. *Nose Leather:* Brick red. *Paw Pads:* Black or dark brown, with same color between toes and extending beyond the paws of the hind legs.

SMOKE: Charcoal grey color with silver undercoat across head, shoulders, legs, tail and underside. All markings jet black, with sufficient contrast against ground color for pattern to be plainly visible. Nose, lips, and eyes outlined in jet black. Upper throat area, chin, and around nostrils lightest in color. *Nose Leather:* Black. *Paw Pads:* Black with black between the toes and extending beyond the paws of the hind legs.

EXOTIC SHORTHAIR

AUTHOR'S NOTE—*The Exotic Shorthair looks like a Persian with short hair. In the sixties the Persian was crossed with the American Shorthair. The result is a sweet, gentle cat with a sharp wit and a plush coat.*

Point Score

Head (including size and shape of eyes, ear shape and set)	30	Coat	20
		Color	20
Type (including shape, size, bone and length of tail)	20	Eye color	10

HEAD: Round and massive, with great breadth of skull. Round face with round underlying bone structure. Well set on a short, thick neck.

NOSE: Short, snub, and broad. With break.

CHEEKS: Full.

JAWS: Broad and powerful.

CHIN: Full and well developed.

EARS: Small, round-tipped, tilted forward, and not unduly open at the base. Set far apart, and low on the head, fitting into (without distorting) the rounded contour of the head.

EYES: Large, round and full. Set far apart and brilliant, giving a sweet expression to the face.

BODY: Of cobby type, low on the legs, deep in the chest, equally massive across shoulders and rump, with a short, well-rounded middle piece. Large or medium in size. Quality the determining consideration rather than size.

BACK: Level.

LEGS: Short, thick and strong. Forelegs straight.

PAWS: Large, round and firm. Toes carried close, five in front and four behind.

TAIL: Short, but in proportion to body length. Carried without a curve and at an angle lower than the back.

COAT: Dense, plush, soft in texture, full of life. Stands out from body due to density, not flat or close-lying. Medium in length, slightly longer than other shorthairs but not long enough to flow.

DISQUALIFY: Locket or button. Kinked or abnormal tail. Incorrect number of toes.

Exotic Shorthair Colors

White, Black, Blue, Red, Cream, Chinchilla, Shaded Silver, Shell Cameo, Shaded Cameo, Black Smoke, Blue Smoke, Cameo Smoke, Classic Tabby Pattern, Mackerel Tabby Pattern, Patched Tabby Pattern, Brown Patched Tabby, Blue Patched Tabby, Silver Patched Tabby, Silver Tabby, Red Tabby, Brown Tabby, Blue Tabby, Cream Tabby, Cameo Tabby, Tortoiseshell, Calico, Dilute Calico, Blue-Cream, Bi-Color, Van Bi-Color, Van Calico, Van Blue-Cream and White. *See American Shorthair for color definitions. Also:*

CHINCHILLA GOLDEN: Undercoat rich warm cream. Coat on back, flanks, head and tail sufficiently tipped with seal brown to give golden appearance. Legs may be slightly shaded with tipping. Chin and ear tufts, stomach and chest, cream. Rims of eyes, lips, and nose outlined with seal brown. *Nose Leather:* Deep rose. *Paw Pads:* Seal brown. *Eye Color:* Green or blue-green.

SHADED GOLDEN: Undercoat rich warm cream with a mantle of seal brown tipping shading down from sides, face and tail from dark on the ridge to cream on the chin, chest, stomach, and under the tail.

Cream tabby *Exotic Shorthair*, female.

Legs to be the same tone as the face. The general effect to be much darker than a Chinchilla. Rims of eyes, lips, and nose outlined with seal brown. *Nose Leather:* Deep rose. *Paw Pads:* Seal brown. *Eye Color:* Green or blue-green.

SHELL TORTOISESHELL: Undercoat white. Coat on the back, flanks, head, and tail to be delicately tipped in black and well-defined patches of red- and cream-tipped hairs as in the pattern of the Tortoiseshell [see American Shorthair]. Face and legs may be slightly shaded with tipping. Chin, ear tufts, stomach, and chest white to very slightly tipped. Blaze of red or cream tipping on face is desirable. *Eye Color:* Brilliant copper.

SHADED TORTOISESHELL: Undercoat white. Mantle of black tipping and clearly defined patches of red- and cream-tipped hairs as in the pattern of the Tortoiseshell [see American Shorthair]. Shading down the sides, face, and tail from dark on the ridge to slightly tipped or white on the chin, chest, stomach, legs, and under the tail. The general effect is to be much darker than the Shell Tortoiseshell. Blaze of red or cream tipping on the face is desirable. *Eye Color:* Brilliant copper.

SMOKE TORTOISESHELL: White undercoat, deeply tipped with black, with clearly defined, unbrindled patches of red- and cream-tipped hairs as in the pattern of the Tortoiseshell [see American Shorthair]. Cat in repose appears Tortoiseshell. In motion, the white undercoat is clearly apparent. Face and ears Tortoiseshell pattern with narrow band of white at the base of the hairs next to the skin that may be seen only when hair is parted. White ruff and ear tufts. Blaze of red or cream tipping on face is desirable. *Eye Color:* Brilliant copper.

Note: Cats possessing more than a couple of small body spots should be shown in the regular Bi-Color class.

HAVANA BROWN

AUTHOR'S NOTE—*The Havana Brown is actually brown. They were arduously bred in the fifties from Siamese, Russian Blues and black Shorthairs to achieve that beautiful brown coat. This is a bright, active love of a cat that looks much like a Burmese. When getting to know members of the breed, one discovers them to be quite distinctive from other breeds. They are affectionate and playful and make ideal pets.*

Point Score

Head	20	Whiskers	5
Coat	10	Body and neck	15
Color (40)		Eyes	5
Coat color, paw pads, nose		Legs and feet	5
leather	25	Tail	5
Eyes	10		

GENERAL: The overall impression of the ideal Havana Brown is a cat of medium size with a rich, solid color and good muscle tone. Due to its distinctive muzzle shape, color and large forward-tilted ears, it is comparable to no other breed.

HEAD: The head is slightly longer than it is wide, with a distinct stop at the eyes. The break at the whisker pad is about the same width overall. A strong chin forms a straight line with the nose. Allowance will be made for stud jowls in the male.

COAT: The coat is medium in length, smooth, and lustrous.

BODY AND NECK: Body and neck are medium in length, firm and

Havana Brown.

muscular. The general conformation is mid-range between the short-coupled, thick-set and svelte breeds.

EYES: Oval-shaped.

EARS: Ears are large, wide set, round-tipped, slightly tilted forward, not flaring, giving an alert appearance. They have little hair inside or out.

LEGS AND FEET: Medium in length, ending in oval paw pads.

TAIL: Medium to medium-long, tapering.

COLOR: Rich, warm, mahogany-toned brown. Solid to the roots; free from tabby markings or barring in the adult. *Nose Leather:* Brown with a rosy cast. *Paw Pads:* Having a rosy tone. *Eyes:* Ranging from chartreuse to green with the greener shades preferred. *Whiskers:* Brown complementing the coat.

DISQUALIFY: Kinked tail; locket or button; incorrect eye, whisker, nose leather or paw pad color.

HIMALAYAN

AUTHOR'S NOTE—*The Himalayan looks like a colorpoint Persian. To the rest of the world it is a Colorpoint Longhair or a Persian, but in the United States it is a Himalayan. They were crossbred in the fifties from the Persian and the Siamese. Since both the long Persian hair and the Siamese colorpoints are recessive traits, it was a difficult task. Mrs. Marguerita Goforth gets the credit. She named them for other similarly colored animals, as the Himalayan rabbit. Mrs. Goforth kept the beautiful Persian fur, the beautiful Persian voice and body, and the special Siamese color and sense of humor. Here is a bright, quick-to-learn, yet docile cat.*

Point Score

Head (including size and shape		Body color	10
of eyes, ear shape		Point color	10
and set)	30	Eye color	10
Type (including shape, size,		Balance	5
bone, and length of tail)	20	Refinement	5
Coat	10		

HEAD: Round and massive, with great breadth of skull. Round face with round underlying bone structure. Well set on a short, thick neck.

NOSE: Short, snub and brown. With "break."

CHEEKS: Full.

JAWS: Broad and powerful.

CHIN: Full and well developed.

EARS: Small, round-tipped, tilted forward, and not unduly open at the base. Set far apart, and low on the head, fitting into (without distorting) the rounded contour of the head.

EYES: Large, round and full. Set far apart and brilliant, giving a sweet expression to the face.

BODY: Of cobby type—low on the legs, deep in the chest, equally massive across shoulders and rump, with a short, well-rounded middle piece. Large or medium in size. Quality the determining consideration rather than size.

BACK: Level.

LEGS: Short, thick and strong. Forelegs straight.

PAWS: Large, round and firm. Toes carried close, five in front and four behind.

TAIL: Short, but in proportion to body length. Carried without a curve and at an angle lower than the back.

COAT: Long and thick, standing off from the body. Of fine texture, glossy and full of life. Long all over the body, including the shoulders. The ruff immense and continuing in a deep frill between the front legs. Ear and toe tufts long. Brush very full.

Blue Point
Himalayan, male.

COLOR: *Body:* Even, free of barring with subtle shading when allowed. Allowance to be made for darker coloring on older cats. Shading should be subtle with definite contrast between points. *Points:* Mask, ears, legs, feet, tail dense and clearly defined. All of the same shade, and free of barring. Mask covers entire face including whisker pads and is connected to ears by tracings. Mask should not extend over top of head. No ticking or white hairs in points.

PENALIZE: Lack of pigment in nose leather and/or paw pads in part or in total. Any resemblance to Peke-Face.

DISQUALIFY: Locket or button. Any tail abnormality. Crossed eyes. Incorrect number of toes. White toes. Eyes other than blue. Apparent weakness in hindquarters. Deformity of skull and/or mouth.

Himalayan Colors

SEAL POINT: Body even pale fawn to cream, warm in tone, shading gradually into lighter color on the stomach and chest. *Points:* Deep seal brown. *Nose Leather:* Same color as points. *Paw Pads:* Same color as points. *Eye Color:* Deep vivid blue.

CHOCOLATE POINT: Body ivory with no shading. *Points:* Milk-chocolate color, warm in tone. *Nose Leather:* Cinnamon pink. *Paw Pads:* Cinnamon pink. *Eye Color:* Deep vivid blue.

BLUE POINT: Body bluish white, cold in tone, shading gradually to white on stomach and chest. *Points:* Blue. *Nose Leather:* Slate-colored. *Paw Pads:* Slate-colored. *Eye Color:* Deep vivid blue.

LILAC POINT: Body glacial white with no shading. *Points:* Frosty grey with pinkish tone. *Nose Leather:* Lavender-pink. *Paw Pads:* Lavender-pink. *Eye Color:* Deep vivid blue.

FLAME (RED) POINT: Body creamy white. *Points:* Delicate orange flame. *Nose Leather:* Flesh or coral pink. *Paw Pads:* Flesh or coral pink. *Eye Color:* Deep vivid blue.

CREAM POINT: Body creamy white with no shading. *Points:* Buff cream with no apricot. *Nose Leather:* Flesh pink or salmon coral. *Paw Pads:* Flesh pink or salmon coral. *Eye Color:* Deep vivid blue.

TORTIE POINT: Body creamy white or pale fawn. *Points:* Seal brown with unbrindled patches of red and cream. Blaze of red or cream on face is desirable. *Nose Leather:* Seal brown with flesh and/or coral pink mottling to conform with colors of points. *Paw Pads:* Seal brown with flesh and/or coral pink mottling to conform with colors of points. *Eye Color:* Deep vivid blue.

BLUE-CREAM POINT: Body bluish white or creamy white, shading gradually to white on the stomach and chest. *Points:* Blue with patches of cream. *Nose Leather:* Slate blue, pink, or a combination of slate blue and pink. *Paw Pads:* Slate blue, pink or a combination of slate blue and pink. *Eye Color:* Deep vivid blue.

JAPANESE BOBTAIL

AUTHOR'S NOTE—*Japan has had a cat for centuries on the streets, in the houses and temples, and recorded in the art of Japanese culture. It is a Japanese Bobtail. The Japanese love the tricolors best because they bring good luck. They call them Mi-Ke and keep little good-luck replicas of them with a paw raised. These cats can be recognized by their charming personalities and, of course, by their bobbed tails, which can be any shape imaginable.*

Point Score

Head	20	Color and markings	20
Type	30	Coat	10
Tail	20		

GENERAL: The Japanese Bobtail should present the overall impression of a medium-sized cat with long clean lines and bone structure, well-muscled but straight and slender rather than massive in build. The unique set of its eyes, combined with high cheekbones and a long parallel nose, lend a distinctive Japanese cast to the face, especially in profile, quite different from the other Oriental breeds. According to the CFA standards, its short tail should resemble a bunny tail with the hair fanning out in all directions to create a pom-pom appearance, which effectively camouflages the underlying bone structure of the tail.

HEAD: Although the head appears long and finely chiselled, it forms almost a perfect equilateral triangle with gentle curving lines, high cheekbones, and a noticeable whisker break, the nose long and well defined by two parallel lines from tip to brow with a gentle dip at, or just below, eye level.

EARS: Large, upright and expressive, set wide apart but at right angles to the head rather than flaring outward, and giving the impression of being tilted forward in repose.

MUZZLE: Fairly broad and rounding into the whisker break; neither pointed nor blunt.

Japanese Bobtail.

EYES: Large, oval rather than round, but wide and alert; set into the skull at a rather pronounced slant when viewed in profile. The eyeball shows a shallow curvature and should not bulge out beyond the cheekbone or the forehead.

BODY: Medium in size, long and lean but shapely and well muscled.

LEGS: In keeping with the body, long, slender and high, but not dainty or fragile in appearance; the hind legs noticeably longer than the forelegs, but deeply angulated or bent when the cat is standing relaxed so that the torso remains nearly level rather than rising toward the rear. When standing, the cat's forelegs and shoulders form two continuous straight lines close together.

PAWS: Oval. Toes: five in front and four behind.

COAT: Medium length, soft and silky but without a noticeable undercoat. Relatively non-shedding.

TAIL: The furthest extension of the tailbone from the body should be approximately two to three inches, even though the tailbone, if straightened out to its full length, might be four or five inches long. The tail is usually carried upright when the cat is relaxed. Hair on tail somewhat longer and thicker than body hair, growing outward in all directions to create a pom-pom or bunny-tail effect, which appears to commence at the base of the spine and which camouflages the underlying bone structure of the tail. The tailbone is usually strong and rigid rather than jointed (except at the base), and may be either straight or composed of one or several curves and angles.

COLOR: In keeping with Japan's traditional Mi-Ke (mee-kay) cats, which are tri-colored (black, red, and white), the preferred breeding colors are those that tend to produce tri-colored females. In bi-colors and tri-colors, any color may predominate, with preference given to bold, dramatic markings and vividly contrasting colors. Nose leather, paw pads, and eye color should harmonize generally with coat color.

PENALIZE: Short round head, cobby build.

DISQUALIFY: Tailbone absent or extending too far beyond body; tail lacking in pom-pom or fluffy appearance; delayed bobtail effect (*i.e.*, the pom-pom being preceded by an inch or two of normal tail with close-lying hair, rather than appearing to commence at the base of the spine).

Japanese Bobtail Colors

WHITE: Pure glistening white.

BLACK: Dense, coal black, sound from roots to tip of fur. Shiny and free from any tinge of rust on tips.

RED: Deep, rich, clear, brilliant red, the deeper and more glowing in tone the better.

BLACK AND WHITE.

RED AND WHITE.

MI-KE (**Tri-Color**): Black, red, and white, or tortoiseshell with white.

TORTOISESHELL: Black, red, and cream.

OTHER JAPANESE BOBTAIL COLORS (OJBC) include the following categories and any other color or pattern or combination thereof except coloring that is point-restricted (*i.e.*, Siamese markings) or unpatterned agouti (*i.e.*, Abyssinian coloring). "Patterned" categories denote and include any variety of tabby striping or spotting with or without areas of solid (unmarked) color, with preference given to bold, dramatic markings and rich, vivid coloring. *Other Solid Colors:* Blue or cream. *Patterned Self-Colors:* Red, black, blue, cream, silver, or brown. *Other Bi-Colors:* Blue and white or cream and white. *Patterned Bi-Colors:* Red, black, blue, cream, silver, or brown combined with white. Patterned Tortoiseshell: Blue-cream. Patterned Blue-cream. *Dilute Tri-Colors:* Blue, cream, and white. *Patterned Dilute Tri-Colors:* Patterned Mi-Ke (Tri-Color).

KORAT

AUTHOR'S NOTE—*The silver-blue Korat is the native cat of the Korat Province of Thailand. In fact it is the true Siamese cat, since the colorpoint Siamese breed was probably imported to Siam by the royal family. Like the Japanese Bobtails, these cats are considered good luck. Sometime before the eighteenth century the Korat was described and pictured in* The Cat-Book Poems, *now in the Bangkok National Museum. It is therefore one of the oldest recorded breeds in history. They aren't very talkative, but these cats are keenly aware of everything in their surroundings. They are alert, attentive and listen to everything going on.*

Point Score

Head (23)			Body (25)	
Broad head	5		Body	15
Profile	5		Legs and feet	5
Breadth between eyes	5		Tail	5
Ear set and placement	5		Coat (12)	
Chin and jaw	3			
			Short	4
			Texture	4
Eyes (15)			Close lying	4
Size	5		Color (25)	
Shape	5		Body color	20
Placement	5		Eye color	5

GENERAL: The Korat is a rare cat even in Thailand, its country of origin. Because of its unusually fine disposition, it is greatly loved by the Thai people, who regard it as a "good luck" cat. Its general appearance is of a silver-blue cat with a heavy silver sheen, medium-sized, hard-bodied, and muscular. All smooth curves with huge eyes, luminous, alert, and expressive. Perfect physical condition, alert appearance.

HEAD: When viewed from the front, or looking down from just back of the head, the head is heart-shaped with breadth between and across the eyes. The eyebrow ridges forming the upper curves of the heart, and the sides of the face gently curving down to the chin, complete the heart shape. Undesirable: Any pinch or narrowness, especially between or across the eyes.

NOSE: Well-defined profile with a slight stop between forehead and nose, which has a lion-like downward curve just above leather. Undesirable: Nose that appears either long or short in proportion to the head.

CHIN AND JAW: Strong and well developed, making a balancing line for the profile and properly completing the heart shape. Neither overly squared nor sharply pointed, nor a weak chin that gives the head a pointed look.

EARS: Large, with a rounded tip and large flare at base, set high on head, giving an alert expression. Inside ears sparsely furnished. Hairs on outside of ears extremely short and close.

BODY: Semi-cobby (that is, neither short-coupled like the Manx nor long like the Siamese), muscular, supple, with a feeling of hard-coiled "spring" power and unexpected weight. Back carried in a curve. Males, renowned in Thailand for their prowess as fighters, must look the part—powerful and fit. Females should be smaller and dainty; medium and curved describe the body size and shape.

LEGS: Well proportioned to body. Distance along back from nape of neck to base of tail appears to be equal to distance from base of tail to floor. Front legs slightly shorter than back legs.

PAWS: Oval. Toes: five in front and four behind.

TAIL: Medium in length, heavier at the base, tapering to a rounded tip. Non-visible kink permitted.

Korat, female.

EYES: Large and luminous. Particularly prominent with an extraordinary depth and brilliance. Wide open and oversized for the face. Eye aperture, which shows as well rounded when fully open, has an Asian slant when closed or partially closed. Undesirable: Small or dull-looking eyes.

COAT: Single. Hair is short to medium in length, glossy and fine, lying close to the body. The coat over the spine is inclined to break as the cat moves.

COLOR: Silver-blue all over, tipped with silver, the more silver tipping the better. Without shading or tabby markings. Where the coat is short, the sheen of the silver is intensified. Undesirable: Coats with silver tipping on only the head, legs, and feet. *Nose Leather:* Dark blue or lavender. *Lips:* Dark blue or lavender. *Paw Pads:* Dark blue ranging to lavender with a pinkish tinge. *Eye Color:* Luminous green preferred, amber cast acceptable. Kittens and adolescents have yellow or amber to amber-green eyes. Color is not usually true until the cat is mature, usually two to four years of age.

DISQUALIFY: Visible kink. Incorrect number of toes. White spot or locket. Any color but silver blue.

MAINE COON

AUTHOR'S NOTE—*No cat ever mated with a raccoon, but the Maine Coon Cat often looks as if it did. The brown tabby varieties have rings on their big bushy tails like raccoon's. The people of Maine began Maine Coon contests in the 1860s in Skowhegan and in 1895 won Best Cat at Madison Square Garden. After a long hiatus, the breed was revived in the fifties. These large cats have heavy coats (for the Maine weather) and almost snowshoe feet for the winter. Their humorous personalities are perfect for the long New England winter evenings.*

Point Score

Head (30)		Legs and feet	5
Shape	15	Tail	5
Ears	10		
Eyes	5	Coat (20)	
Body (35)		Color (15)	
Shape	20	Body color	10
Neck	5	Eye color	5

GENERAL: Originally a working cat, the Maine Coon is solid, rugged and can endure a harsh climate. A distinctive characteristic is its smooth, shaggy coat. With an essentially amiable disposition, it has adapted to varied environments.

HEAD SHAPE: Medium in width and medium-long in length with a squareness to the muzzle. Allowance should be made for broadening in older studs. Cheekbones high. Chin firm and in line with nose and upper lip. Nose medium-long in length; slight concavity when viewed in profile.

EARS: Large, well-tufted, wide at base, tapering to appear pointed. Set high and well apart.

EYES: Large, wide set. Slightly oblique setting.

NECK: Medium-long.

BODY SHAPE: Muscular, broad-chested. Size medium to large. Females may be smaller than males. The body should be long with all parts in proportion to create a rectangular appearance. Allowance should be made for slow maturation.

LEGS AND FEET: Legs substantial, wide set, of medium length and in proportion to the body. Paws large, round, well-tufted. Five toes in front; four in back.

TAIL: Long, wide at base and tapering. Fur long and flowing.

COAT: Heavy and shaggy; shorter on the shoulders and longer on the stomach and britches. Frontal ruff desirable. Texture silky with coat falling smoothly.

PENALIZE: A coat that is short or even overall.

DISQUALIFY: Delicate bone structure. Undershot chin. Crossed eyes. Kinked tail. Incorrect number of toes. Buttons, lockets, or spots.

Maine Coon Cat Colors

EYE COLOR: Eye color should be shades of green, gold, or copper, though white cats may also be either blue- or odd-eyed. There is no relationship between eye color and coat color.

Solid Color Class

WHITE: Pure glistening white. *Nose Leather:* Pink. *Paw Pads:* Pink.

BLACK: Dense coal black, sound from roots to tip of fur. Free from any tinge of rust on tips or smoke undercoat. *Nose Leather:* Black. *Paw Pads:* Black or brown.

BLUE: One level tone from nose to tip of tail. Sound to the roots. *Nose Leather:* Blue. *Paw Pads:* Blue.

RED: Deep, rich, clear, brilliant red; without shading, markings or ticking. Lips and chin the same color as coat. *Nose Leather:* Brick red. *Paw Pads:* Brick red.

CREAM: One level shade of buff cream, without markings. Sound to the roots. *Nose Leather:* Pink. *Paw Pads:* Pink.

Tabby Color Class

CLASSIC TABBY PATTERN: Markings dense, clearly defined and broad. Legs evenly barred with bracelets coming up to meet the body markings. Tail evenly ringed. Several unbroken necklaces on neck and upper chest, the more the better. Frown marks on forehead form intricate letter "M." Unbroken line runs back from outer corner of eye. Swirls on cheeks. Vertical lines over back of head extend to shoulder markings, which are in the shape of a butterfly with both upper and lower wings distinctly outlined and marked with dots in-

Maine Coon, female.

side outline. Back markings consist of a vertical line down the spine from butterfly to tail with a vertical stripe paralleling it on each side, the three stripes well separated by stripes of the ground color. Large solid blotch on each side to be encircled by one or more unbroken rings. Side markings should be the same on both sides. Double vertical row of buttons on chest and stomach.

MACKEREL TABBY PATTERN: Markings dense, clearly defined and all narrow pencillings. Legs evenly barred with narrow bracelets coming up to meet the body markings. Tail barred. Necklaces on neck and chest distinct, like so many chains. Head barred with an "M" on the forehead. Unbroken lines running back from the eyes. Lines running down the head to meet the shoulders. Spine lines run together to form a narrow saddle. Narrow pencillings run around the body.

SILVER TABBY: Ground color pale, clear silver. Markings dense black. White trim around lip and chin allowed. *Nose Leather:* Brick red desirable. *Paw Pads:* Black desirable.

RED TABBY: Ground color red. Markings deep, rich red. White trim around lip and chin allowed. *Nose Leather:* Brick red desirable. *Paw Pads:* Brick red desirable.

BROWN TABBY: Ground color brilliant coppery brown. Markings dense black. Back of leg black from paw to heel. White trim around lip and chin allowed. *Nose Leather:* Brick red desirable. *Paw Pads:* Black or brown desirable.

BLUE TABBY: Ground color pale, bluish ivory. Markings a very deep blue affording a good contrast with ground color. Warm fawn overtones or patina over the whole. White trim around lip and chin allowed. *Nose Leather:* Old rose desirable. *Paw Pads:* Rose desirable.

CREAM TABBY: Ground color very pale cream. Markings of buff or cream sufficiently darker than the ground color to afford good contrast, but remaining within the dilute range. White trim around lip and chin allowed. *Nose Leather:* Pink desirable. *Paw Pads:* Pink desirable.

CAMEO TABBY: Ground color off-white. Markings red. *Nose Leather:* Rose. *Paw Pads:* Rose.

PATCHED TABBY PATTERN: A Patched Tabby (torbie) is an established silver, brown, or blue tabby with patches or red and/or cream.

Tabby with White Class

TABBY WITH WHITE: Color as defined for Tabby with or without white on the face. Must have white on bib, belly, and all four paws.

White on one-third of body is desirable. Colors accepted are silver, red, brown, blue, and cream.

PATCHED TABBY WITH WHITE (Torbie with White): Color as described for Patched Tabby (torbie) but with distribution of white markings as described in Tabby with White. ("Color as described for Patched Tabby [Torbie] with or without white on face. Must have white on bib, belly, and all four paws. White on one-third of body desirable.") Colors to be accepted are silver, brown and blue.

Parti-Color Class

TORTOISESHELL: Black with unbrindled patches of red and cream. Patches clearly defined and well broken on both body and extremities. Blaze of red or cream on face is desirable.

TORTOISESHELL WITH WHITE: Color as defined for Tortoiseshell with or without white on the face. Must have white on bib, belly, and all four paws. White on one-third of body is desirable.

CALICO: White with unbrindled patches of black and red. White predominant on underparts.

DILUTE CALICO: White with unbrindled patches of blue and cream. White predominant on underparts.

BLUE-CREAM: Blue with patches of solid cream. Patches clearly defined and well broken on both body and extremities.

BI-COLOR: A combination of a solid color with white. The colored areas predominate, with the white portions being located on the face, chest, belly, legs, and feet. Colors accepted are red, black, blue, and cream.

Other Maine Coon Colors Class

CHINCHILLA: Undercoat pure white. Coat on back, flanks, head and tail sufficiently tipped with black to give the characteristic sparkling silver appearance. Legs may be slightly shaded with tipping. Chin and ear tufts, stomach and chest, pure white. *Rims of Eyes, Lips and Nose:* Outlined with black. *Nose Leather:* Brick red. *Paw Pads:* Black.

SHADED SILVER: Undercoat white with a mantle of black tipping shading down from sides, face and tail from dark on the ridge to white on the chin, chest, stomach and under the tail. Legs to be the same tone as the face. The general effect to be much darker than a chinchilla. *Rims of Eyes, Lips and Nose:* Outlined with black. *Nose Leather:* Brick red. *Paw Pads:* Black.

SHELL CAMEO (Red Chinchilla): Undercoat white, the coat on the back, flanks, head and tail to be sufficiently tipped with red to give the characteristic sparkling appearance. Face and legs may be very slightly shaded with tipping. Chin, ear tufts, stomach and chest, white. *Nose Leather:* Rose. *Rims of Eyes:* Rose. *Paw Pads:* Rose.

SHADED CAMEO (Red Shaded): Undercoat white with a mantle of red tipping shading down the sides, face, and tail from dark on the ridge to white on the chin, chest, stomach, and under the tail. Legs to be the same tone as face. The general effect to be much redder than the Shell Cameo. *Nose Leather:* Rose. *Rims of Eyes:* Rose. *Paw Pads:* Rose.

BLACK SMOKE: White undercoat, deeply tipped with black. Cat in repose appears black. In motion the white undercoat is clearly apparent. Points and mask black with narrow band of white at base of hairs next to skin, which may be seen only when the fur is parted. Light silver frill and ear tufts. *Nose Leather:* Black. *Paw Pads:* Black.

BLUE SMOKE: White undercoat, deeply tipped with blue. Cat in repose appears blue. In motion the white undercoat is clearly apparent. Points and mask blue, with narrow band of white hairs next to skin, which may be seen only when fur is parted. White frill and ear tufts. *Nose Leather:* Blue: *Paw Pads:* Blue.

CAMEO SMOKE (Red Smoke): White undercoat, deeply tipped with red. Cat in repose appears red. In motion the white undercoat is clearly apparent. Points and mask red with narrow band of white at base of hairs next to skin, which may be seen only when fur is parted. White frill and ear tufts. *Nose Leather:* Rose. *Rims of Eyes:* Rose. *Paw Pads:* Rose.

MALAYAN

AUTHOR'S NOTE—*The Malayan is separated from its twin, the Burmese, by color only. It is the most recently accepted breed by the CFA (1980). The Burmese comes in a sable brown, while the Malayans are color dilutions in shades of Champagne (a warm, honey beige with slight shadings), blue (a soft grey tinged with beige), and platinum (a mother-of-pearl color combining soft shades of silver, mauve and fawn). They share with the Burmese a compact, sturdy, bulldog appearance and surprising weight for their size. In temperament they*

*are strong-willed and expect their owners to provide a cuddly lap
and lots of affection—which they return full measure. Although registered as a separate breed, Malayans occur naturally out of Burmese
parents and may have Burmese littermates.*

Point Score

Head (25)			Legs and feet	5
Roundness of head	7		Tail	5
Breadth between eyes	4			
Full face with proper profile	8		Coat (10)	
Ear set and placement	6		Short	4
			Texture	4
Eyes (5)			Close lying	2
Placement and shape	5			
			Color (30)	
Body (30)			Body color	25
Torso	15		Eye color	5
Muscle tone	5			

GENERAL: The overall impression of the ideal Malayan would be
a cat of medium size and rich solid color; with substantial bone structure, good muscular development and a surprising weight for its size.
Perfect physical condition with excellent muscle tone. There should
be no evidence of obesity, paunchiness, weakness or apathy.

HEAD: Pleasingly rounded without flat planes whether viewed
from front or side. Face full, with considerable breadth between the
eyes, tapering slightly to a short, well-developed muzzle. In profile
there should be a visible nose break.

EARS: Medium in size and set well apart on a rounded skull; alert,
tilting slightly forward, broad at base with slightly rounded tips.

EYES: Set far apart and with rounded aperture.

BODY: Medium in size, muscular in development, and presenting
a compact appearance. Allowance to be made for larger size in males.
An ample, rounded chest, with back level from shoulder to tail.

LEGS: Well proportioned to body.

PAWS: Round. Toes: five in front and four behind.

TAIL: Straight, medium in length.

COAT: Fine, glossy, satin-like in texture, short and close lying.

PENALIZE: Green eyes.

DISQUALIFY: Kinked or abnormal tail. Locket or button. Incorrect
number of toes. Blue eyes.

Malayan Colors

CHAMPAGNE: The mature specimen should be a warm honey beige, shading to a pale gold-tan underside. Slight darkening on ears and face permissible but lesser shading preferred. A slight darkening in older specimens allowed, the emphasis being on evenness of color. *Nose Leather:* Light warm brown. *Paw Pads:* Warm pinkish tan. *Eye Color:* Ranging from yellow to gold, the greater the depth and brilliance the better.

BLUE: The mature specimen should be a medium blue with warm fawn undertones, shading almost imperceptibly to a slightly lighter hue on the underparts, but otherwise without shadings or markings of any kind. *Nose Leather:* Slate grey. *Paw Pads:* Slate grey. *Eye Color:* Ranging from yellow to gold, the greater the depth and brilliance the better.

PLATINUM: The mature specimen should be a pale, silvery grey with pale fawn undertones, shading almost imperceptibly to a slightly lighter hue on the underparts, but otherwise without shadings or markings of any kind. *Nose Leather:* Lavender-pink. *Paw Pads:* Lavender-pink. *Eye Color:* Ranging from yellow to gold, the greater the depth and brilliance the better.

Malayan.

MANX

AUTHOR'S NOTE—*The cats from the Isle of Man in the Irish Sea have no tails. The Manx also have long, powerful hind legs and double coats that distinguish them from other breeds. They are very distinctive in appearance. As a matter of fact, there are Manx with tails; those with the longest tails are called "Taily," then "Stumpy," "Riser" and a pure tailless "Rumpy." The tailed cats are important because when "Rumpies" are bred together for three generations the kittens do not survive. Manx are wonderful mousers and are said to be good swimmers.*

Point Score

Head and ears	25	Legs and feet	15
Eyes	5	Coat	10
Body	25	Color and markings	5
Taillessness	15		

GENERAL: The overall impression of the Manx cat is that of roundness: round head with firm, round muzzle and prominent cheeks, broad chest, substantial short front legs, short back which arches from shoulders to a round rump, great depth of flank, and rounded, muscular thighs. The heavy, glossy double coat accentuates the round appearance. With regard to condition, the Manx presented in the show ring should evidence a healthy physical appearance, feeling firm and muscular, neither too fat nor too lean. The Manx should be alert, clear of eye, with a glistening, clean coat.

HEAD AND EARS: Round head with prominent cheeks and a jowly appearance. Head is slightly longer than it is broad. Moderately rounded forehead, pronounced cheekbones and jowliness (jowliness more evident in adult males) enhance the round appearance. Definite whisker break, with large, round whisker pads. In profile there is a gentle nose dip. Well-developed muzzle, slightly longer than broad, with a strong chin. Short, thick neck. Ears wide at the base, tapering gradually to a rounded tip, with sparse interior furnishings. Medium in size in proportion to the head, widely spaced and set slightly outward.

EYES: Large, round and full, set at a slight angle toward the nose (outer corners slightly higher than inner corners). Ideal eye color conforms to requirements of coat color.

BODY: Solidly muscled, compact and well balanced, medium in size with sturdy bone structure. The Manx is stout in appearance, with broad chest and well-sprung ribs; surprisingly heavy when lifted. The constant repetition of curves and circles gives the Manx the appearance of great substance and durability, a cat that is powerful without the slightest hint of coarseness. Males may be somewhat larger than females. Flank (fleshy area of the side between the ribs and hip) has greater depth than in any other breed, causing considerable depth to the body when viewed from the side. The short back forms a smooth, continuous arch from shoulders to rump, curving at the rump to form the desirable round look. Shortness of back is unique to the Manx, but is in proportion to the entire cat and may be somewhat longer in the male.

TAILLESSNESS: Absolute in the perfect specimen, with a decided hollow at the end of the backbone where, in the tailed cat, a tail would begin. A rise of the bone at the end of the spine is allowed and should not be penalized unless it is such that it stops the judge's hand, thereby spoiling the tailless appearance of the cat. The rump is extremely broad and round.

LEGS AND FEET: Heavily boned, forelegs short and set well apart to emphasize the broad, deep chest. Hind legs much longer than forelegs, with heavy, muscular thighs and substantial lower legs. Longer hind legs cause the rump to be considerably higher than the shoulders. Hind legs are straight when viewed from behind. Paws are neat and round, with five toes in front and four behind.

COAT: Double coat is short and dense, with a well-padded quality due to the longer, open outer coat and the close, cottony undercoat. Texture of outer guardhairs is somewhat hard; appearance is glossy. Coat may be thicker during cooler months of the year.

TRANSFER TO AOV [ANY OTHER VARIETY]: Definite, visible tail joint; long, silky coat.

DISQUALIFY: Evidence of poor physical condition; incorrect number of toes; evidence of hybridization; weak hindquarters causing inability to stand or walk properly.

Manx Colors

White, Black, Blue, Red, Cream, Chinchilla, Shaded Silver, Black Smoke, Blue Smoke, Classic Tabby Pattern, Mackerel Tabby Pattern, Patched Tabby Pattern, Brown Patched Tabby, Blue Patched Tabby, Silver Patched Tabby, Silver Tabby, Red Tabby, Brown Tabby, Blue

Tabby, Cream Tabby, Tortoiseshell, Calico, Dilute Calico, Blue-Cream. *See American Shorthair for color definitions, but where the American Shorthair Eye Color reads "Brilliant gold" or "gold," Manx Eye Color should read "Brilliant copper" or "copper."*

BI-COLOR: White with unbrindled patches of black, or white with unbrindled patches of blue, or white with unbrindled patches of red, or white with unbrindled patches of cream. Cats with no more white than a locket and/or button do not qualify for this color class. Such cats shall be judged in the color class of their basic color with no penalty for such locket and/or button. *Eye Color:* Brilliant copper.

OMC (OTHER MANX COLORS): Any other color or pattern with the exception of those showing hybridization resulting in the colors chocolate, lavender, the Himalayan pattern, or these combinations with white, etc. *Eye Color:* Appropriate to the predominant color of the cat.

White *Manx*, female.

ORIENTAL SHORTHAIR

AUTHOR'S NOTE—*The Oriental Shorthair was created by cross-ing the Siamese with shorthair solid colors and Russian Blues. It is a Siamese cat that is "self-colored," which means solid-colored with no point color contrast. The most popular colors are those of the Siamese points, such as chocolate or lilac. There is even an all-lavender-tone Siamese cat. This hybrid breed includes many coat varieties. It is quite similar in nature to the Siamese; however, it is felt that its voice is softer.*

Point Score

Head (25)		Muscle tone	5
Long, flat profile	7	Legs and feet	5
Wedge, fine muzzle, size	6	Tail	3
Ears	5		
Chin	4	Coat (10)	
Width between eyes	3	Color (30)	
Eyes (10)		Body color, uniform density	
		of coloring, proper foot	
Shape, size, slant, and		pads, and nose leather	20
placement	10	Eye color	10
Body (25)			
Structure and size, including			
neck	12		

GENERAL: The ideal Oriental Shorthair is a svelte cat with long, tapering lines, very lithe but muscular. Excellent physical condition. Eyes clear. Neither bony nor flabby. Not fat.

HEAD: Long tapering wedge, in good proportion to body. The total wedge starts at the nose and flares out in straight lines to the tips of the ears forming a triangle, with no break at the whiskers. No less than a width of an eye between the eyes. When the whiskers are smoothed back, the underlying bone structure is apparent. Allowance must be made for jowls in the stud cat.

SKULL: Flat. In profile, a long straight line is seen from the top of the head to the tip of the nose. No bulge over eyes. No dip in nose.

NOSE: Long and straight. A continuation of the forehead with no break.

MUZZLE: Fine, wedge-shaped.

CHIN AND JAW: Medium size. Tip of chin lines up with tip of nose in the same vertical plane. Neither receding nor excessively massive.

EARS: Strikingly large, pointed, wide at the base, continuing the lines of the wedge.

EYES: Almond-shaped, medium size. Neither protruding nor recessed. Slanted toward the nose in harmony with lines of wedge and ears. Uncrossed.

BODY: Long and svelte. A distinctive combination of fine bones and firm muscles. Shoulders and hips continue the same sleek lines of tubular body. Hips never wider than shoulders. Abdomen tight. Males may be somewhat larger than females.

NECK: Long and slender.

LEGS: Long and slim. Hind legs higher than front. In good proportion to body.

PAWS: Dainty, small and oval. Toes: five in front and four behind.

TAIL: Long, thin at the base and tapered to a fine point.

COAT: Short, fine-textured, glossy, lying close to body.

PENALIZE: Crossed eyes.

EYE COLOR: Green. White Orientals may have blue or green eye color, but not odd-eye.

DISQUALIFY: Any evidence of illness or poor health. Weak hind legs. Mouth breathing due to nasal obstruction or poor occlusion. Emaciation. Visible kink. Miniaturization. Lockets and buttons.

Oriental Shorthair Colors

Solid Colors Class

WHITE: Pure glistening white. *Nose Leather* and *Paw Pads:* Pink.

EBONY: Dense coal black, sound from roots to tip of fur. Free from any tinge of rust on tips or smoke undercoat. *Nose Leather:* Black. *Paw Pads:* Black or brown.

BLUE: Blue, lighter shade preferred, one level tone from nose to tip of tail. Sound to the roots. A sound darker shade is more acceptable than an unsound lighter shade. *Nose Leather:* Blue. *Paw Pads:* Blue.

CHESTNUT: Rich chestnut brown, sound throughout. *Whiskers* and *Nose Leather:* Same color as coat. *Paw Pads:* Cinnamon.

LAVENDER: Frost grey with a pinkish tone, sound and even throughout. *Nose Leather* and *Paw Pads:* Lavender pink.

RED: Deep, rich, clear, brilliant red; without shading, markings or ticking. Lips and chin the same color as coat. *Nose Leather:* Brick red. *Paw Pads:* Brick red.

CREAM: One level shade of buff cream, without markings. Sound to the roots. Lighter shades preferred. *Nose Leather:* Pink. *Paw Pads:* Pink.

CARAMEL: Light caramel, sound throughout. *Whiskers, Nose Leather* and *Paw Pads:* Same as coat color.

Shaded Colors Class

EBONY SILVER: Undercoat white. Coat on back, flanks, head and tail sufficiently tipped with ebony to give the characteristic sparkling appearance. Face and legs may be shaded with tipping. Rims of eyes, lips, and nose outlined with ebony tipping color. *Nose Leather:* Brick red. *Paw Pads:* Black.

BLUE SILVER: Undercoat white. Coat on back, flanks, head and tail sufficiently tipped with blue to give the characteristic sparkling appearance. Face and legs may be shaded with tipping. Rims of eyes, lips and nose outlined with blue tipping color. *Nose Leather:* Old rose. *Paw Pads:* Rose.

CHESTNUT SILVER: Undercoat white. Coat on back, flanks, head and tail sufficiently tipped with chestnut to give the characteristic sparkling appearance. Face and legs may be shaded with tipping. Rims of eyes, lips and nose outlined with chestnut tipping color. *Nose Leather:* Pink. *Paw Pads:* Cinnamon.

LAVENDER SILVER: Undercoat white. Coat on back, flanks, head and tail sufficiently tipped with lavender to give the characteristic sparkling appearance. Face and legs may be shaded with tipping. Rims of eyes, lips and nose outlined with lavender tipping color. *Nose Leather:* Pink. *Paw Pads:* Lavender-pink.

CAMEO: Undercoat white. Coat on the back, flanks, head and tail sufficiently tipped with red to give the characteristic sparkling appearance. Face and legs may be shaded with tipping. *Nose Leather:* Rose. *Paw Pads:* Rose.

Smoke Colors Class

EBONY SMOKE: White undercoat, deeply tipped with black. Cat in repose appears black. In motion the white undercoat is clearly apparent. Points and mask, black with narrow band of white at base of hairs next to skin, which may be seen only when the fur is parted. *Nose Leather:* Black. *Paw Pads:* Black.

BLUE SMOKE: White undercoat, deeply tipped with blue. Cat in repose appears blue. In motion the white undercoat is clearly apparent. Points and mask blue, with narrow band of white at base of hairs next to skin, which may be seen only when fur is parted. *Nose Leather:* Blue. *Paw Pads:* Blue.

CHESTNUT SMOKE: White undercoat, deeply tipped with chestnut brown. Cat in repose appears chestnut brown. In motion the white undercoat is clearly apparent. Points and mask chestnut brown, with narrow band of white at base of hairs next to skin, which may be seen only when fur is parted. *Nose Leather:* Chestnut. *Paw Pads:* Cinnamon.

LAVENDER SMOKE: White undercoat, deeply tipped with lavender. Cat in repose appears lavender. In motion the white undercoat is clearly apparent. Points and mask lavender with narrow band of white at base of hairs next to skin, which may be seen only when fur is parted. *Nose Leather:* Lavender-pink. *Paw Pads:* Lavender-pink.

CAMEO SMOKE (Red Smoke): White undercoat, deeply tipped with red. Cat in repose appears red. In motion the white undercoat is clearly apparent. Points and mask red with narrow band of white at base of hairs next to skin, which may be seen only when fur is parted. *Nose Leather:* Rose. *Rims of Eyes:* Rose. *Paw Pads:* Rose.

PARTI-COLOR SMOKE: White undercoat deeply tipped with ebony, chestnut, blue or lavender with clearly defined, unbrindled patches of red- and cream-tipped hairs as in the pattern of the Parti-color [see below]. Cat in repose appears Parti-color. In motion, the white undercoat is clearly apparent. Face and ears Parti-color pattern with narrow band of white at the base of the hairs next to the skin, which may be seen only when hair is parted. Blaze of red or cream tipping on face is desirable.

Tabby Colors Class

CLASSIC TABBY PATTERN: Markings dense, clearly defined and broad. Legs evenly barred with bracelets coming up to meet the body markings. Tail evenly ringed. Several unbroken necklaces on neck and upper chest, the more the better. Frown marks on forehead form intricate letter "M." Unbroken line runs back from outer corner of eye. Swirls on cheeks. Vertical lines over back of head extend to shoulder markings, which are in the shape of a butterfly with both upper and lower wings distinctly outlined and marked with dots inside outline. Back markings consist of a vertical line down the spine from butterfly to tail with a vertical stripe paralleling it on each side, the three stripes well separated by stripes of the ground color. Large solid blotch on each side to be encircled by one or more unbroken rings. Side markings should be the same on both sides. Double vertical row of buttons on chest and stomach.

MACKEREL TABBY PATTERN: Markings dense, clearly defined, and all narrow pencillings. Legs evenly barred with narrow bracelets coming up to meet the body markings. Tail barred. Necklaces on neck and chest distinct, like so many chains. Head barred with an "M" on the forehead. Unbroken lines running back from the eyes. Lines running down the head to meet the shoulders. Spine lines run together to form a narrow saddle. Narrow pencillings run around body.

SPOTTED TABBY PATTERN: Markings on the body to be spotted. May vary in size and shape, with preference given to round, evenly distributed spots. Spots should not run together in a broken mackerel pattern. A dorsal stripe runs the length of the body to the tip of the tail. The stripe is ideally composed of spots. The markings of the face and forehead shall be typically tabby markings, underside of the body to have "vest buttons." Legs and tail are barred.

Lavender
Oriental Shorthair.

TICKED TABBY PATTERN: Body hairs to be ticked with various shades of marking color and ground color. Body when viewed from top to be free from noticeable spots, stripes, or blotches, except for darker dorsal shading. Lighter underside may show tabby markings. Face, legs, and tail must show distinct tabby striping. Cat must have at least one distinct necklace.

PATCHED TABBY PATTERN: A Patched Tabby (torbie) is an established silver, ebony, chestnut, blue or lavender tabby with patches of red and/or cream.

EBONY TABBY: Ground color brilliant coppery brown. Markings dense black. Lips and chin the same shade as the rings around the eyes. Back of leg black from paw to heel. *Nose Leather:* Black, or brick red rimmed with black. *Paw Pads:* Black or brown.

BLUE TABBY: Ground color, including lips and chin, pale bluish ivory. Markings a very deep blue affording a good contrast with ground color. Warm fawn overtones or patina over the whole. *Nose Leather:* Blue, or old rose rimmed with blue. *Paw Pads:* Rose.

CHESTNUT TABBY: Ground color is warm fawn, markings are bright chestnut. *Nose Leather:* Chestnut, or pink rimmed with chestnut. *Paw Pads:* Cinnamon.

LAVENDER TABBY: Ground color is pale lavender. Markings are rich lavender affording a good contrast with the ground color. *Nose Leather:* Lavender, or pink rimmed with lavender. *Paw Pads:* Lavender-pink.

RED TABBY: Ground color red. Markings deep, rich red. Lips and chin red. *Nose Leather:* Brick red. *Paw Pads:* Brick red.

CREAM TABBY: Ground color, including lips and chin, very pale cream. Markings of buff or cream sufficiently darker than the ground color to afford good contrast, but remaining within the dilute color range. *Nose Leather:* Pink. *Paw Pads:* Pink.

SILVER TABBY: Ground color, including lips and chin, pale, clear silver. Markings dense black. *Nose Leather:* Black or brick red rimmed with black. *Paw Pads:* Black.

CAMEO TABBY: Ground color off-white. Markings red. *Nose Leather:* Rose. *Paw Pads:* Rose.

Parti-color Colors Class

TORTOISESHELL: Black with unbrindled patches of red and cream. Patches clearly defined and well broken on both body and extremities. Blaze of red or cream on face is desirable.

BLUE-CREAM: Blue with patches of solid cream. Patches clearly defined and well broken on both the body and extremities.

CHESTNUT-TORTIE: Chestnut brown with unbrindled patches of red and cream. Patches clearly defined and well broken on both body and extremities. Blaze of red or cream on face is desirable.

LAVENDER-CREAM: Lavender with patches of solid cream. Patches clearly defined and well broken on both body and extremities.

PERSIAN

AUTHOR'S NOTE—*No one knows where the Persian came from. Of course there were long-haired cats in Persia during ancient times. But the Persian and Angora were crossed frequently around the turn of the century, making our Persian a different cat from the ancient one. The Persian came to the United States during that period. The Persian is one of the most beautiful, dignified, popular and successful breeds. Although quite docile in appearance, Persians make insistent demands for one's attention.*

Point Score

Head (including size and shape		Balance	5
of eyes, ear shape and set)	30	Refinement	5
Type (including shape, size,		Color	20
bone and length of tail)	20	Eye color	10
Coat	10		

In all tabby varieties, the 20 points for color are to be divided 10 for markings and 10 for color.

HEAD: Round and massive, with great breadth of skull. Round face with round underlying bone structure. Well set on a short, thick neck.

EARS: Small, round-tipped, tilted forward, and not unduly open at the base. Set far apart, and low on the head, fitting into (without distorting) the rounded contour of the head.

EYES: Large, round and full. Set far apart and brilliant, giving a sweet expression to the face.

NOSE: Short, snub, and broad. With "break."

CHEEKS: Full.

JAWS: Broad and powerful.

CHIN: Full and well developed.

BODY: Of cobby type, low on the legs, deep in the chest, equally massive across shoulders and rump, with a short, well-rounded middle piece. Large or medium in size. Quality the determining consideration, rather than size.

BACK: Level.

LEGS: Short, thick and strong. Forelegs straight.

PAWS: Large, round and firm. Toes carried close, five in front and four behind.

TAIL: Short, but in proportion to body length. Carried without a curve and at an angle lower than the back.

COAT: Long and thick, standing off from the body. Of fine texture, glossy and full of life. Long all over the body, including the shoulders. The ruff immense and continuing in a deep frill between the front legs. Ear and toe tufts long. Brush very full.

DISQUALIFY: Locket or button. Kinked or abnormal tail. Incorrect number of toes.

Persian Colors

WHITE: Pure glistening white. *Nose Leather:* Pink. *Paw Pads:* Pink. *Eye Color:* Deep blue or brilliant copper. Odd-eyed whites shall have one blue and one copper eye with equal color depth.

BLACK: Dense coal black, sound from roots to tip of fur. Free from any tinge of rust on tips, or smoke undercoat. *Nose Leather:* Black. *Paw Pads:* Black or brown. *Eye Color:* Brilliant copper.

BLUE: Blue, lighter shade preferred, one level tone from nose to tip of tail. Sound to the roots. A sound darker shade is more acceptable than an unsound lighter shade. *Nose Leather:* Blue. *Paw Pads:* Blue. *Eye Color:* Brilliant copper.

RED: Deep, rich, clear, brilliant red; without shading, markings or ticking. Lips and chin the same color as coat. *Nose Leather:* Brick red. *Paw Pads:* Brick red. *Eye color:* Brilliant copper.

CREAM: One level shade of buff cream, without markings. Sound to the roots. Lighter shades preferred. *Nose Leather:* Pink. *Paw Pads:* Pink. *Eye Color:* Brilliant copper.

CHINCHILLA: Undercoat pure white. Coat on back, flanks, head, and tail sufficiently tipped with black to give the characteristic sparkling silver appearance. Legs may be slightly shaded with tipping. Chin and ear tufts, stomach and chest, pure white. *Rims of Eyes, Lips and Nose:* Outlined with black. *Nose Leather:* Brick red. *Paw Pads:* Black. *Eye Color:* Green or blue-green.

SHADED SILVER: Undercoat white with a mantle of black tipping shading down from sides, face, and tail from dark on the ridge to white on the chin, chest, stomach, and under the tail. Legs to be the same tone as the face. The general effect to be much darker than a Chinchilla. *Rims of Eyes, Lips and Nose:* Outlined with black. *Nose Leather:* Brick red. *Paw Pads:* Black. *Eye Color:* Green or blue-green.

CHINCHILLA GOLDEN: Undercoat rich warm cream. Coat on back, flanks, head and tail sufficiently tipped with seal brown to give golden appearance. Legs may be slightly shaded with tipping. Chin and ear tufts, stomach and chest, cream. *Rims of Eyes, Lips and Nose:* Outlined with seal brown. *Nose Leather:* Deep rose. *Paw Pads:* Seal brown. *Eye Color:* Green or blue-green.

SHADED GOLDEN: Undercoat rich warm cream with a mantle of seal brown tipping shading down from sides, face, and tail from dark on the ridge to cream on the chin, chest, stomach, and under the tail. Legs to be the same tone as the face. The general effect to be much darker than a Chinchilla. *Rims of Eyes, Lips and Nose:* Outlined with seal brown. *Nose Leather:* Deep rose. *Paw Pads:* Seal brown. *Eye Color:* Green or blue-green.

SHELL CAMEO (Red Chinchilla): Undercoat white, the coat on the back, flanks, head, and tail to be sufficiently tipped with red to give the characteristic sparkling appearance. Face and legs may be very slightly shaded with tipping. Chin, ear tufts, stomach, and chest, white. *Nose Leather:* Rose. *Rims of Eyes:* Rose. *Paw Pads:* Rose. *Eye Color:* Brilliant copper.

SHADED CAMEO (Red Shaded): Undercoat white with a mantle of red tipping shading down the sides, face, and tail from dark on the ridge to white on the chin, chest, stomach, and under the tail. Legs to be the same tone as face. The general effect to be much redder than the Shell Cameo. *Nose Leather:* Rose. *Rims of Eyes:* Rose. *Paw Pads:* Rose. *Eye Color:* Brilliant copper.

SHELL TORTOISESHELL: Undercoat white. Coat on the back, flanks, head, and tail to be delicately tipped in black with well-defined patches of red- and cream-tipped hairs as in the pattern of the Tortoiseshell. Face and legs may be slightly shaded with tipping. Chin, ear tufts, stomach, and chest, white to very slightly tipped. Blaze of red or cream tipping on face is desirable. *Eye Color:* Brilliant copper.

SHADED TORTOISESHELL: Undercoat white. Mantle of black tipping and clearly defined patches of red- and cream-tipped hairs as in the pattern of the Tortoiseshell. Shading down the sides, face, and tail

Black and white *Persian*, female.

from dark on the ridge to slightly tipped or white on the chin, chest, stomach, legs, and under the tail. The general effect is to be much darker than the Shell Tortoiseshell. Blaze of red or cream tipping on the face is desirable. *Eye Color:* Brilliant copper.

BLACK SMOKE: White undercoat, deeply tipped with black. Cat in repose appears black. In motion the white undercoat is clearly apparent. Points and mask black with narrow band of white at base of hairs next to skin, which may be seen only when the fur is parted. Light silver frill and ear tufts. *Nose Leather:* Black. *Paw Pads:* Black. *Eye Color:* Brilliant copper.

BLUE SMOKE: White undercoat, deeply tipped with blue. Cat in repose appears blue. In motion the white undercoat is clearly apparent. Points and mask blue with narrow band of white at base of hairs next to skin, which may be seen only when fur is parted. White frill and ear tufts. *Nose Leather:* Blue. *Paw Pads:* Blue. *Eye Color:* Brilliant copper.

CAMEO SMOKE (**Red Smoke**): White undercoat, deeply tipped with red. Cat in repose appears red. In motion the white undercoat is clearly apparent. Points and mask red with narrow band of white at base of hairs next to skin, which may be seen only when fur is parted.

White frill and ear tufts. *Nose Leather:* Rose. *Rims of Eyes:* Rose. *Paw Pads:* Rose. *Eye Color:* Brilliant copper.

SMOKE TORTOISESHELL: White undercoat deeply tipped with black with clearly defined, unbrindled patches of red- and cream-tipped hairs as in the pattern of the Tortoiseshell. Cat in repose appears Tortoiseshell. In motion, the white undercoat is clearly apparent. Face and ears Tortoiseshell pattern with narrow band of white at the base of the hairs next to the skin, which may be seen only when hair is parted. White ruff and ear tufts. Blaze of red or cream tipping on face is desirable. *Eye Color:* Brilliant copper.

CLASSIC TABBY PATTERN: Markings dense, clearly defined and broad. Legs evenly barred with bracelets coming up to meet the body markings. Tail evenly ringed. Several unbroken necklaces on neck and upper chest, the more the better. Frown marks on forehead form intricate letter "M." Unbroken line runs back from outer corner of eye. Swirls on cheeks. Vertical lines over back of head extend to shoulder markings, which are in the shape of a butterfly with both upper and lower wings distinctly outlined and marked with dots inside outline. Back markings consist of a vertical line down the spine from butterfly to tail with a vertical stripe paralleling it on each side, the three stripes well separated by stripes of the ground color. Large solid blotch on each side to be encircled by one or more unbroken rings. Side markings should be the same on both sides. Double vertical row of buttons on chest and stomach.

MACKEREL TABBY PATTERN: Markings dense, clearly defined, and all narrow pencillings. Legs evenly barred with narrow bracelets coming up to meet the body markings. Tail barred. Necklaces on neck and chest distinct, like so many chains. Head barred with an "M" on the forehead. Unbroken lines running back from the eyes. Lines running down the head to meet the shoulders. Spine lines run together to form a narrow saddle. Narrow pencillings run around body.

PATCHED TABBY PATTERN: A Patched Tabby (torbie) is an established silver, brown, or blue tabby with patches of red and/or cream.

BROWN PATCHED TABBY: Ground color brilliant coppery brown with classic or mackerel tabby markings of dense black with patches of red and/or cream clearly defined on both body and extremities; a blaze of red and/or cream on the face is desirable. Lips and chin the same shade as the rings around the eyes. *Eye Color:* Brilliant copper.

BLUE PATCHED TABBY: Ground color, including lips and chin, pale bluish ivory with classic or mackerel tabby markings of deep blue affording a good contrast with ground color. Patches of cream clearly defined on both body and extremities; a blaze of cream on the face is desirable. Warm fawn overtones or patina over the whole. *Eye Color:* Brilliant copper.

SILVER PATCHED TABBY: Ground color, including lips and chin, pale silver with classic or mackerel tabby markings of dense black with patches of red and/or cream clearly defined on both body and extremities. A blaze of red and/or cream on the face is desirable. *Eye Color:* Brilliant copper or hazel.

SILVER TABBY: Ground color, including lips and chin, pale, clear silver. Markings dense black. *Nose Leather:* Brick red. *Paw Pads:* Black. *Eye Color:* Green or hazel.

RED TABBY: Ground color red. Markings deep, rich red. Lips and chin red. *Nose Leather:* Brick red. *Paw Pads:* Pink. *Eye Color:* Brilliant copper.

BROWN TABBY: Ground color brilliant coppery brown. Markings dense black. Lips and chin the same shade as the rings around the eyes. Back of leg black from paw to heel. *Nose Leather:* Brick red. *Paw Pads:* Black or brown. *Eye Color:* Brilliant copper.

BLUE TABBY: Ground color, including lips and chin, pale bluish ivory. Markings a very deep blue affording a good contrast with ground color. Warm fawn overtones or patina over the whole. *Nose Leather:* Old rose. *Paw Pads:* Rose. *Eye Color:* Brilliant copper.

CREAM TABBY: Ground color, including lips and chin, vary pale cream. Markings of buff or cream sufficiently darker than the ground color to afford good contrast, but remaining within the dilute color range. *Nose Leather:* Pink. *Paw Pads:* Pink. *Eye Color:* Brilliant copper.

CAMEO TABBY: Ground color off-white. Markings red. *Nose Leather:* Rose. *Paw Pads:* Rose. *Eye Color:* Brilliant copper.

TORTOISESHELL: Black with unbrindled patches of red and cream. Patches clearly defined and well broken on both body and extremities. Blaze of red or cream on face is desirable. *Eye Color:* Brilliant copper.

CALICO: White with unbrindled patches of black and red. White predominant on underparts. *Eye Color:* Brilliant copper.

DILUTE CALICO: White with unbrindled patches of blue and cream. White predominant on underparts. *Eye Color:* Brilliant copper.

BLUE-CREAM: Blue with patches of solid cream. Patches clearly defined and well broken on both body and extremities. *Eye Color:* Brilliant copper.

BI-COLOR: Black and white, blue and white, red and white, or cream and white. White feet, legs, undersides, chest and muzzle. Inverted "V" blaze on face desirable. White under tail and white collar allowable. *Eye Color:* Brilliant copper.

PERSIAN VAN BI-COLOR: Black and white, red and white, blue and white, cream and white. White cat with color confined to the extremities: head, tail, and legs. One or two small colored patches on body allowable.

PEKE-FACE RED AND PEKE-FACE RED TABBY: The Peke-Face cat should conform in color, markings and general type to the standards set forth for the Red and Red Tabby Persian cat. The head should resemble as much as possible that of the Pekingese dog from which it gets its name. Nose should be very short and depressed, or indented between the eyes. There should be a decidedly wrinkled muzzle. Eyes round, large, and full, set wide apart, prominent and brilliant.

PERSIAN VAN CALICO: White cat with unbrindled patches of black and red confined to the extremities: head, tail, and legs. One or two small colored patches on body allowable.

PERSIAN VAN BLUE-CREAM AND WHITE: White cat with unbrindled patches of blue and cream confined to the extremities: head, tail, and legs. One or two small colored patches on body allowable. *Note:* Cats possessing more than a couple of small body spots should be shown in the regular Bi-Color class.

REX

AUTHOR'S NOTE—*One cannot mistake a Rex. They are small-to-medium, lean, curly-coated cats. They were the result of a spontaneous mutation born to Domestic Shorthairs during the fifties. They appeared in England, Germany and the United States. There are two recessive Rex genes, the Cornish and the Devon, that cannot breed together to produce a Rex. But both genes cause the cat to have a curly undercoat (downy coat) with no topcoat (guardhairs). Most cats have only a topcoat. The Rex is a quiet lap cat with a personality as soft and cuddly as its fur.*

Point Score

Head (25)

Size and shape	5	Ears	5
Muzzle and nose	5	Profile	5
Eyes	5		

Body (30)		Coat (40)	
Size	3	Texture	10
Torso	10	Length	5
Legs and paws	5	Wave, extent of wave	20
Tail	5	Close lying	5
Bone	5		
Neck	2	Color (5)	

GENERAL: The Rex cat, a spontaneous mutation of the domestic cat, has accentuated the characteristic features of the breed to create a longer, slighter and more agile creature than its ancestors. Its arched back and muscular hind legs develop the flexibility for high jumps, quick starts and amazing speed. At ease its relaxed appearance is contradictory to its capacity for sudden and fast movements. When handled it feels firm and because of its short coat, warm to the touch.

HEAD: Comparatively small and narrow; length about one-third greater than the width. A definite whisker break.

MUZZLE: Narrowing slightly to a rounded end.

EARS: Large, wide at base, come to a modified point at the top. Placed high on the head and erect.

EYES: Medium to large in size, oval in shape and slanting slightly upward. A full eye's width apart. Color should be clear, intense and appropriate to coat color.

White *Rex*, female.

NOSE: Roman. Length is one-third length of head. In profile a straight line from end of nose to chin with considerable depth and squarish effect.

CHEEKS: Lean and muscular.

CHIN: Strong, well developed.

BODY: Small to medium, males proportionately larger. Torso long and slender. Back is arched with lower line of the body following the upward curve.

SHOULDERS: Well knit.

RUMP: Rounded, well muscled.

LEGS: Very long and slender. Hips well muscled, somewhat heavy in proportion to the rest of the body. The Rex stands high on its legs.

PAWS: Dainty, slightly oval. Toes: five in front and four behind.

TAIL: Long and slender, tapering toward the end and extremely flexible.

NECK: Long and slender.

BONE: Fine and delicate.

COAT: Short, extremely soft, silky, and completely free of guard-hairs. Relatively dense. A tight, uniform marcel wave, lying close to the body and extending from the top of the head across the back, sides, and hips, continuing to the tip of the tail. The fur on the undersides of the chin and on chest and abdomen is short and noticeably wavy.

CONDITION: Firm and muscular.

DISQUALIFY: Kinked or abnormal tail. Incorrect number of toes. Any coarse hair or guardhairs. Evidence of hybridization resulting in the colors chocolate, lavender, the Himalayan pattern or these combinations with white.

Rex Colors

White, Black, Blue, Red, Cream, Chinchilla, Shaded Silver, Black Smoke, Blue Smoke, Classic Tabby Pattern, Mackerel Tabby Pattern, Patched Tabby Pattern, Brown Patched Tabby, Silver Tabby, Red Tabby, Brown Tabby, Blue Tabby, Cream Tabby, Tortoiseshell, Calico, Dilute Calico, Blue-Cream, Blue Patched Tabby, Silver Patched Tabby. *See American Shorthair for color definitions. Also:*

BI-COLOR: White with unbrindled patches of black, or white with unbrindled patches of blue, or white with unbrindled patches of red, or white with unbrindled patches of cream. Cats with no more white than a locket and/or button do not qualify for this color class. Such cats shall be judged in the color class of their basic color with no penalty for such locket and/or button. *Eye Color:* Gold.

ORC (OTHER REX COLORS): Any other color or pattern with the exception of those showing evidence of hybridization resulting in the colors chocolate, lavender, the Himalayan pattern, or these combinations with white, etc. *Eye Color:* Appropriate to the predominant color of the cat.

RUSSIAN BLUE

AUTHOR'S NOTE—*In the cat world, "blue" is a rich grey tinted with blue. In the case of the Russian Blue, the undercoat of this warm, plush cat is "blue" and the outer coat is tipped with silver. Russian Blues originated in Archangel, northern Russia. It's a cold, Arctic climate that would cause a cat to develop a double coat. These Russians came to America at the turn of the century via England. There is one other feature that would help one recognize these quiet, retiring animals. They have bright green eyes blazing from their blue-grey heads.*

Point Score

Head and neck	20	Coat	20
Body type	20	Color	20
Eye shape	5	Eye color	10
Ears	5		

GENERAL: The good show specimen has good physical condition, is firm in muscle tone, and alert.

HEAD: Top of skull flat and long. The face is broad across the eyes due to wide eye-set and thick fur.

EARS: Rather large and wide at the base. Tips more pointed than rounded. The skin of the ears is thin and translucent, with very little inside furnishing. The outside of the ear is scantily covered with short, very fine hair, with leather showing through. Set far apart, as much on side as on the top of the head.

EYES: Set wide apart. Aperture rounded in shape.

NECK: Long and slender, but appearing short due to thick fur and high placement of shoulder blades.

NOSE: Medium in length.

Russian Blue, male.

CHIN: Perpendicular with the end of the nose and with level under-chin. Neither receding nor excessively massive.

BODY: Fine-boned, long, firm and muscular, lithe and graceful in outline and carriage.

LEGS: Long and fine-boned.

PAWS: Small, slightly rounded. Toes: five in front and four behind.

TAIL: Long, but in proportion to the body. Tapering from a moderately thick base.

COAT: Short, dense, fine and plush. Double coat stands out from body due to density. It has a distinct, soft and silky feel.

COLOR: Even, bright blue throughout. Lighter shades of blue preferred. Guardhairs distinctively silver-tipped, giving the cat a silvery sheen or lustrous appearance. A definite contrast should be noted between ground color and tipping. Free from tabby markings. *Nose Leather:* Slate-grey. *Paw Pads:* Lavender-pink or mauve. *Eye Color:* Vivid green.

DISQUALIFY: Kinked or abnormal tail. Locket or button. Incorrect number of toes.

SCOTTISH FOLD

AUTHOR'S NOTE—*The Scottish Fold appeared in Perthshire, Scotland, in the sixties. The mutation is an unusual recessive gene that causes the ears to fold down in the middle. These cats have a wonderfully intense look. Everything about them is round—their heads, eyes, even their cobby bodies. (*Cobby *means short legs, stocky body, a generally thick look.)*

Point Score

Ears	30	Head	15
Tail	20	Body	10
Eyes	15	Color	10

GENERAL: The Scottish Fold cat occurred as a spontaneous mutation in farm cats in Scotland. The breed has been established by crosses to British Shorthair and domestic cats in Scotland and England. In America the outcross is the American and British Shorthair. All bona fide Scottish Fold cats trace their pedigree to Susie, the first fold-ear cat discovered by the founders of the breed, William and Mary Ross.

HEAD: Well rounded with a firm chin and jaw. Muzzle to have well-rounded whisker pads. Head should blend into a short neck. Prominent cheeks with a jowly appearance in males.

EYES: Wide open with a sweet expression. Large, well rounded and separated by a broad nose. Eye color to correspond with coat color.

NOSE: Nose to be short with a gentle curve. A brief stop is permitted but a definite nose break considered a fault. Profile is moderate in appearance.

EARS: Fold forward and downward. Small, the smaller, tightly folded ear preferred over a loose fold and large ear. The ears should be set in a caplike fashion to expose a rounded cranium. Eartips to be rounded.

BODY: Medium, rounded and even from shoulder to pelvic girdle. The cat should stand firm on a well-padded body. There must be no hint of thickness or lack of mobility in the cat due to short, coarse legs. Toes to be neat and well rounded with five in front and four behind.

Overall appearance is that of a well-rounded cat with medium bone; fault cats obviously lacking in type. Females may be slightly smaller.

TAIL: Tail should be medium to long but in proportion to the body. Tail should be flexible and tapering. Longer, tapering tail preferred.

COAT: Short, dense and resilient.

DISQUALIFY: Kinked tail. Tail that is foreshortened. Tail that is lacking in flexibility due to abnormally thick vertebrae.

Scottish Fold Colors

White, Black, Blue, Red, Cream, Chinchilla, Shaded Silver, Shell Cameo, Shaded Cameo, Black Smoke, Blue Smoke, Cameo Smoke, Classic Tabby Pattern, Mackerel Tabby Pattern, Patched Tabby Pattern, Silver Tabby, Red Tabby, Brown Tabby, Blue Tabby, Cream Tabby, Cameo Tabby, Tortoiseshell, Calico, Dilute Calico, Blue-Cream, Bi-Color. *See American Shorthair for color definitions.*

OSFC (OTHER SCOTTISH FOLD COLORS): Any other color or pattern with the exception of those showing evidence of hybridization resulting in the colors chocolate and lilac or the Himalayan pattern or these combinations with white. *Eye Color:* Appropriate to the dominant color of the cat.

White *Scottish Fold.*

SIAMESE

AUTHOR'S NOTE—*The famous Siamese cat was first known as the Royal Cat of Siam because it lived with the royal family and the priests. No one knows how it came to the royal family. The colorpoint gene is recessive, causing conjecture that these cats may have been bred from a mutant by some enterprising person. A drawing of a Seal Point appears in* The Cat-Book Poems *in the Bangkok Museum. The book first appeared in 1350, indicating a long history for this breed. In the 1880s the King of Siam gave a pair to Mr. Owen Gould, British Consul-General, who got them started in England. Mrs. Rutherford B. Hayes, wife of the nineteenth American President, had the first American Siamese on record in the late 1870s. These are truly unique cats. The colorpoints are beautiful, the coat texture is magnificent, their minds approach cat genius and their voices are unequaled on the face of the earth.*

Lilac Point *Siamese*, male.

Point Score

Head (20)		Muscle tone	10
Long flat profile	6	Legs and feet	5
Wedge, fine muzzle, size	5	Tail	3
Ears	4		
Chin	3	Coat (10)	
Width between eyes	2	Color (30)	
		Body color	10
Eyes (10)		Point color—matching	
Shape, size, slant and		points of dense color,	
placement	10	proper footpads and	
		nose leather	10
Body (30)		Eye color	10
Structure and size,			
including neck	12		

GENERAL: The ideal Siamese is a svelte, dainty cat with long, tapering lines, very lithe but muscular.

HEAD: Long, tapering wedge. Medium size in good proportion to body. The total wedge starts at the nose and flares out in straight lines to the tips of the ears forming a triangle, with no break at the whiskers. No less than the width of an eye between the eyes. When the whiskers are smoothed back, the underlying bone structure is apparent. Allowance must be made for jowls in the stud cat.

SKULL: Flat. In profile, a long straight line is seen from the top of the head to the tip of the nose. No bulge over eyes. No dip in nose.

EARS: Strikingly large, pointed, wide at base, continuing the lines of the wedge.

EYES: Almond-shaped. Medium size. Neither protruding nor recessed. Slanted toward the nose in harmony with lines of wedge and ears. Uncrossed.

NOSE: Long and straight. A continuation of the forehead with no break.

MUZZLE: Fine, wedge-shaped.

CHIN AND JAW: Medium size. Tip of chin lines up with tip of nose in the same vertical plane. Neither receding nor excessively massive.

BODY: Medium size. Dainty, long, and svelte. A distinctive combination of fine bones and firm muscles. Shoulders and hips continue same sleek lines of tubular body. Hips never wider than shoulders. Abdomen tight.

NECK: Long and slender.

LEGS: Long and slim. Hind legs higher than front. In good proportion to body.

PAWS: Dainty, small, and oval. Toes: five in front and four behind.

TAIL: Long, thin, tapering to a fine point.

COAT: Short, fine textured, glossy. Lying close to body.

CONDITION: Excellent physical condition. Eyes clear. Muscular, strong and lithe. Neither flabby nor bony. Not fat.

COLOR: *Body:* Even, with subtle shading when allowed. Allowance should be made for darker color in older cats as Siamese generally darken with age, but there must be definite contrast between body color and points. *Points:* Mask, ears, legs, feet, tail dense and clearly defined. All of the same shade. Mask covers entire face including whisker pads and is connected to ears by tracings. Mask should not extend over the top of the head. No ticking or white hairs in points.

PENALIZE: Improper (*i.e.*, off-color or spotted) nose leather or paw pads. Soft or mushy body.

DISQUALIFY: Any evidence of illness or poor health. Weak hind legs. Mouth breathing due to nasal obstruction or to poor occlusion. Emaciation. Visible kink. Eyes other than blue. White toes and/or feet. Incorrect number of toes. Malocclusion resulting in either undershot or overshot chin.

Siamese Colors

SEAL POINT: Body even pale fawn to cream, warm in tone, shading gradually into lighter color on the stomach and chest. Points deep seal brown. *Nose Leather:* Same color as points. *Paw Pads:* Same color as points. *Eye Color:* Deep vivid blue.

CHOCOLATE POINT: Body ivory with no shading. Points milk-chocolate color, warm in tone. *Nose Leather:* Cinnamon-pink. *Paw Pads:* Cinnamon-pink. *Eye Color:* Deep vivid blue.

BLUE POINT: Body bluish white, cold in tone, shading gradually to white on stomach and chest. Points deep blue. *Nose Leather:* Slate-colored. *Paw Pads:* Slate-colored. *Eye Color:* Deep vivid blue.

LILAC POINT: Body glacial white with no shading. Points frosty grey with pinkish tone. *Nose Leather:* Lavender-pink. *Paw Pads:* Lavender-pink. *Eye Color:* Deep vivid blue.

*   *   *

SOMALI

AUTHOR'S NOTE—*There have been random, long-hair mutations in Abyssinian litters for years. In the seventies these handsome rareties were finally bred to create the Somali. They retain all the characteristic Abyssinian traits, such as the agouti coloring (each hair is individually striped with brown or black) and that active, assertive, spirited personality.*

Point Score

Head (25)			Coat (25)		
Skull	6		Texture		10
Muzzle	6		Length		15
Ears	7		Color (25)		
Eye shape	6		Body Color		10
Body (25)			Ticking		10
Torso	10		Eye color		5
Legs and feet	10				
Tail	5				

GENERAL: The overall impression of the Somali is that of a well-proportioned medium-to-large cat, firm muscular development, lithe, showing an alert, lively interest in all surroundings, with an even disposition and easy to handle. The cat is to give the appearance of activity, sound health and general vigor.

HEAD: A modified, slightly rounded wedge without flat planes; the brow, cheek, and profile lines all showing a gentle contour. A slight rise from the bridge of the nose to the forehead, which should be of good size with width between the ears flowing into the arched neck without a break.

MUZZLE: Shall follow gentle contours in conformity with the skull, as viewed from the front profile. Chin shall be full, neither undershot nor overshot, having a rounded appearance. The muzzle shall not be sharply pointed and there shall be no evidence of snipiness, foxiness, or whisker pinch. Allowance to be made for jowls in adult males.

EARS: Large, alert, moderately pointed, broad and cupped at the base. Ear set on a line toward the rear of the skull. Inner ear shall have horizontal tufts that reach nearly to the other side of the ear; tufts desirable.

EYES: Almond-shaped, large, brilliant and expressive. Skull aperture neither round nor Oriental. Eyes accented by dark lidskin, encircled by light-colored area. Above each, a short, dark, vertical pencil stroke with a dark pencil line continuing from the upper lid toward the ear.

BODY: Torso medium long, lithe and graceful, showing well-developed muscular strength. Ribcage is rounded; back is slightly arched, giving the appearance of a cat about to spring; flank level with no tuck-up. Conformation strikes a medium between the extremes of cobby and svelte lengthy types.

LEGS AND FEET: Legs in proportion to torso; feet oval and compact. When standing, the Somali gives the impression of being nimble

Somali.

and quick. Toes: five in front and four in back.

TAIL: Having a full brush, thick at the base and slightly tapering. Length in balance with torso.

COAT: Texture very soft to the touch, extremely fine and double-coated. The more dense the coat, the better. Length: A medium-length coat, except over shoulders, where a slightly shorter length is permitted. Preference is to be given to a cat with ruff and breeches, giving a full-coated appearance to the cat.

PENALIZE: Color faults: Cold grey or sandy tone to coat color; mottling or speckling on unticked areas. Pattern faults: Necklaces, leg bars, tabby stripes or bars on body, lack of desired markings on head and tail. Black roots on body.

DISQUALIFY: White locket or groin spot, or white anywhere on body other than on the upper throat, chin and nostrils. Any skeletal abnormality. Wrong color paw pads or nose leather. Unbroken necklace. Incorrect number of toes. Kinks in tail.

Somali Colors

RUDDY: Overall impression of an orange-brown or ruddy tipped with black. Color has radiant or glowing quality. Darker shading along the spine allowed. Underside of body and inside of legs and chest to be an even ruddy tone, harmonizing with the top coat; without ticking, barring, necklaces or belly marks. *Nose Leather:* Tile red. *Paw Pads:* Black or brown, with black between toes and extending upward on rear legs. Toe tufts on front and rear feet black or dark brown. White or off-white on upper throat, lips and nostrils only. Tail continuing the dark spine line ending at black at the tip. Complete absence of rings on tail. Preference given to unmarked ruddy color. Ears tipped with black or dark brown. *Eye Color:* Gold or green—the more richness and depth of color the better.

RED: Warm glowing red ticked with chocolate brown. Deeper shades of red preferred. Ears and tail tipped with chocolate brown. *Paw Pads:* Pink with chocolate brown between toes, extending slightly beyond paws. *Nose Leather:* Rosy pink. *Eye Color:* Gold or green—the more richness and depth of color the better.

PLEASE NOTE: The Somali is extremely slow in showing mature ticking and allowances should be made for kittens and young cats.

* * *

TURKISH ANGORA

AUTHOR'S NOTE:—*The Turkish Angora hails from Ankara (Angora), Turkey. It has been there for many centuries, watching the comings and goings of the rest of the world. The zoo in Ankara has been carefully preserving the white Angora, at least in this century. In the sixties, Colonel and Mrs. Walter Grant brought two pairs to America, establishing the Turkish Angora here. Many colors are now accepted, including the classical white.*

Point Score

Head	35
Body	30
Color	20
Coat	15

GENERAL: Solid, firm, giving the impression of grace and flowing movement.

HEAD: Size, small to medium. Wedge-shaped. Wide at top. Definite taper toward chin. Allowance to be made for jowls in stud cat.

EARS: Wide at base, long, pointed, and tufted. Set high on the head.

EYES: Large, almond-shaped to round. Slanting upward slightly.

NOSE: Medium-long, gentle slope. No break.

NECK: Slim and graceful, medium length.

CHIN: Gently rounded. Tip to form a perpendicular line with the nose.

JAW: Tapered.

BODY: Small-to-medium size in female, slightly larger in male. Torso long, graceful and lithe. Chest, light framed. Rump slightly higher than front. Bone, fine.

LEGS: Long. Hind legs longer than front.

PAWS: Small and round, dainty. Tufts between toes.

TAIL: Long and tapering, wide at base, narrow at end, full. Carried lower than body but not trailing. When moving, relaxed tail is carried horizontally over the body, sometimes almost touching the head.

White *Turkish Angora*, female.

COAT: Body coat medium-long, long at ruff. Full brush on tail. Silky with a wavy tendency. Wavier on stomach. Very fine and having a silk-like sheen.

BALANCE: Proportionate in all physical aspects with graceful, lithe appearance.

PENALIZE: Kinked or abnormal tail.

DISQUALIFY: Persian body types.

Turkish Angora Colors

WHITE: Pure white, no other coloring. *Paw Pads:* Pink. *Nose Leather:* Pink. *Lips:* Pink. *Eye Color:* Blue, amber, or odd-eyed.

BLACK: Dense coal black, sound from roots to tip of fur. Free from any tinge of rust on tips or smoke undercoat. *Nose Leather:* Black. *Paw Pads:* Black or brown. *Eye Color:* Amber.

BLUE: Blue, lighter shade preferred, one level tone from nose to tip of tail. Sound to the roots. A sound darker shade is more acceptable than an unsound lighter shade. *Nose Leather:* Blue. *Paw Pads:* Blue. *Eye Color:* Amber.

CREAM: One level shade of buff cream, without markings. Sound to the roots. Lighter shade preferred. *Nose Leather:* Pink. *Paw Pads:* Pink. *Eye Color:* Brilliant copper.

RED: Deep, rich, clear, brilliant red; without shading, markings, or ticking. Lips and chin the same color as coat. *Nose Leather:* Brick red. *Paw Pads:* Brick red. *Eye Color:* Brilliant copper.

BLACK SMOKE: White undercoat, deeply tipped with black. Cat in repose appears black. In motion the white undercoat is clearly apparent. Points and mask black with narrow band of white at base of hairs next to skin, which may be seen only when the fur is parted. *Nose Leather:* Black. *Paw Pads:* Black. *Eye Color:* Amber.

BLUE SMOKE: White undercoat, deeply tipped with blue. Cat in repose appears blue. In motion the white undercoat is clearly apparent. Points and mask blue, with narrow band of white at base of hairs next to skin, which may be seen only when fur is parted. *Nose Leather:* Blue. *Paw Pads:* Blue. *Eye Color:* Amber.

CLASSIC TABBY PATTERN: Markings dense, clearly defined and broad. Legs evenly barred with bracelets coming up to meet the body markings. Tail evenly ringed. Several unbroken necklaces on neck and upper chest, the more the better. Frown marks on forehead form intricate letter "M." Unbroken line runs back from outer corner of eye. Swirls on cheeks. Vertical lines over back of head extend to shoulder markings, which are in the shape of a butterfly with both upper and lower wings distinctly outlined and marked with dots inside outline. Back markings consist of a vertical line down the spine from butterfly to tail with a vertical strip paralleling it on each side, the three stripes well separated by stripes of the ground color. Large solid blotch on each side to be encircled by one or more unbroken rings. Side markings should be the same on both sides. Double vertical row of buttons on chest and stomach.

MACKEREL TABBY PATTERN: Markings dense, clearly defined, and all narrow pencillings. Legs evenly barred with narrow bracelets coming up to meet the body markings. Tail barred. Necklaces on neck and chest distinct, like so many chains. Head barred with an "M" on the forehead. Unbroken lines running back from the eyes. Lines running down the head to meet the shoulders. Spine lines run together to form a narrow saddle. Narrow pencillings run around body.

SILVER TABBY: Ground color, including lips and chin, pale clear silver. Markings dense black. *Nose Leather:* Brick red. *Paw Pads:* Black. *Eye Color:* Green or hazel.

RED TABBY: Ground color red. Markings deep rich red. Lips and chin red. *Paw Pads:* Pink. *Nose Leather:* Brick red. *Eye Color:* Amber.

BROWN TABBY: Ground color brilliant coppery brown. Markings dense black. Lips and chin the same shade as the rings around the eyes. Back of leg black from paw to heel. *Nose Leather:* Brick red. *Paw Pads:* Black or brown. *Eye Color:* Amber.

BLUE TABBY: Ground color, including lips and chin, pale bluish ivory. Markings a very deep blue affording a good contrast with ground color. Warm fawn overtones or patina over the whole. *Nose Leather:* Old rose. *Paw Pads:* Rose. *Eye Color:* Amber.

CREAM TABBY: Ground color, including lips and chin, very pale cream. Markings of buff or cream sufficiently darker than the ground color to afford good contrast, but remaining within the dilute color range. *Nose Leather:* Pink. *Paw Pads:* Pink. *Eye Color:* Brilliant copper.

TORTOISESHELL: Black with unbrindled patches of red and cream. Patches clearly defined and well broken on both body and extremities. Blaze of red or cream on face is desirable. *Eye Color:* Brilliant copper.

CALICO: White with unbrindled patches of black and red. White predominant on underparts. *Eye Color:* Amber.

DILUTE CALICO: White with unbrindled patches of blue and cream, white predominant on underparts. *Eye Color:* Brilliant copper.

BLUE-CREAM: Blue with patches of solid cream. Patches clearly defined and well broken on both body and extremities. *Eye Color:* Brilliant copper.

BI-COLOR: Black and white, blue and white, red and white, or cream and white. White feet, legs, undersides, chest and muzzle. Inverted "V" blaze on face desirable. White under tail and white collar allowable. *Eye Color:* Amber.

Glossary

Abbreviations

     ACA: American Cat Association
    ACFA: American Cat Fanciers' Association
    CCA: Canadian Cat Association
  CCFF: Crown Cat Fanciers' Federation
    CFA: Cat Fanciers' Association
    CFF: Cat Fanciers' Federation
    UCF: United Cat Federation

Ailurophile: A lover of cats.

Ailurophobe: A detester of cats, or one who fears them.

Altered: A cat that has been surgically sterilized.

Angora: Ancient name of the capital city of Turkey (Ankara). Archaic term for first longhair cats seen in Europe. Recognized by CFA as Turkish Angora.

Barring: Linear markings of the tabby (striped) coat pattern.

Blaze: Color marking from forehead to nose. Usually white or contrasting color of the coat.

Break: Where the nose meets the forehead. Usually applied to snubbed or pugged noses of some Persians, indicating an indentation.

Brindling: Wrong-colored hairs intermingling with those of the correct color.

Brush: Profuse tail of a long-haired cat.

Butterfly: Distinctive markings found on the shoulders of well-marked tabbies.

Button: A patch of color anywhere on the body, usually in white or contrasting color to the coat.

Cat Fancy: All persons and cats involved in any aspect of breeding, exhibiting, and/or promoting pedigreed cats.

Champion: A cat that has won six winner's ribbons with at least four different judges. The title must be approved by the registration body with jurisdiction over the cat.

Classic: Most typical coat pattern of tabby markings. It is referred to as "marbled" in England.

Cobby: A type of cat body—short-legged, sturdy, broad-chested, somewhat square in appearance.

Condition: The health and fitness of a cat.

Crossbreed: A cat that is the result of two separate pure breeds.

Double coat: A long topcoat of hair and a dense undercoat of shorter hair. Found on such breeds as Manx, Russian Blue and Somali.

Foreign: A body type found on various short-haired breeds. Refers to a long, narrow body associated with grace and delicacy.

Frill: Sometimes referred to as the *ruff*, it is the hair around the head that frames the face.

Gloves: Base of paws colored white in contrast to body color. Required on Birman.

Grand Champion: According to CFA Show Rules, this is a Champion cat that has won the equivalent of seven Grand Ribbons by accumulating points in Best Champion competition.

Grand Premier: The equivalent of Grand Champion for a neutered or spayed cat.

Guardhair: Long, stiff outer hair protecting the undercoat.

Hairball: An accumulation of hair in the cat's stomach caused by constant licking of the coat. If an obstruction is formed, it must be removed surgically.

Haw: A third eyelid at the side or lower lid of the eye. This membrane keeps the eye clean and moist by sliding across, horizontally, from the inner corner.

Heat: The female's estrus cycle, when she is most receptive to the male for mating.

Hot: An incorrect reddish color.

In-breeding: Mating cats closely related to each other.

Kink: A congenital tail defect. It is usually a shortened, bent tail.

Kitten: Any cat younger than eight months of age.

Locket: A patch of color under the neck that is white or in contrast to the color of the coat.

Mackerel: A tabby coat pattern resembling the skeleton of a fish.

Mask: Fur on the cat's face that is a darker color than that of the rest of the coat.

Muzzle: The cat's nose and jaws.

Neuter: A cat that has been surgically sterilized.

Nose leather: The outer skin of the nose.

Oriental: A descriptive term for some cats' eyes, *e.g.*, the Siamese. Also some short-haired varieties.

Pads: The soft tufts of skin under the paws.

Patched: Random markings of different coloring.

Pedigree: An official record establishing a cat's lineage for no fewer than three generations of pure breeding. Recorded in the "stud book" of a registry organization.

Peke-faced: Resembling the face of a Pekingese dog. Short, depressed nose, indented between the eyes. Wrinkled muzzle.

Pencilling: Pencil-like marks on the faces of tabbies.

Points: The dark coloring on the cat's extremities, which include the head, legs, ears and tail, as on a Chocolate Point Siamese. Also, marks earned in cat shows according to breed standards.

Premier: A neutered cat that has won the title of Champion in competition.

Queen: A female cat used for breeding.

Ruff: *See* Frill.

Rumpy: A Manx cat with no trace of a tail.

Self: Fur colored the same all over.

Short-coupled: Having a short, compact body.

Snub: Short nose type, such as that of the Persian.

Spaying: The surgical sterilization of a female cat. The most effective procedure is the *ovariohysterectomy.*

Spraying: The male cat's urinating to mark territory or to attract a female. The odor is acrid and pungent.

Squint: Eyes that point inward; *i.e.,* "crosseyed." Common in Siamese cats, although it is a disqualification.

Standard: Aesthetic ideal established for each breed by official cat clubs belonging to the various registry organizations, such as the CFA. One hundred points given for established characteristics (or "Standard") are earnable for each breed.

Stud: Male cat used for breeding.

Stud book: The official record of breeding kept by a registry organization.

Stumpy: A Manx that is not completely tailless.

Tabby: Markings of a specific coat type involving stripes, spots or variations of stripes.

Tapered: Refers to a long, narrowing tail.

Ticking: Several bands of contrasting color on each hair of the fur. Most often seen in the Abyssinian.

Tufts: Slight clumps of hair growing from between the toes or the ears.

Type: Manner of description of physical characteristics.

Undercoat: Shorter, softer hair lying under the topcoat.

Wedge: A head shape of various breeds, such as the Siamese. A requirement of the Standard.

Whip: A long, tapering tail.

Whiskers: Long facial hairs protruding from the sides of the muzzle.

Cat Registry Organizations

CAT FANCIERS' ASSOCIATION, INC.
Walter A. Friend, Jr., President
1309 Allaire Avenue
Ocean, NJ 07712

AMERICAN CAT ASSOCIATION, INC.
Susie Page
10065 Foothill Boulevard
Lake View Terrace, CA 91342

AMERICAN CAT FANCIERS' ASSOCIATION, INC.
Edward Rugenstein
P.O. Box 203
Point Lookout, MO 65726

CAT FANCIERS' FEDERATION, INC.
Ms. Barbara Haley
9509 Montgomery Road
Cincinnati, OH 45242

CROWN CAT FANCIERS' FEDERATION
Mrs. Martha Underwood
1379 Tyler Park Drive
Louisville, KY 40204

UNITED CAT FEDERATION, INC.
David Young
6621 Thornwood Street
San Diego, CA 92111

TICA—International Cat Association
Bob Mullen
211 East Olive, Suite 201
Burbank, CA 91502

CANADIAN CAT ASSOCIATION
Donna Aragona
14 Nelson Street W., Suite 5
Brampton, Ontario
Canada L6X 1B7

Publications of Interest to Cat Owners

Publications of Interest to Cat Owners

ALL CATS MAGAZINE (Pet Pride)
Suite 7
15113 Sunset Boulevard
Pacific Palisades, CA 90272

ANIMAL NEWS
2002 Fourth Street
Santa Rosa, CA 95404

ANIMALS MAGAZINE
MSPCA
350 South Huntington Avenue
Boston, MA 02130

CAT FANCIERS' ASSOCIATION YEARBOOK
Marna Fogarty
Deer Lane
South Londonderry, VT 05155

CAT FANCY MAGAZINE
P.O. Box 2431
Boulder, CO 80321

CATS MAGAZINE
P.O. Box 83048
Lincoln, NE 68501

CAT-TAB Newspaper
7700 Old Dominion Drive
McLean, VA 22101

CAT WORLD
P.O. Box 127
Golden, CO 80401

FELINE PRACTICE
Journal of Feline Medicine and Surgery for the Practitioner
P.O. Box 4457
Santa Barbara, CA 93103

KIND MAGAZINE (a youth publication)
Humane Society of the United States
Dept. CM
2100 L Street NW
Washington, DC 20037

PET GAZETTE
P.O . Box 1369
Vancouver, WA 98666

TODAY'S ANIMAL HEALTH
1905 Sunnycrest Drive
Fullerton, CA 92635

Suggested Reading

BEHAVIOR

Beadle, Muriel. *The Cat*. New York: Simon and Schuster, 1977.

Burghardt, Gordon M. and Bekoff, Marc. *The Development of Behavior*. New York: Garland STPM Press, 1978.

Burton, Maurice and Burton, Robert. *Inside the Animal World*. New York: Quadrangle/The New York Times Book Co., 1977.

Caras, Roger. *Panther!* New York: Little, Brown & Company, 1969.

Ewer, R. F. *The Carnivores*. Ithaca, NY: Cornell University Press, 1973.

Guggisberg, C. A. W. *Wild Cats of the World*. New York: Taplinger Publishing Co., 1975.

Hafez, E. S. E. *The Behaviour of Domestic Animals*. Third Edition. London: Bailliere Tindall. U.S. Distributor: Lea & Febiger, Philadelphia. 1975.

Hediger, H. *The Psychology and Behavior of Animals in Zoos and Circuses*. New York: Dover Publications, Inc., 1968.

Kirk, Mildred. *The Everlasting Cat*. New York: The Overlook Press/The Viking Press, 1977.

Leyhausen, Paul. *Cat Behavior: The Predatory and Social Behavior of Domestic and Wild Cats*. New York: Garland STPM Press, 1979.

Lorenz, Konrad and Leyhausen, Paul. *Motivation of Human and Animal Behavior*. New York: Van Nostrand Reinhold, 1973.

Manolson, Frank. *My Cat's in Love*. New York: St. Martin's Press, 1970.

Roots, Clive. *Animals of the Dark*. New York: Praeger Publishers, 1974.

Sankhala, Kailash. *Tiger!* New York: Simon and Schuster, 1977.

Schaller, George B. *The Serengeti Lion*. Chicago: The University of Chicago Press, 1972.

Siegal, Mordecai. *Mordecai Siegal's Happy Pet/Happy Owner Book: How to Recognize and Handle the Emotional Problems of Your Pet.* New York: Rawson Associates Publishers, Inc., 1978.

Wilson, Edward O. *Sociobiology: The New Synthesis.* Cambridge, MA: The Belknap Press of Harvard University Press, 1975.

CAT CARE, TRAINING AND HEALTH

Agricultural Research Service. "Nutritive Value of Foods." Home and Garden Bulletin Number 72. United States Department of Agriculture. Washington, DC: Superintendent of Documents, U.S. Government Printing Office, 1977.

American Academy of Pediatrics, Subcommittee on Accidental Poisoning, 1973–1976. "Handbook of Common Poisonings in Children." HEW Publication No. (FDA) 76-7004. Washington, DC: Superintendent of Documents, U.S. Government Printing Office, 1976.

Carr, William H. A. *The New Basic Book of the Cat.* New York: Charles Scribner's Sons, 1978.

Catcott, E. J., DVM, Ph.D. *Feline Medicine & Surgery.* Second Edition. Santa Barbara, CA: American Veterinary Publications, Inc., 1975.

Dolensek, Emil P., DVM, and Burn, Barbara. *A Practical Guide to Impractical Pets.* New York: The Viking Press, 1976.

Firestone, Judy. *Cat Catalog.* New York: Workman Publishing Company, 1976.

Fogarty, Marna. *The Cat Fanciers' Association Annual Yearbook*, 1976, 1977, 1978, 1979 Editions. Red Bank, NJ: The Cat Fanciers' Association, Inc., 1976, 1977, 1978, 1979.

Follis, T. B., DVM, Ph.D. *Veterinary Guide to Cat Care.* St. Louis: The Purina Cat Care Center, 1975.

Fontana, Vincent J., MD, F.A.A.P. *A Parents' Guide to Child Safety.* New York: Thomas Y. Crowell, 1973.

Gerstenfeld, Sheldon L., VMD. *Taking Care of Your Cat.* Reading, MA: Addison-Wesley Publishing Company, 1979.

Getty, Robert, DVM, Ph.D. *Sisson and Grossman's The Anatomy of the Domestic Animals.* Fifth Edition. Volumes 1 and 2. Philadelphia: W. B. Saunders Company, 1975. ·

Greer, Milan. *The Fabulous Feline.* New York: The Dial Press, 1961.

Johnson, Norman H., DVM, with Galin, Saul. *The Complete Kitten and Cat Book.* New York: Harper & Row, 1979.

Joshua, Joan O. *Cat Owner's Encyclopedia of Veterinary Medicine.* Neptune City, NJ: t.f.h. Publications, Inc., 1977.

Kearny, Mathilde. *Angell Memorial Guide to Animal First Aid.* Framingham, MA: American Humane Education Society. Massachusetts Society for the Prevention of Cruelty to Animals, 1976.

Kirk, Robert W., DVM. *First Aid for Pets*. New York: A Sunrise Book/E.P. Dutton, 1978.

Kirk, Robert W., BS, DVM, and Bistner, Stephen I., BS, DVM. *Handbook of Veterinary Procedures and Emergency Treatment*. Second Edition. Philadelphia: W. B. Saunders Company, 1975.

Lippmann, Margrit. *Cat Training*. Neptune City, NJ: t.f.h. Publications, Inc., 1974.

Loeb, Jo and Loeb, Paul. *You Can Train Your Cat*. New York: Simon and Schuster, 1977.

McGinnis, Terri, DVM. *Dog and Cat Good Food Book*. San Francisco: Taylor & Ng, 1977.

McGinnis, Terri, DVM. *The Well Cat Book*. San Francisco: The Bookworks, and New York: Random House, Inc., 1975.

Meins, Betty and Floyd, Wanita. *Groom Your Cat*. Neptune City, NJ: t.f.h. Publications, Inc., 1972.

Meins, Betty and Floyd, Wanita. *Show Your Cat*. Neptune City, NJ: t.f.h. Publications, Inc., 1972.

Mellentin, Robert W. "Gaines Basic Guide to Canine Nutrition with a Chapter on the Nutritional Requirements of Cats" by Patricia P. Scott, Ph.D. Fourth Edition. White Plains, NY: Gaines Professional Services, 1977.

Miller, Harry. *The Common Sense Book of Kitten and Cat Care*. New York: Bantam Books, Inc., 1966.

Morris, Mark L., Jr., DVM, Ph.D., and Teeter, Stanley M., DVM. *The Guide to Nutritional Management of Small Animals*. Topeka, KS: Mark Morris Associates, 1976.

Morris, Mark L., Jr., DVM, Ph.D. *Feline Dietetics*. Topeka, KS: Mark Morris Associates, 1976.

Moyes, Patricia. *How to Talk to Your Cat*. New York: Holt, Rinehart and Winston, Inc., 1978.

Ralston Purina Company. "Your Kitten's First Year." St. Louis: Grocery Products Division, Ralston Purina Company, 1975.

Sautter, Frederic J. and Glover, John A. *Behavior, Development, and Training of the Cat*. New York: Arco Publishing Company, 1978.

Schneck, Stephen with Norris, Dr. Nigel. *The Complete Home Medical Guide for Cats*. Briarcliff Manor, NY: Stein and Day/Publishers/Scarborough House, 1976.

Siegmund, O. H. *The Merck Veterinary Manual*. Fourth Edition. Rahway, NJ: Merck & Co., Inc., 1973.

Thomas, Bernice. *The Truth About Cats*. New York: Thomas Congdon Books/ E. P. Dutton, 1979.

Whitney, Leon F., DVM. *The Complete Book of Cat Care*. New York: Doubleday and Company, 1950.

Whitney, Leon F., DVM. *Training You to Train Your Cat*. New York: Doubleday and Company, 1968.

BREED AND MISCELLANEOUS BOOKS

Brearley, Joan McDonald. *All About Himalayan Cats*. Neptune City, NJ: t.f.h. Publications, Inc., 1976.

Caras, Roger. *The Roger Caras Pet Book*. New York: Holt, Rinehart and Winston, Inc., 1976.

Cat Fanciers' Association, Inc. *Show Rules, May 1980*. Red Bank, NJ: Cat Fanciers' Association, Inc., 1980.

Cisin, Catherine. *An Ocelot in Your Home*. Neptune City, NJ: t.f.h. Publications, Inc., 1968.

Denlinger, Milo G. *The Complete Siamese Cat*. New York: Howell Book House, 1952.

Eastman Kodak. *How to Make Good Pictures*. Rochester, NY: Eastman Kodak Company, 1967.

Eustace, May. *100 Years of Siamese Cats*. New York: Charles Scribner's Sons, 1978.

Gebhardt, Richard H.; Pond, Grace; and Raleigh, Dr. Ivor. *A Standard Guide to Cat Breeds*. New York: McGraw-Hill Book Company, 1979.

Lauder, Phyllis. *The Siamese Cat*. New York: Charles Scribner's Sons, 1971.

Loxton, Howard and Warner, Peter. *Guide to the Cats of the World*. Oxford, England: Elsevier Phaidon/Phaidon Press Ltd., 1975.

Naples, Marge. *This Is the Siamese Cat*. Second Edition. Neptune City, NJ: t.f.h. Publications, Inc., 1978.

Ramsdale, Jeanne. *Persian Cats and Other Longhairs*. Neptune City, NJ: t.f.h. Publications, Inc., 1976.

Wilson, Meredith D. *Encyclopedia of American Cat Breeds*. Neptune City, NJ: t.f.h. Publications, Inc., 1978.

Wolfgang, Harriet. *Short Haired Cats*. Neptune City, NJ: t.f.h Publications, Inc., 1976.

Index

PHOTO CREDITS